Referees, Docs, and God

(Journal of a Country Doctor)

By Donald L. Martin, M.D.

Fairway Press
Lima, Ohio

REFEREES, DOCS, AND GOD
(JOURNAL OF A COUNTRY DOCTOR)

FIRST EDITION
Copyright © 1990 by
Donald L. Martin, M.D.

To protect their identity the names of each patient and of many other persons referred to in this book have been changed by the author. The author acknowledges that the material of this book is based on his own recollection of these events.

7733 / ISBN 1-55673-274-0

Dedication:
To my family, friends and patients in the eastern Kentucky hills and in the rolling land of southern Indiana, without whose loyalty and trust this book could not have been written.

Table of Contents

Part One: This I Have Seen

Table of Contents

Part Two: This I Believe

5. A Country Doctor's Ideas and Philosophy

Introduction

Referees spend their time observing and making judgment calls. And so this book is about observing life as I have seen it and drawing some conclusions. This book is about doctors for obvious reasons. I have doctored, been doctored, and observed doctors for over forty years. And finally, this book has references to religious matters. I have made a spiritual voyage from rigid Christian orthodoxy to the open seas of conviction brought about by personal experience rather than by indoctrination.

It seems to me that referees, docs, and God have something in common. Mistakes by any of these three entities simply are not tolerated. At the present time the NCAA tournament is in progress and the refs better be alert and please everyone and make no mistakes. They must be super human. Even if they are obviously right and the call is against one's team we yell out uncomplimentary phrases at the referee. But if the referee does make a mistake for one reason or another, then, woe be to the man. We don't expect the players to get a hundred percent of their shots, but we expect that from the referees.

And now let's turn to the doctors. We expect them to bat 1,000 and make no mistakes especially if it has to do with us or our family. Why not? The doctor is intelligent or he could not have graduated from medical school. He has been to school eight years and was in residency training for three to four years. He may have had thirty years of experience out in the trenches so to speak. People with those credentials ought not to make a mistake we insist. And then when the fees and the hospital bills are high, sometimes outrageously high, we are in no mood to accept an error. The doctor simply must be right. The truth as I see it from the doctor's point of view, is that no matter how intelligent and knowledgeable and dedicated the doctor is, and regardless of the fact that he is doing his best, that will not be good enough every time.

Now, lastly of course, we can't permit God to make a mistake either. However, many do blame God for a series of misfortunes which they resent. It is amazing to me that we expect God to keep us on easy street simply because we have been faithful. God didn't even allow Jesus to be on easy street, how can we expect to be treated any differently?

I am at the lake house on a hot, sultry June night alone. I am relaxed maybe for the first time in my forty-two years of medical practice. Three weeks ago I said good-bye to the hospital. I gave it all to my new friend and colleague, Dr. Daniel Anderson. A great big burden has rolled off my tired shoulders. At first I wasn't sure how I would handle this or if I could take it in my stride. A workaholic has problems when he decelerates. To my amazement, I love it! Office practice continues to be brisk and full and rewarding. To be able to walk away at night and have the emergency room doctor care for my practice is literally medical heaven. To have Dr. Andersoon look after my inpatient work and to bear the full brunt of responsibility for the night and day hospital work, I especially appreciate. It was a tremendous challenge to me during the forty years to manage the hospital practice but now I am thrilled to give it to someone else.

For years it seemed I was driven to be on the go continually. The phone calls, the trips to the emergency room at night, code blue in the coronary unit, and on and on and on. I enjoyed it, loved it, couldn't seem to do otherwise. Now I am a bit weary. I have seen plenty, done plenty, made some great saves, made some mistakes. Oh, the practice of medicine and surgery, the glory, the joy, the triumphs, and yet the tension, the pressure, the disenchantments, the disappointments. I have seen so many brave people suffer and die. So many good people suffer and die as well as complainers and the unlovely and the bitter suffer and die. I don't want to see anymore.

I am on third base heading for home plate. I want and expect this part of the trip to be the best. Why not? To score a run is fun. I feel that my experience is something I want to share for whatever it is worth. Whoever you are, I think some of what I say may get your attention. You may disagree with many of my beliefs, ideas, and conclusions. I expect that. But I hope you will read it and not throw it in the fire. What the world needs so desperately, I believe, is for all of us to listen to each other. God gave us two ears and one mouth. Does that tell you something? So I will put pen to paper and hope you might say that I did not live in vain nor write for naught.

What I have attempted to do in this journal is to literally "bare my soul," tell it like I have seen it, experienced it, and believed it. I am undressing intellectually, spiritually, and emotionally. This is not easy. Most of us go around most of our lives with our defenses in place and with our masks on, for reasons that are obvious.

I want also to make it clear that the statements I make come from the seed bed of my own experience and also from that of others. A doctor, you must remember, hears a lot of stories, enters into a lot of private lives, hears everything, sees almost everything, but not quite. Do not assume that my statements and conclusions have come simply out of my own personal life, far from it. They have come also and perhaps principally from listening to the joys, the frustrations, the anger, the struggling, the triumphs and tragedies of my fellow man. Let me say this to those who know me personally, to my close friends, to my family and to my patients. I hope that you can accept me despite the likelihood that some of you may find some of my beliefs and conclusions offensive and contrary to your beliefs and practices.

Those who are open to change, those who are open to grow, those who really listen to others, know that to do so one has to take the stance that convictions and beliefs are in a sense tentative. That is, new information or experience may and does often cause us to make changes in our convictions and beliefs. If God in his mercy spares my life, I may be in some ways a different person in five years than I am now. Convictions that I have uttered in this journal may no longer stand or may have been modified. The safest place for the ship of life is to be tied to the dock or anchored in the bay but the excitement of a voyage at sea can never be had by staying put. Have a happy voyage in the time that you have left.

Part One:

This I Have Seen

—1—
Homeplace

Homeplace is a rural center located fifteen miles from Hazard, Kentucky, in the heart of the coal fields. It has performed a number of functions through the years including a demonstration farm, woodworking shop, hospital and clinic activities, and a community center for folk dancing, scout meetings, Sunday School classes, and other activities. Homeplace was founded in 1930, by Mr. E. O. Robinson of Cincinnati, Ohio. He established the fund to operate this community center shortly before his death. The hospital opened in 1948, and closed in 1968. The clinic is operative to this day.

Flight for Life

Jane arrived at our little hospital in the Kentucky mountains on a clear summer day in the early 1950's. Ambulance case. First time I ever laid eyes on her. She, like many mountain

15

girls who had moved away, had come back home to deliver her baby. First pregnancy, full term, in active labor, bleeding vaginally, in great pain, steady pain, and unrelenting. She was examined at once knowing that there was a critical matter at hand. The baby was dead. The placenta had separated prematurely. The usual procedure was to wait for a vaginal delivery and hope there was not excessive bleeding, but her labor did not progress, her bleeding continued, her pain worsened, and her abdomen slowly and ominously grew firmer. The decision to terminate labor by section, even with the dead baby, was made for us, if we were to save Jane. Blood donors from the family were rounded up and multiple units were cross matched. We had no blood bank. I called Dr. Keith Cameron, my associate, and we went to surgery along with our OR team at once. General anesthesia, longitudinal incision, uterus entered and the dead baby delivered. The placenta was removed along with huge blood clots. Bleeding continued from the empty uterus. The patient was getting shocky, blood transfusions were started. The uterus continued to bleed. Why? Why? "Let's close the uterus and get out of here, Keith. She'll settle down surely." But every time we put in a stitch anywhere, blood continued to come even from the needle cuts in the tissue. On to the skin we went, quickly, as we sewed up layer after layer. The blood pressure was steadily falling despite pumping in blood. There was even blood coming from around the skin sutures. Blood continued to flow from the vagina steadily. The uterus was failing to clamp properly. Pitocin drip was started, trying to get that uterus to clamp. And so there we were. Pitocin going, blood going, shock position, no let up in the situation. "Keith, what on earth are we dealing with here?" A light flashed in my mind. Could she have that syndrome recently described at a medical meeting I attended? Afibrinogenemia. It is now known as DIC Syndrome. Maybe it was. We drew some blood and put it into a tube to see if it would clot. It would not. This confirmed our suspicion and the horror of watching her bleed to death in front of our eyes loomed before us. We needed a miracle. "Keith, stay here with her while

16

I drop out and call the University of Louisville Medical School Obstetrical Service." I went to our newly installed telephone. We operated the hospital the first year without telephone service, believe it or not. Luckily I got the obstetrical chief on the phone right away. I described the situation to him. He confirmed my suspicion. "Was there an airport near?" "Yes, fifteen miles away." "I'll send you six bottles of fibrinogen." "That ought to do it." The precious cargo was on the way to Bowman Field Airport. A small plane and pilot were waiting. The weather was good. The 200 mile flight was made without incident. At the Hazard Airport a taxi was waiting to come on to Homeplace. Jane was still alive, waiting on the operating table, still bleeding, still in shock, transfusions going in her arms, and bleeding continued from the skin sutures and steadily from the vagina. It was running out as fast we we were putting it in. The fibrinogen arrived by taxi. That driver crossed two mountains at breakneck speed despite the coal trucks he encountered and the steep cliffs he went around. Saline was added to the fibrinogen and it was started into the vein. One, two, three bottles were put in, and she still continued to bleed. Four, five, six bottles were put in and her bleeding began to slow and within a few moments it was controlled almost like turning off the water spigot. Thank God! Thanks to U. of L.! Thanks to the Red Cross! Thanks to the pilot! Thanks to the taxi driver and also thanks to the circulating nurse, the scrub nurse and the nurse anesthetist and the family who donated the ten units of blood that we had used!

Her blood pressure began to rise, her pulse slowed, a blush of pink returned to her pale cheeks and the situation was under control. She was out of the OR and into recovery and then on to her family. She was alive, gloriously alive! The young mother now had a future and another chance.

I have never seen her since she left. I would like to see her. I would like to put my arms around her. I would like to tell her how wonderful it was to save a life and to restore a young wife to her husband and family.This to me is the bottom line of what being a doctor is all about. Some of my medical school classmates, upon hearing about my working under difficult circumstances in Appalachia, for love more than money, thought I had rocks in my head. As I sit back and reflect tonight, would I do it again? Yes, a thousand times yes.

■————————————————————————————■

Homeplace Happenings

There was no place like Homeplace, we always said through the years and these stories, all gospel truth may prove the point. Homeplace, nestled in the mountains of Perry County, Kentucky, county seat, Hazard. In those days it was on Kentucky 15, main artery to Jackson, Campton, Winchester, and Lexington, but the artery was arteriosclerotic, hard, twisted and often clogged with coal trucks heavily laden. Homeplace was truly Homeplace to hundreds of mountain people. They loved us and we loved them. We never closed, night and day, seven days a week, 365-days-a-year and we were open for clinics and emergencies, hospitalizations, deliveries, caesarean sections, appendectomies, heart attacks, strokes, broken legs, cut-up bodies, gunshot wounds, and bloody miscarriages by the dozens, with the patients sometimes in shock from blood loss. Dr. Keith Cameron and I were associated together for twenty years and one of us was always there, or at least not over fifty yards from the hospital. Because of this security to the patient, especially in emergencies, we became a popular place and we went heavy duty day and night, on and on, but we were young and vigorous, eager to work and be involved and we were, sometimes a lot more than we wished. We were relatively isolated, and consultation was unavailable except by telephone. On occasion, one of us dropped out of surgery to call and consult and get advice about a messy situation.

One day in the mid-fifties, we took Lucy to surgery. She was a mountain lady with an acute abdomen. Our preoperative diagnosis was a perforated peptic ulcer. We put her to sleep, opened her abdomen, and sure enough there was peritonitis, but it was not due to a perforated peptic ulcer.It was perforated cancer of the colon just at the liver edge. Wow! Thirty-six years old! Not supposed to happen. I had never seen such as this before nor since in years of exposure to sick folk. I dropped out of surgery and called my surgeon mentor at the Veterans Hospital in Louisville, Kentucky, Dr. Ellis Duncan. He advised me. I followed his instruction, we made it through, and she recovered. I did a drainage procedure at the site of perforation and then I did a cecostomy to divert the fecal stream, irrigated the abdomen thoroughly and closed. We put her on intravenous Chloromycetin, a marvelous drug to fight peritonitis, which was a death-dealing condition in the pre-antibiotic days. She sailed through beautifully. Wow! Later we rescheduled her for a right hemi-colectomy and carried that out without incident. Dr. Duncan flew to Hazard from Louisville and gave us a hand and assisted me as I proceeded. Believe it or not she had two primary cancers, one at the perforation and one in the cecum. When I left the mountains, she was well, hale, and hardy!

Gracie was a mountain girl living and working in Chicago. So many mountain people were transplanted in order to find work. At every opportunity, they would return to the mountains for a visit. Gracie got sick and went to Cook County Hospital emergency room. She was diagnosed as having acute appendicitis and was told that surgery would be scheduled in a short time. She "lowed as how" that if she was going to be operated on that it wouldn't be at Cook County Hospital, but it would be at Homeplace. Believe it or not, she went to the Greyhound Bus Station and bought a ticket to Ary, Kentucky, and ten hours later at about eight o'clock in the morning a Greyhound bus fully loaded came up the driveway from the highway to the hospital parking lot. Out came Gracie, all bent over with pain, carrying a suitcase and obviously walking with difficulty. I examined her and her abdomen was "red hot" and appendicitis was the most likely diagnosis. Within an hour, she was in the operating room and the gangrenous appendix on the edge of perforation was removed. She did fine and went back to Chicago. That is loyalty or stupidity depending on whether you were commenting as a mountaineer or a Chicagoan.

On another similar occasion, the Greyhound bus left the highway to climb up the hospital hill road and deposited a patient at our doorstep. The patient was very pregnant. As a matter of fact, she was in hard labor. She had hailed the bus at Quicksand, twenty miles downstream and had to get to the hospital as quickly as possible. Once the driver realized the implications of her predicament, he was about the unhappiest driver in all the fleet. He couldn't put her off and yet he was fearful she would deliver the baby en route. He didn't stop for customers, believe you me, for he raced to the hospital and deposited his cargo as quickly as he could. We took her at once to the delivery room and she pushed it out pronto. Close! Too close!

Mary got sick with an earache. Her mother didn't believe in doctors because she believed God would always heal if one had enough faith, so she kept the child away from the doctor. Her pain increased in the ear and the neighbors became aware of the problem, hearing the child moan and at times yell out! They called Mary's dad who was working in Columbus, Ohio. He came home and brought her in to the hospital despite the mother's protestations. By the time I saw her she had been sick the best part of a week and the otitis media had blossomed into acute mastoiditis and there was a huge abscess behind the ear, overlying the mastoid bone. The process had broken through the bone into the surrounding tissues. We took her to surgery and widely incised the abscess and put in drains. We started intravenous penicillin and sulfadiazine. She got better and as a matter of fact she got a lot better and her dad left for Columbus to return to work. No sooner had he gone than the mother pulled the IV out, grabbed up the daughter and took her home against our pleas. The neighbors called Dad again and he came home and brought her back. By this time it was too late. She had developed meningitis from the inadequately treated mastoiditis. Treatment was of no avail. She died. The mother blamed the hospital and the doctors. She was convinced the Lord allowed her death as an indication of his displeasure over seeking medical attention.

Peggy came to the hospital with difficult breathing due to a severe case of tonsillitis. The tonsils were huge and met in the midline obliterating the swallowing space. Her adenoids were likewise involved and blocked her breathing space. As a result, she made a loud noise with her respiratory efforts. We admitted her to the hospital and started intravenous penicillin and oxygen. Nevertheless, she got worse and by midnight the nurse became alarmed. I was called and I came over to the hospital at once. I found her gasping for air, unresponsive, and turning blue. I yelled orders to the nurse for a tracheotomy set and I did the procedure right in her bed where she lay. It was now or never. Endotracheal intubation was unheard of then. Without anesthesia, I opened her trachea and inserted the tube, she drew in quickly several deep breaths, and her pink color was restored. Soon she was conscious and wondering what on earth was going on. What was going on was her life-saving operation! She fully recovered and she went home in good condition.

I was leaving the clinic one day about 5:30 after a hard day when a car full of people drove up to the parking lot. Traditionally, in the mountains, when someone is brought to the hospital for anything really significant, plenty of family accompany. The door opened and people came out and among them was a young girl about nine and she was holding her right arm up. She couldn't lower it because a huge stick was stuck in her axilla (armpit). No one seemed real excited, not even the girl, but after one glance at her I sure got uptight. I led her to the emergency room and put her on the table and got everyone out except her mother. I took her things off to better survey the situation. It was a sapling stick, about one-and-one-half inches in diameter and a test gentle movement of the stick immediately revealed the terrible truth that the stick was embedded very deep. To my horror, I found that the object had penetrated her axilla, gone through her neck completely, and one could easily feel the point of the stick on the other side of her neck. As a matter of fact, you could see where the stick had emerged from the deep structures as the skin of her neck was tented out over the sharp stick edge almost ready to punch through. Her vital signs were good. There was no bleeding and she didn't seem in great distress. She was not even complaining especially and the entire family was rather calm and stoic. This demonstration of the acceptance of hardship and trouble was replayed over and over again among the mountain people, and so I did what I did from time to time during my twenty-year stay in hill country. I went to the phone and called my dear friend, Farra Van Meter, M.D. and heard his cheery voice and usual comment, "and what kind of mess do you have for me today, Don?" Traditionally, my calls to Dr. Van Meter were reserved for four alarm medical fires, so to speak, and he braced himself when he heard my voice on these occasions. He hesitated in disbelief when I described the situation, "but send her on, Don, I will get Jim Redd and we will do what we can." So off she went in the car fully loaded with her people. The news I received from Lexington two days later was good. After a five-hour operation, they removed the stick and cleaned out the bark and debris. Miraculously, the stick had dissected its way with almost a surgeon's precision between all the vital structures in the neck without damage. It could have punctured muscles, windpipe, esophagus, jugular veins, common carotid arteries or her spine but it missed them all. No major damage. She fully recovered. How did the accident happen? You won't believe it. She was playing in a field where small saplings had been cut across obliquely with a machete. The cut-off trees were about two feet tall. She had fallen and impaled herself on one of the saplings and screamed until she was heard. Instead of trying to lift her off the stick, they gently sawed the tree off at the ground level and brought her, stick in place, to the doctor and all kept their cool real good. City folks often have a stereotype uncomplimentary view of mountaineers, but I want to tell you, brother, they have some excellent qualities. I know. I lived and worked with them and learned to love them.

I had been at Homeplace only a short time when I was confronted with an overwhelming obstetrical disaster. Obstetrical nightmares were not uncommon in those days for two reasons. First and foremost, the mountain women had no means of contraception. The unstructured and disorganized life of many of the mountain folk living up the hollows simply didn't include the use of condoms, diaphragms or observing the so-called rhythym method of birth control. There was no birth control pill and to sterilize anybody took an act of Congress in those days. Consequently, families often included ten to fifteen "head of younguns" along with grandma and grandpa and maybe Aunt Mary. As a result of multiparity the uterus became exhausted and like an auto tire with too many miles something bad might happen during the pregnancy or later. Alice came in the clinic one day in hard labor. Pregnancy number thirteen, I had never laid eyes on her before. When you live at the end of nowhere up a hollow and the trip out means going in and out of the creek many times by jeep travel or by walking, you don't make too many trips to the doctor during the prenatal period. As a matter of fact, you don't go at all and so with Alice and perhaps one-half of my deliveries in the early fifties, such was the case. She had been in bed about thirty minutes with frequent pain and hard labor and I knew that I should stick close. Suddenly she screamed, "Doctor I am dying, I can't stand it." I examined her and found to my horror that her abdomen was extremely tender, very hard and there was no fetal movement or heartbeat obtained. The diagnosis was a ruptured uterus, dead baby, hemorrhage, shock and potential death to the mother. We took her to surgery and put her to sleep. The abdomen was opened and our suspicions were confirmed. The baby was lying free in the abdominal cavity — dead. Blood was everywhere. Alice was in shock with blood pressure fifty and pulse extremely weak. Fluids were going. We needed blood and there was no blood bank, no Red Cross. Over the next hour, we managed to get twelve units of blood rounded up for her. Where did we get it? The hospital staff were the donors. Even those of us in the operating room one by one dropped out and gave a unit. We kept her alive. The uterus was removed. The tear into the uterus had gone right through the blood vessels that supplied the left side of the uterus and had torn the vessels off at their roots so to speak. This made hemorrhage control virtually impossible with the standard procedure. The only hope was to ligate the internal iliac artery on that side which supplied all of the structures in the pelvis. I did this and it helped, but not enough, for she continued to bleed unacceptably. I was fearful of ligating the other internal iliac, thinking that if we did that she would lose her blood supply to the entire pelvis and that the damage to the structures would be intolerable. While I was deliberating, Alice suddenly worsened, her blood pressure fell, her pulse became imperceptible and she was gone. Later I learned that ligation of both internal iliac arteries would be an acceptable alternative in such a situation but at the time this was considered too risky. Practicing medicine and surgery was indeed and still is a very stressful occupation. If you are rough and tough like a drill sergeant such ordeals may be tolerated with relative ease. But if you are a loving and caring person by nature, such events are not borne easily, I can tell you that for sure.

■———————————————————■

The Rattlesnake and the Pussycat

An ambulance from Breathitt County came full speed up the hill to Homeplace Hospital one day and deposited a man in deep shock and in bad shape. His right hand was swollen badly and a tourniquet was on his arm. His eyes were closed and he was unresponsive. His pulse was minimal and his blood pressure was zero. He had been bitten by a rattlesnake two hours previously or perhaps longer. By the time he reached us he was in shock and his life was hanging in the balance. In addition to that, he was drunk. He had been in the woods hunting squirrels according to his half-drunk buddy, who said he leaned over to pet a pussycat and it turned out to be a coiled rattlesnake. He was bitten on the thumb and evidently took on a good quantity of venom since it was an early morning snake bite. This is the worst time for a snake bite because the snake has a full load of venom in his pouch early in the morning. By the end of the day many snakes have emptied out their venom and the depleted reservoir gives only a partial dose of venom to the victim and one stands a much better chance of survival. The man was admitted to the hospital and resuscitative measures were immediately started. He was given several units of plasma to combat his shock. Intravenous anti-venom vials were injected one after another until he perhaps had as many as twelve. More plasma, oxygen, attention to the wound was given. The wound was incised allowing the blood to bleed freely and so relieved the swollen tissues of some of the venom. Soon we began to get some response and there was a perceptible pulse and his blood pressure began to rise. More plasma was given and more anti-venom injected and there was further improvement. He, finally, after a period of two hours, became aware and gradually regained consciousness. He made it through the first twenty-four hours and it would appear that he might survive. The initial insult to him from the venom was one of shock due to blood volume loss. He simply bled into his body tissues all over including the skin, the muscles, the stomach, the intestines, the kidneys and colon. He passed blood rectally and passed blood through his urine in great quantities. His skin was hemorrhagic and black and blue in many places. This bleeding tendency was brought about by the effect of the snake venom on the blood coagulation system. He became intensely jaundiced over the next few days because of the hemolytic effect of the venom on the red blood cells. The venom simply broke the cells up and destroyed them releasing the hemoglobin into the tissues and plasma. Later his kidneys failed because of the insult to them from the broken down red blood cells. He was then given unit after unit of blood in order to restore the blood loss. Eventually his kidneys began to function again and after a week his jaundice began to clear. His bitten hand was a mess and for a time we thought amputation might be necessary but he weathered the storm and his hand and arm were saved. After two weeks he was up and about and was released.

In twenty years at Homeplace Hospital, I treated three rattlesnake bites. During the same time I treated, I am sure, over a hundred copperhead bites. They were rather nasty and painful and caused a great deal of local tissue reactions but in no cases were they life-threatening. In a number of places in our area, snake-handling was a part of church service activity. It was believed that if you had enough faith the rattlesnake would not bite you when you handled it. If you were bitten, if you had enough faith, then you didn't need medical care. It didn't always work that way. Some people were bitten and some people did die.

We have all recognized the fact that there is some good in the worst of us and some bad in the best of us. I guess this is probably true, as my years of experience in dealing with people tends to bear this out and I imagine that this applies to snakes, too. The worst of the critters is the rattlesnake, by far, but he seems to be a gentleman in some ways in as much as he stays high up on the ridges away from people and seldom comes into the valleys unless it is real dry and he is forced to do that in order to obtain water. He lives on small animals such as mice, squirrels, moles, ground squirrels and frogs, and after killing them he dislocates his jaws and swallows them whole and the digestive process goes on slowly. Furthermore, the rattlesnake is equipped with a great alarm system. He sounds off by shaking his tail violently prior to biting and gives his intended victim a chance to escape, at least as far as a human is concerned. Before he takes on a squirrel I am not quite sure whether he sends the alarm on not. And so you see the snake kills for food or for protection while man kills for pleasure, anger, money, women, or just about anything

26

he decides is worth the effort. Snakes we fear, but men can be infinitely worse.

The copperhead snake, although better in terms of hurting the human, is far worse in terms of his disposition. He tends to live not up on the ridges like the rattlesnake but down in the valleys around barns and near people's homes and near civilization. As a matter of fact, he likes gardens especially and when children and adults come into the garden to gather vegetables, they are bitten every now and then and the copperhead gives no warning. He slips up on you and gets you on your blind side, so to speak. Mountain folk say that a copperhead will cross a highway to bite you if necessary.

In the fifteen years that I have been in Salem, Indiana, the only snake bite that I encountered was that of a black snake. The boy who had received the bite on the finger came to the office in a semi-hysterical state thinking that probably the end was coming. When I assured him that he was perfectly all right and would suffer no difficulties he immediately got well. Though I haven't encountered any poisonous snakebites in Indiana, I have dealt with some people who were about as dangerous, I think, as rattlesnakes in some ways. As a matter of fact, perhaps more so. A rattlesnake as I say has his gentlemanly qualities but there are some people who have unfortunately, not a trace of this quality in them. The vast majority of patients are great people, dependable, appreciative, pay their bills and bring the doctor a tremendous amount of satisfaction.

Polly

Perhaps my most vivid and unforgettable character from my beloved Kentucky mountains was Polly. I have on the wall at my office, in a frame, a dollar bill with the caption "Polly" under it. I see it every day and it gives me a good warm satisifed feeling inside. Polly is alive today because of the efforts of a number of medical people and I was privileged to play a pivotal role in the drama.

My dear friend and colleague, Denzil Barker, M.D. of Hindman, Kentucky, delivered Polly of her first born. It was either a home delivery or an office delivery. It was certainly not a hospital delivery. There were no major problems at the time of delivery but a few days afterward she had a sharp hemorrhage and she came to our hospital by ambulance and was admitted. We gave her blood and examined her under anesthesia and did a general gentle curettage of the uterus. She settled down and went home with minimal bleeding. A few days later she was back bleeding again, and this time we thought it advisable to have a gynecological consultation and so off to Lexington, Kentucky, she was sent by ambulance on a four-and-a-half hour trip over treacherous winding roads. At the Lexington hospital a few sutures were taken into the friable and oozing cervix and vaginal packing was inserted and she settled down once more. She was allowed to go home. The same scenario was repeated a third time and she was back into Homeplace Hospital with heavy bleeding. Back to Lexington, Kentucky, she went and on this occasion she had a total hysterectomy and things once again were under control. A few days after her return home, believe it or not, once again a very sharp vaginal hemorrhage recurred and she was brought back by ambulance to Homeplace where her vagina was packed quickly and then she was transported by ambulance again to Lexington. It was necessary for me to ride with Polly in order to keep pressure on the vaginal packing and to keep the bleeding under some degree of control. Despite this she continued to ooze and bleed and the blood clotted and ran onto the floor of the ambulance. I got motion sick during the process and felt absolutely miserable. Polly was in semi-shock and despite this she was very much concerned about my condition. She was a very sweet natured mountain girl and she was not alarmed, not even upset. She even sang or tried to sing some of the old mountain tunes as the ambulance sped along. She, on more than one occasion, squeezed my hand and told me how much she appreciated my going along with her in an attempt to save her life. I think we both cried a time or two during this drama.

We arrived at Good Samaritan Hospital, Lexington, Kentucky, and Polly was in bad shape. Lots of blood loss, deep shock, condition critical. To surgery we went. An attempt to deal with the problem from the vaginal approach was useless, and so the abdomen was opened and there was oozing from both adnexal areas at the uterine vessels. There was evidence of infection and any attempt at suturing was futile. The tissues were entirely too friable to deal with from a surgical point of view. The only chance was to pack the pelvis with heavy gauze packing and hope for the best. This was done and a great deal of packing was left in the pelvis and brought out through the abdominal wound. Blood was given, lots of it. She made it through the surgery by the skill of the surgeon and by the grace of God. Post operatively, at the appropriate time the packing was cautiously removed she did not bleed. Antibiotics had been given in massive amounts. Almost by miracle, she recovered without major infection.

She went home and was restored to health and was able to go on and raise her son and keep the family going. When in 1969, I left Homeplace the first time, she came over to see me on the last day in the office and as she said good-bye she said, "Doc Martin, I didn't have time to go to town to get you nothing, so here take this." She put something in my hand. I hugged her and she was gone. I have never seen her since. After she left I opened my hand and there was a crushed up dollar bill. That dollar is precious to me. I wouldn't sell it for $5,000. It is in my office and framed to remind me of the event. It reminds me of the successful effort to save a life. It reminds me of the appreciation expressed by a simple mountain woman in the only way she knew how. It reminds me of the joy that is produced by loving and helping a fellow traveler in this earth. That is the bottomline of what doctoring is all about.

Death in the Mountains

A funeral service in the Kentucky mountains in 1955, was a far cry from such a service in Salem, Indiana, in 1989. In the hill country, emotions are expressed uninhibited. If the death is untimely and perhaps tragic and unexpected, the out-pouring of grief is awesome to behold to someone not used to this sort of thing. In Salem, one's emotions are suppressed and subdued and the atmosphere is altogether different in the local funeral homes. In such instances at times there is light conversation, even smiling and laughing. Not so in Appalachia. There one's grief is openly expressed and one's sorrow is uninhibited. To do otherwise in mountain culture would be disrespectful of the departed one and the family. Now this is mainly true of the folk in the hills and the hollows. The county seat people would be less apt to show their emotions so vividly as the rural people.

I shall never forget the death of a young husband and father in 1955. He died of leukemia and left a young wife and a baby. During the time of his terminal illness I was his physician and I found myself being absorbed into the grief of the family and finding it hard to disassociate myself from their emotions. I attended the funeral. The service began at 10:00 in the morning and the church house was full and people were standing outside. It was summer time. The service ended about 1:30 in the afternoon and during this time at least six preachers participated, each one giving a thirty-minute speech or sermon. Customarily in the hill country, each and every preacher present at a funeral would be called upon to speak. People came and went from the building during this time without any embarrassment. There was much emotion with crying and wailing at times and shouts of amen (to the preacher) were heard.

Generally speaking, hill country people were more apt to show their emotions in many phases of life than their county seat cousins. If they are sad, they cry and moan. I shall never forget the visitation in a home up Williams Branch near Homeplace where two young people were lying in their caskets in their home and the neighbors from far and wide were coming and going. The family had lived in Chicago and had left the hill country in order to find work. The children were integrated into Chicago society as best as could be. One day in Lake Michigan they were both drowned. They were teenagers. They were brought home and I knew the family and paid my respects. The outpouring of emotion was beyond description at this home during this most tragic circumstance.

When I go back to visit the hill country and see my friends and my patients, I am welcomed with open arms and love and hugs. When the mountain folks like you they love you and are demonstrative. If you are disliked, you had better give space. I happen to be very comfortable in this kind of setting and found it rewarding to interact with people of this nature. If one is uncomfortable in such a setting, he has no place in Appalachia.

How the Preacher Got Saved

They say that if you shake a tree in Kentucky the Baptists will fall all over the ground. Knott County, Kentucky, was no exception to that rule, although the Baptists were not all of the same variety. There were the Old Regular Baptists, the United Baptists, the Missionary Baptists (Southern Baptists), and maybe others. These were the big three anyhow.

A preacher came to Hindman many years ago, having been born and reared in Tennessee and having graduated from Southern Baptist Theological Seminary in Louisville. He was called to a small and struggling Missionary Baptist Church in Hindman, the county seat. The Old Regular Baptist congregations were the dominant group for sure. Regular Baptists believed in predestination. This meant that those souls who made it to heaven and those sent to hell were predetermined to be that way. Before one was born he was elected to salvation or to damnation and there was nothing that could be done to change that. For that reason there was no urgency or obligation to be a missionary or to carry the good message of God anywhere. However, the Baptists educated in seminaries said otherwise. They believed that it was necessary to confront people with the good news of God so that they might be in a position to make their own decision. Thus, they felt responsible to evangelize and preach the good news and accordingly were called Missionary Baptists. The Regular Baptist preachers were all laymen. They worked for a living like anyone else and preached sermons, weddings and funerals as the opportunity arose. They did not have special theological education and simply studied their Bible and did the preaching.

The preacher was a real missionary for sure. He was convinced that it was the church's responsibility to preach the gospel, start Sunday schools, hold vacation Bible schools and generally be aggressive. Under his leadership, Sunday schools and churches were begun in many areas of the county. During a Sunday school contest nationwide, the Hindman Baptist Church won first place and on the crucial Sunday there were 1,700 in Sunday school among the mother church and all the missions.

A number of town people were touched by the preacher's influence and were brought into the church fellowship. There was one young man who resisted his efforts repeatedly. Billy simply resisted the efforts of the preacher to reach him with the message of the church and of Christ.

Every few years a flood hit the town and it was often devastating. This was true all through Appalachia. One spring one of the extra big flood waters rose into the church and in to the main street buildings and crossed the highway and it was a real mess. The preacher put on his baptismal outfit which sort of resembled a set of overalls except that it was rubber and was waterproof. He was wading around in the waters trying to help rescue people and various items. He got out a little far and the water was swifter than he had anticipated. Suddenly he was swept off his feet and his baptismal outfit was filled with water and he was pulled into the flood waters for sure. Billy happened to be alongside the preacher at the time and he quickly grabbed the preacher and slowly and surely pulled him from what might have been his death to safety. Fantastic! The preacher got saved. Billy went on his way. He didn't come into the church fellowship, but he did a compassionate and courageous deed!

■────────────────■

"Take it Out, Doc!"

One of the more interesting and challenging aspects of doctoring is presented when a patient comes along with a foreign body of some sort in his body space or cavity. Every doctor has his collection of tales about this sort of thing. I'll tell a few stories to illustrate the point.

One night at Homeplace the nurse called me over to the hospital saying that a man was there with something in his ear and he simply couldn't stand it any longer. It was then 3:00 in the morning. I dutifully got up as I had done more than a thousand times before and would again another thousand or more times if I lived. I went to the emergency room and this guy was holding his ear and was pacing the floor saying in no uncertain terms, "Take it out, doc." I looked in the ear with my trusty otoscope and what did I see but a tiny winged insect beating its wings and trying to execute a take off but the runway was inadequate somehow. He was just plain stuck. I ran a jet stream of water into that ear canal and flushed out that dude and I had me one grateful patient real fast. How nice if all problems had a simple solution like that or would it? Maybe life would be too dull that way.

Kiddies aged three to six put lots of things up their noses, I mean way up to the point that no one could manage to retrieve them; beans, corn, limas, crayons, plastic pieces, you name it. Some kid will manage to get it in but can't get it out and so a trip to the doctor is necessary. The parents are embarrassed and sometimes mad. The kid is very upset. It takes a bunch of people to hold a four year old still enough to extract a nasal foreign body without removing a portion of the nose. Usually we are successful by using a small hemostat and grasping the object. Given a good light and a steady hand, a child held down tightly, and we are usually successful.

Then there was the bizarre tale of the child who said he had swallowed some coins but the x-rays said otherwise. The x-ray was read revealing an odd appearing metallic foreign body in the stomach the identity of which was uncertain. We waited for two or three days and re-x-rayed. There was no change and the foreign object had not advanced out of the stomach. So he was scheduled for a procedure in which the specialist passed an instrument into the stomach and had a look to see what was going on and remove it if possible. This was done and the object was removed and low and behold it turned out to be coins just as the child had said. The four coins were pennies stuck together face to face making an object too big to pass out of the stomach. Amazing!

My father was one of the first patients of a new dentist. My father had a gold crown to fix. In the process of trying it in place and then removing it, it flipped into his throat and he gagged and managed to aspirate that crown with the attached bridge. He came back to Salem and we got him x-rayed and sure enough the foreign body was in the trachea. It had to be removed at once. I called up my chest surgeon friend at Louisville North Hospital and it was removed by bronchoscopy. This was an embarrassment for the dentist, a problem for my dad, and a neat triumph for the surgeon.

One night at Homeplace Hospital I admitted a patient with an appendiceal abscess. He was quite sick and vomiting repeatedly and in a lot of pain. He had a mass which could easily be felt in the right lower quadrant of his abdomen. We operated late that night. When we got the area exposed, I put my hand in the abdomen and felt the area. It didn't feel like any appendiceal abscess I ever felt before. As a matter of fact, I never felt anything like this before. After we enlarged the incision in order to get better visibility we saw an obstruction at the ileo-cecal junction (the junction of the small and large intestine). Something was moving inside the intestine at this area and the intestine was distended to the size of a tennis ball. It had to be a ball of round worms all knotted up. We were instructed never to open the bowel when worms were present for fear that an overlooked and left behind worm might work its way out through the suture line in the intestine and crawl out into the peritoneal cavity. We had no choice, however, but to open and remove the worms anyhow. The patient had intestinal obstruction and simply could not live unless this was done. So we opened the intestine and removed all the worms. They were at least six inches long and there were many of them. When we got them all out we put some worm killing medicine in the bowel just in case some which might be left behind would be killed. We sewed up the bowel and closed the wound. There was no problem post operatively. We were lucky. The patient was lucky. We did the right thing.

Fishhooks are something else when they get into your fingers, your face, your scalp and even the eyelids. One day a young boy came to the emergency room with a fishhook clear through his upper eyelid and miraculously it did not injure the eyeball. He was shook real bad but he was brave and cooperated beautifully while I removed the fishhook with a local anesthetic. One Saturday a fellow came to the office real drunk and very happy. He had not one but two, three pronged fishhooks in his scalp with the attached artificial worm hanging down over his face. We were successful in our surgery despite the fact that he wouldn't hold still and it required a steady hand on my part to get the job done. Usually, victims of fishhooks are more embarrassed than they are hurting. You are supposed to catch a fish not yourself.

"Land at Homeplace? Better Not!"

It was on a Friday afternoon about 5:00 and I was leaving the clinic at Homeplace back in the early 1960's. As I walked out I heard a plane overhead, coming in close, and apparently going to land on our small landing strip on top of the hill near the clinic. I figured it was Victor, our business manager, who was about the only one who could manage to land there. The terrain was strange and difficult and it was no place for a novice. Victor had bulldozed the top of the hill and made a short landing strip for his new love, a single engine airplane. No one else would dare attempt to land there for very good reasons, namely, they didn't have first hand knowledge of the terrain. So I assumed it was Victor coming in for the landing. But as the plane came in lower, I realized that there was a problem, a big one. The plane simply was not coming in properly for a safe landing. I held my breath and then it happened. The pilot, realizing his mistake, tried to gain speed and get out of his predicament but it was too late. The plane hit a tree and went down on the other side of the hill and disappeared. I raced up the hill and on to the landing strip and down to the other side expecting the worst.

To my utter amazement, instead of a bloody and battered pilot in a crashed plane, the guy was on his feet walking to me at a good clip. The plane was a mess. It was nose down in the dirt and the front end crumpled up pretty badly. The pilot was upset but not hysterical. He wasn't hurt very much either. Before I could get a word out he promptly blurted out, "I don't give a damn about the plane, but I am sure nervous about telling my wife." Apparently he was a new pilot and very courageous or foolhardy — depending on how you viewed the situation. He was from New York and had flown in to bring us a piece of medical equipment. His wife had advised and warned him about the hazards of his trip into the mountains of Kentucky with his inexperience, but he came on anyhow. Her last words to her impulsive husband were, "Please be careful and don't take any chances." He made it to the Hazard airport and landed okay. That wasn't easy and he did well considering his lack of experience. He was advised at Hazard to go out to Homeplace by taxi and deliver his package to us. However, he heard about a landing strip at Homeplace and he was determined to try to land there despite the warning from the folk at Hazard.

Well, he learned a valuable lesson or at least I hope he did. I have never seen or heard from him since. He was a risk-taker, he was adventuresome, and actually he was a bit foolish. If he profited by his mistake, he is a wiser man. If he did not, he may be a dead man by now. Well, this is so typical of life for so many of us. I have not had a problem with airplanes or motorcycles, but I have taken some chances and have usually been lucky. Most of us have engaged in very risky behavior in life at one time or another. Some of us have paid heavily for that behavior. Some of us have been lucky and gotten away with it.

Why do we insist on taking chances that put us in jeopardy? Why do we flirt with danger and at times court disaster? Why do motorcyclists hate a helmet required by law? Why do we want the freedoms that could take us to ruin or to an early grave? Well, this is a complex subject and I can't give a complete answer in a sentence for sure. For one thing, there is a conviction on the part of many who take chances that bad things won't happen to them. Smokers just don't think cancer will get them. Tightrope walkers don't believe they will fall. Speeders don't believe they will wreck. And then the other matter. Our risky behavior can be so much fun, bring us joy and exhilaration, enhance our lifestyle, rid us of the monotony. If we don't crash, in short, the rewards can be great. Like the lottery. We bet a thousand dollars which we can't afford but if we win, life starts all over again. And then there is, in many of us, at some place in our life an attitude of rebellion. We say, "to hell with oughts and shoulds, I am going to do what I want to do and that is all there is to it." And so we plunge in.

Risky behavior may be confined to our youth and then we settle down. This is perhaps the usual pattern. It may hit us when we grow older and then we decide to "live it up" before the show is over. Risky behavior may be a life-long pattern. If so, we are apt to have a very bumpy ride.

Now finally, risky living can be of two kinds: Good risks and bad risks. Worthwhile gambles and stupid gambles. Leaving a secure job for a more responsible one in a distant city is likely a good risk. Saying good-bye to a dead marriage and risking an uncertain future is a good risk. But riding a cycle eighty miles an hour without a helmet is not in anyone's best interest, except perhaps the undertaker.

Life has no guarantees. Each of us must make decisions every day. We alone are responsible. The only way to avoid risk is not to come into this world in the first place. But I am glad I am here. I am glad I am a responsible person. I am glad that I have not gone to an early grave because of a stupidity. But tomorrow is another day. I must not let down my guard.

———————————————————

A Dead Body in July and No Morgue

It was July and it was hot. It was at our little hospital in the hills, Homeplace. Jane was dying of cancer. She was suffering and she was skin and bones. Death would come as a relief and a blessing. She knew she was dying. We gave lots of narcotics and it helped. It produced pain relief and sleep. Thank God for morphine. If I had to go through my bag and throw out my pills and medicines one by one, the last one that would go would be morphine for sure.

Jane's family remained faithfully at her bedside like all mountain families customarily did. The room was small and there was no air conditioning. She was from up a hollow at the end of nowhere. Her lifestyle had been simple, unpretentious, and by the standards of upper middle class America, she lived in abject poverty. But she didn't know it. She knew one thing though. She was loved and she was not abandoned.

Her attendants were not there out of any sense of obligation. They expected no inheritance at her death. Someone of her family slept under her bed at night, there was no room for a cot. The mountain people from up the hollows may be poor in these world's goods, but they are rich in love and devotion to family and friends. Through life they take time to visit one another, help one another, and are people-oriented rather than thing-oriented as are many of the upper middle class Americans.

Jane lived on for about three weeks before the end came. She was never left alone during this time that she lived. However, the moment she died everyone disappeared. We assumed they would soon be back and we could learn which funeral home to call. But they didn't come back. Night came and the next morning followed. It was hot July. No morgue. The body we kept in the bed where it had breathed its last. We closed the door to the room. In desperation we sent the sheriff to see if he could locate the family but failed. By the night of the second day, as we were getting desperate as to what to do with the body, here came a pickup truck driven by one of the family members and there were three men in the cab. They brought a hand-made casket into the patient's room and gently placed it on the floor and removed the lid. It was in the shape of the Egyptian casket of old and made of yellow poplar wood. The family explained to us that they had the wood ready at home but that the casket was unmade. Upon death they went home and went to work and made the casket as quickly as possible. They put the casket on the floor beside the bed and gently lowered Jane's body into the newly-made coffin complete with silk-like lining and expert crafting. They put the casket in the pickup and took off. I am sure the burial soon followed and no doubt there was preaching at either the home or at the grave site. It is traditional for mountain preachers to lay it on very heavy at the time of death and plead with the sinners to clean up their lives before death strikes. They don't pull any punches. It is sort of like when the crowd gathers to watch a neighbor's house burn down, the fire insurance agent circulates through the crowd trying to convince them that they need to buy insurance. Not a bad idea come to think of it.

This scenario I had never experienced before or since. But it was their way and I am sure those who participated in this event had observed or participated in it many times before. To prepare the coffin ahead of time before death simply was taboo for one reason or another. You just don't do that. Had we known their intentions, we would not have gotten so shook up as we did. This event illustrates another principle in life that communication and declaring one's intentions in important matters is essential to making life livable and for human relations to be acceptable.

"One More Time, Don"

It was in the early 1960's at Homeplace Hospital. Keith Cameron, M.D. and I were busy, busy, busy with all manner of obstetrical, surgical and medical challenges. We alternated night and weekends on call. Keith had a big and obese patient in labor at the time and we knew the baby was big. The labor was long and difficult. She finally advanced to the point of delivery and was taken to the delivery room. Keith scrubbed up and was able to get the head delivered although it was slow. Finally, the shoulders presented but they were stuck. Shoulder dystocia we call it. Simply it was a big baby and a large mother and not enough room. Keith called for help and I went into the delivery room and assisted. The baby was finally delivered after a hard struggle. Keith cut the cord, gave the baby to me and I took it to the incubator but there was no spontaneous breathing and minimal heartbeat. I knew we were in serious trouble. I gave mouth to mouth breathing, sucked out the airway and gave it stimulants. Nothing was effective and I gave up after a struggle, told Keith the bad news and walked out of the delivery room. Keith sent the nurse for me and requested for me to give it one more try and to do closed chest heart massage along with the mouth-to-mouth breathing. We had no ventilators in those days. Cardiac massage had just come in as an accepted technique of resuscitation. Under these circumstances I did what he asked and after a time, low and behold, the baby was resuscitated. It did well over the next two or three days and we dismissed the baby hoping that it would not be brain damaged because of this ordeal. It turned out later that it was okay.

This case points out several lessons for life. First of all, it shows that we should keep trying and we should not give up on a situation too soon. Secondly, it points out how much the human organism can stand and still make the grade. Thirdly, it points out the fact quite clearly that a team approach to a problem is often better than an individual approach. It also points out the wisdom of taking advice and not being satisfied that you always know all the answers. I was convinced that the baby didn't have a chance when I left the delivery room. Keith was not so sure. His faith prevailed and as a result we were the winners along with the baby and the parents.

■————————————————————■

—2—
University of Louisville, School of Medicine

Student Daze — University of Louisville Medical School 1944-1947

In 1944, World War II was going full blast both in Europe and Southeast Asia. Hundreds of thousands were in uniform defending the nation. Factories were converted into war machine production instead of consumers goods. Women in unprecedented numbers were in factories working every day and America was fighting a "holy war" against the Nazi horror and the Japanese treachery. Daily, American families were informed by special courier of their dead and despite the overall good news of victories on the battlefield and on the high seas, for hundreds and thousands the grief of the lost young man or woman brought agony and pain.

It was my good fortune to be in the United States Navy and be assigned to the University of Louisville Medical School as my duty station. We were in midshipman's uniforms and received Navy pay and subsistence and had few, if any, military obligations beyond rigid classroom attendance requirements. If we flunked out, out to sea we would go. I had strong motivation to make the grade for sure. I wanted to be a doctor and I didn't want to fight and kill in a horrible war. I was a lucky boy, although we Navy and Army boys assigned to medical schools were hated by the fighting men for obvious reasons. Good old fashioned jealously has always been easy to acquire.

The first day in gross anatomy lecture hall, Arch Cole, the professor, was giving us the word and laying down the rules of the road. First off, he was mad at the military for sending fourteen more men than we could comfortably accommodate in the anatomy dissecting room and he admonished us in no uncertain terms that the next year they could not make room for the extra fourteen. You know what he had in mind for the low fourteen in the class. That, I might add, put the fear of God in us and it didn't exactly have a calming effect on our nervous system. One boy from Salt Lake City, Utah, simply failed to show up the next day. Back to Utah he went! Of the four girls in our class of 104, one was so pretty she was picked off quickly and got married. Another girl didn't make the grade and she departed early on. So that left only eleven more students to dispose of one way or another. We all hoped and prayed we wouldn't be included in that number. All the students were good and highly qualified. You had to be to even get into medical school in the first place. We were all top notch A and B students and so the spirit of competition was strong, and in a way it was "dog eat dog" and every man for himself.

We took three subjects only the first year and were in class from 8 a.m. to 5 p.m., five days a week and until noon on Saturday. We took gross anatomy, microscopic anatomy and biological chemistry. We learned the body organs thoroughly by reading about them and then dissecting out the structures in the dissecting room, all afternoon, five days a week. The "gross" lab was on the top floor of the four story building and there was no elevator. It was a big room with plenty of light from side windows and sky lights. We also had spot lights overhead to focus on our work. The first day in the lab was a never-to-be-forgotten experience. We assembled ourselves at our assigned tables where we would work from 1 to 5 p.m., five days a week, to spend a total of at least 600 hours learning the human body from top to bottom inside to outside. Four students were assigned to a table. The cadavers (dead bodies especially preserved and prepared for dissection) were encased in a special coffin-like container designed for easy access so that lids to cover the cadavers were opened and fastened under the tables giving us easy access to our work. We sat on stools and dissected, or stood, as the particular position we were working in required. The preserving fluid had a strange and never-to-be-forgotten odor. We smelled like medical students the entire year wherever we went. The embalming fluid permeated our clothing and hair and we simply had to accept our plight. Every Monday we had an anatomy exam and four times a year we had a major practical exam in which we would go from body to body to identify labeled structures. It was interesting and fascinating to be sure but the pace was fast and we had to cram in knowledge by rote memory very rapidly. Gross anatomy was the "flunk course," and we sweated it out.

In microscopic anatomy we learned what muscles, heart, lungs, brain, intestine, and bone looked like under the microscope and became familiar with the wonders of the body so marvelously engineered and designed to do its complex job day after day for years and years often with minimal care and maintenance. What a fantastic machine the human body was.

In biological chemistry we learned the amazing and complicated chemical reactions that constantly were going on in our bodies night and day, moment by moment, in order to maintain life and good health and ward off the hosts of would-be invaders that would and could destroy the body. Our amazing immune system with all its complex chemical reactions was designed to protect us and did. We students who had a religious upbringing and who were mentally prepared to appreciate the divine, were especially impressed with the marvels of nature and the wisdom of our creator as we learned more and more about the most marvelous and complicated machine ever designed. We were treading on holy ground, as it were, although our anxiety about learning our lessons kept us far more nervous than awestruck.

The initial adjustment period to long hours of study and test preparation was difficult to say the least for many of us. Some of us were compulsive achievers and were always a bit worried that we might flunk if we did not give our best effort. By nature, some students always ran scared. I was one of them. Before every test I was not sure I would pass it and then often ended up with the top grade or near the top. After six weeks of school I, along with others, was having a difficult adjustment period getting into the stride of long hours in school, long hours of night study, and working under lots of stress. I began to show signs of anxiety along with some depressive elements. At that time, I didn't understand what was happening to me. I couldn't relax very well, and as a result I was tired the next day and couldn't function as well during the school hours. This quickly snowballed and it became obvious that unless I could catch a limb on my downhill slide, I could very well hit the bottom of the hill. My religious faith was put to the test and on this occasion was a lifesaver. I simply was able to pray "God, if you really want me to be a doctor, then no way will I fail and if you don't then I don't want to be." I totally was ready to accept whatever answer would be forthcoming and I relaxed immediately. I slept, I was awake the next day and functioning at top efficiency all day and I flourished. I graduated with the highest academic honors in September, 1947, at the University of Louisville School of Medicine.

The relentless pressure continued throughout the second year. We spent long hours in physiology, the study of how our body and each organ system worked. Practical hands-on training was obtained in the laboratory where we anesthetized and operated on animals and observed the effects of drugs upon their organ functioning. We became acquainted with bacteria in the lecture room and observed their growth and reactions to antibiotics in the laboratory. In pathology, we learned what disease did to the body and organs and tissues and the havoc produced by the invasion of the body with bacteria, the many inflammatory conditions, the ravages of cancer, as well as the effects of the long list of enemies of the human organism.

The last two years of school we got hands on experience at the Louisville General Hospital. We were told and soon found out it was true that in making a diagnosis the most important item was the account the patient gave the doctor about his illness. We called this the taking of the medical history. In 1946, we were told that the medical history was worth seventy-five percent, the physical exam fifteen percent, and the tests we ran ten percent in making any given diagnosis. Today, I think testing is of greater importance when we consider the amazing data of information derived from blood analysis, body fluid analysis, x-rays, CAT scans, and not to mention MRI's, cardiac catheterizations, and the list of procedures goes on and on and on. Still, there is no substitute for listening carefully to your patient and asking timely appropriate questions. Sometimes, a patient will not tell it all, out of fear that the truth might require an intensive and involved medical investigation which they fear, and are not prepared to have them done. Occasionally, for the same reason, a patient will simply lie about his or her illness out of fear of the consequences of the truth. This can be disastrous both for the patient, the family and the doctor. A terrible and sometimes fatal mistake can be made if this happens. Who knows better than I?

The scene was the treatment room on men's medical ward at Louisville General Hospital. The wards were "open wards" with fifteen beds on each side of a long room without partitions between the beds. Privacy was unknown, no television, no private bathrooms, very little chance to maintain any personal dignity under such conditions. A dozen medical students along with the resident physician were assembled to carry out and observe a thoracentesis (removal of fluid from around the lung) which needed to be done in order to enable the patient to breathe better and also to analyze the fluid in hopes of making a diagnosis. The patient was a bit apprehensive as the instruments were readied and the chest wall was washed and antiseptic applied. The resident doctor then looked around and flung out the challenge, "Who wants to do this?" No one volunteered. He looked at me and said, "Martin, how about you?" I responded that I would, with as much assurance as I could muster. I don't know who was the most nervous, I or the poor patient. It was a first for both of us. I injected the space between the ribs with procaine for anesthetic effect and then picked up the 100cc. syringe with the number sixteen needle and thrust it into the chest cavity after making a small skin incision. I pulled back on the syringe and yellow fluid came out to my and my patient's relief. From then on, it was easy. We took off a quart of fluid and his breathing immediately improved. We learned and conquered our fears by "doing" and by plunging ahead despite our anxiety and insecurity. The same emotion we experienced with each new procedure we attempted, such as spinal taps, surgical procedures, setting fractures and delivering babies spontaneously and also by forceps extraction. If you mess up the first time around, it is hard to go at it again, but one must if success is to be achieved. It is one thing to fix a broken motor; it is quite another thing to fix the human body. Try it, you may not like it!

And so the learning process went on night and day as we listened to sick folk, examined them, tested them, x-rayed them, looked into them and cut them open to fix them. A Cummins engine model number twenty-five is the same world around but the human being is not the same. Bodies are similar, true, but the body is encased in a personality and that calls for more skill in diagnosing and treating than simply being a mechanic. While it is true that we treat strep throat with penicillin and appendicitis by surgery, the problems of individuality come to the surface as we attempt to diagnose and treat conditions that are more complex and complicated. Here is the area where the so called "art of medicine" comes into play. To gain the information we need, we must understand the patient, need to ask the right questions, we need to be understood by the patient, and finally we need to win the patient's confidence. If possible, we need to convey to the patient that his welfare is our first consideration and this must be genuine and honest. In other words, each patient is a separate world and we have to approach one as such. When the Cummins engine model number twenty-five breaks down, we don't have a personality to dissect or individual variations to contend with as we attempt to diagnose the break down. Not so with a sick person. The anatomy is the same with minor variations and the physiology or functioning of the body is the same, but in order to properly treat and lead the patient to recovery we must contend with individuals, not machines. The stakes are higher in the people-fixing business contrasted with mechanical business. If a mistake is made with the engine or if it is worn out, we replace it. One night at the hospital at about 2:00 in the morning, I was leaving a patient and ran into a colleague who was sweating out a very tough labor case. A breech presentation (butt first), first baby, a diabetic patient, blood pressure up, and the baby's heart beat was slowing ominously, but delivery was near. The labor had been long and tedious. Should he call the surgeon for a quick Caesarean section before a disaster occurred, or should he "cool it" and let her deliver? It was in the days when a Section was a last resort consideration. We looked at each other, both tired and tense where upon he said, "Don, this is a damn stressful occupation we are in." I couldn't have agreed more. I later learned he waited and the delivery was smooth and the baby and mother were okay, but the doc had ten more gray hairs. In September, 1947, medical school was concluded but we had stuffed four academic years into three calendar years because of the war. Our bodies were tired and our minds and emotions somewhat frayed. We had learned by studying, by listening, by observing, by doing, by

49

making mistakes, by trying again, by going on despite our exhaustion, by keeping our cool in a tense situation and at least trying not to reveal our anxieties. Medical school was fascinating and at times boring, at times discouraging and difficult, rarely easy. Always it was challenging. Final exams came and we plowed through them again for the last time and so the week of September 20th, three big things happened in my life, graduation from Louisville Medical School, State Board Examinations, and my marriage to Virginia. I survived, but I must say that I enjoyed the honeymoon more than the state board examination.

Hollywood

The year was 1946. The scene was the City Hospital, later on called Louisville General Hospital, and affectionately referred to by the staff as Louisville "Generous" Hospital. The teaching staff of the University of Louisville was depleted because of the war and so doctors were still in short supply. There was the usual number of embryonic docs, however, who were students at the University. I was a junior student living in "Old Hollywood," the affectionate name for the dorm for working students, interns, and residents. What a place to live! No air conditioning, windows were wide open and in the summer time, noises from the ambulances pierced the midnight hours. Across the driveway was the psychiatric ward and the open windows there permitted the noises from the disturbed psychotic patients to penetrate "Hollywood" night and day. We had fewer drugs to calm the agitated patients in those days and so they often shouted until they fell asleep in exhaustion.

There was only one hall telephone to a floor. It rang incessantly all night it seemed and the first doc to wake up finally in disgust would answer and then call whoever to the phone. Ugh!! What a system! Imagine trying to sleep on those hot summer nights in such conditions. How I ever existed for two years that way is still an amazement to me. Every fourth night I was on duty in the emergency room of the hospital and often I was up much of the night working. No chance to make up for lost sleep either. The next morning in the hospital amphitheater during a lecture on who knows what, I slept with my head in my hand and my elbow on the arm rest. I would wake up with a start during the perfunctory applause at the end of the lecture, but we had note takers to keep in edited order all that was said and I got by.

Book learning was surely important but without our hands-on experience on the wards and in the clinics and especially in the emergency room we would have been sorry docs indeed. For working all night every fourth night, I got my room, such as it was, my food in the hospital cafeteria, such as it was, and my uniforms washed and ironed, such as they were. Of all the jobs available to medical students in the hospital, the emergency room appointment was the most coveted. To make a real soldier, battle experience in the front lines either made you or broke you and so the emergency room exposed us to the worst and the most and at times coming at us so fast we could hardly keep up. After two years of that, we fledgling "shave tail" doctors felt like we had seen it all and done it all. We emergency room docs regarded ourselves as the marine corps of medicine and were rightfully proud of our knowledge and prestige. And so like every learning experience, we learned by doing, we learned by making mistakes, and we learned by trying again and not giving up. We tried to learn patience by repeated exposures to alcoholics, the lacerated, the beat up, the yelling of obscenities, and trying to suture up these people while three or four cops held them on the table. We tried to learn compassion for the poor, the hopeless, and the handicapped. Often it wasn't an easy task and finally we tried to learn to quickly assess a situation of major trauma and multiple victims, to do first things first, and organize our work and save lives and relieve suffering and calm the hysterical. We learned and learned and learned. It was demanding and at times confusing and frustrating and it took commitment and determination to go on but I loved it. I had found my place. I was going to be a doctor. I was determined to be a good doctor.

Alcoholic Antics

I have usually managed to get along with most of my patients. As a matter of fact, I find it easy to relate to most people. Some I easily love and get close to. I tend to accept people as basically honest with me and genuine until proven otherwise. This attitude, of course, has caused me embarrassment on occasion as the drug dependent and dope dealers have sold me a bill of goods. Nevertheless, my basic attitude of acceptance has brought to my patients and to me a great deal of satisfaction and pleasure. People, I find, are hungry for love and acceptance, want someone to shut up and listen and be genuinely interested in them and upbeat. I try to do that and I think for the most part I do. Nevertheless, there is one class of patients that all doctors are exposed to during their career that I find difficult and hard to accept and love. I am referring to the alcoholic who is also self-centered, gets nasty during drinking sprees and who invariably hauls me out of bed on a cold winter night to come the emergency room and suture up his lacerated hide while he yells and carries on in his accustomed disgusting manner. And the icing on the cake is, of course, that he always manages to find money for his booze and cigarettes but never any money for me or the hospital. Now, I will be the first to admit that if I had an alcohol problem myself or if I had a family member who did, I might be more tolerant. But I don't and so I am not.

First Case: I was suturing up a drunk sailor one night in the emergency room at LGH (Louisville General Hospital) and I had spent at least an hour or more on his head and various other parts of his anatomy and after I had finished the suture job we had a few parting words not fit to print. He had been held rigidly on the table by the police during that hour and he did not like doctors and needles and hospitals one little bit. The cop then led him out to the paddy wagon when suddenly he broke loose and ran. They quickly caught the poorly coordinated grand member of Uncle Sam's navy and in the fight and struggle which followed the good ole cops found it necessary to whack him over the head a few times and managed to rip open the head wounds I had struggled to suture together. So back in they came rather sheepishly and presented me with their bloody sailor washed up once again on the shores of LGH emergency room for the second time. I managed to put him back together again and I am not sure who was the most disgusted and disgruntled that Saturday morning at 2:00, the police, the sailor, or me. It didn't matter, we simply got on with the job.

Second Case: I was struggling one night with an equally unappreciative alcoholic, and I walked away when my suture job was finished to get to the next patient, when I found myself in a very awkward and scarey situation. The guy was mad as a hornet at me and had picked up a metal chair and was coming at me swinging the chair like a pendulum on a clock. He was obviously more mean than he was drunk. He backed me into a corner and I wondered what on earth I was to do next. Quickly, I dropped to the floor and crawled out of my predicament and beat it out of the room before he knew what had happened to me. By that time security caught up with him and led him away cursing.

Third Case: One Friday night a fight broke out in a nearby tavern. One of the characters broke the bottom off of a beer bottle and jammed the cut end into the face of his victim like a biscuit cutter would cut out dough for a biscuit. It was across his nose, the eyes, the forehead and the cheek and left bits and pieces of glass deep into the wound and puncturing the eye in the process. It was a terrible mess for the plastic surgeons. The eye was damaged beyone repair unfortunately. The fighters in that scenario were fueled by alcohol quite naturally.

I am confident in saying that most of the trauma on Friday and Saturday nights was fueled by alcohol. The beautiful and gorgeous females and debonair and handsome men seen on the whiskey and beer advertisements on billboards and magazines of our nation give the impression of the association of spirits with wealth, success, and seduction. The doc in the emergency room at LGH saw the flip side of that coin. It was blood and guts, despair, horror and disease.

Unforgettable Cases at Louisville General Hospital

There are always the cases you never forget in any tour of duty as a doctor. These are few and far between and lifted out by one's memory from the hundreds of routine "run of the mill" situations that are so frequently encountered. One night about midnight the police ambulance came screaming into the emergency room receiving area with a young man that had a stab wound at the fifth rib interspace to the left of the breast bone. Just underneath this area was the heart. The victim was in bad shape by his appearance. He was semiconscious, his skin was cold and clammy, his blood pressure was 50/30 and his pulse imperceptible. The heart sounds by stethoscope were distant. A quick chest x-ray revealed a large heart shadow. It was obvious beyond a doubt that this man had a stab wound of the heart muscle and had cardiac tamponade. That is, blood had filled the space around the heart because with each heart beat, blood was pushed out through the lacerated heart muscle into the pericardinal space or the space around the heart muscle. As a result, the heart could hardly contract due to the pressure build-up around it. The surgical resident was notified immediately and he was taken at once to surgery. He was quickly put to sleep and the chest prepared and opened. The chest cavity was entered and the ribs were spread apart by the rib retractors. The heart was identified and there was almost no movement of the heart whatsoever due to the pressure. The pericardial space was entered after the pericardium or the sac around the heart, was opened. Blood filled the cavity and it was sucked out. There was plenty of it and the heart then began to contract more forcibly and as it did blood spurted out through the one centimeter laceration of the heart muscle. The surgeon put his finger over the wound and as he did he put three fairly heavy silk sutures through the stab wound and tied them securely. He closed the opening tightly and expertly. The patient was cured. The pericardium was closed, drains were left in the chest and the chest cavity was closed. Another life had been saved and he would live to fight again, no doubt.

Late one afternoon a man was brought into the examination room on a stretcher. He was conscious but having convulsive seizures one after another. He was literally dying of respiratory paralysis because we were helpless to do anything about his continuous seizure activity. He simply couldn't get his breath because of the repeated seizures. We had no muscle paralyzing agents in those days and no respirators. He died right before our eyes as we helplessly looked on. He was aware of what was happening almost to the end. Someone had spiked his drink with a lethal dose of strychnine powder. Today, if that situation arose, we would put the patient on a respirator and paralyze his convulsive muscles with appropriate drugs and his life doubtless could be saved.

George was a frequent attender in the emergency room of the General Hospital. His heart was damaged beyond repair by a defective valve and it had begun to fail. He had frequent bouts of heart failure resulting in marked shortness of breath and wheezing respiration and great apprehension. He would come straight to the emergency room and be brought into the exam room by wheelchair. He would be terribly short of breath and wheezing audibly. Immediately upon his arrival, we all knew who it was. We would get the oxygen ready and start it, load up the aminophylline syringes, two or three of them and start injecting by vein. The aminophylline usually would give him relief after one, two or three syringe-fulls were given. We did not dilute the drug. We gave it straight. We called this cardiac asthma in contrast to allergic asthma that so many people have. In this situation the failing heart would allow the pressure in the circulating blood through the lungs to increase and expand the vessels. The traffic jam of blood, so to speak, and consequently the outpouring of fluid into the air spaces caused the air tubes to constrict and contract and as a result the patient had a terrible time trying to get his breath and exchange the air. The aminophylline that we gave by vein allowed the air tubes to relax and once again establish an exchange of air and a life would be saved. We then injected a drug that would make the kidneys kick into gear double time or triple time and get rid of the fluid build-up in the lung tissues. The patient would be relieved until the next attack would hit. We all saw George repeatedly during the year and always in the same condition and always responding. It got harder and harder, though, to give him relief. One night I injected the third vial of aminophylline and George did not respond. His heart fluttered and then quit. In those days we knew nothing of CPR. When the heart quit, it was all over and it was all over for ole George. We hated to see him go. We had learned to love him.

One morning about 7:00 as I was going off duty, ambulances roared into the emergency room area with twenty burned victims, bad ones, adults and kids, many had their clothes burned off entirely, some only partly. All the cases had extensive potentially lethal burns. One boy about fifteen years of age broke loose as he was being lifted out of an ambulance and he ran stark naked into the parking lot in front of Hollywood. He had at least ninety percent total body burns. He was corralled and admitted to the hospital where he died in a few hours. Many did die but several survived. The tragedy occurred when people gathered around a large overturned gasoline truck on the edge of Louisville. The police, in vain, attempted to keep the curious away from the accident when, without warning, the explosion occurred and the fire engulfed everyone near. It was truly a "hell" of a way to die.

―――――――――――――――――――

A Toothpick Can Be Powerful

Ordinarily we do not regard a toothpick as anything more than a handy item if we have meat stuck between our teeth. But let me tell you a wild tale about a toothpick that may change your mind.

The scene was the morgue of the Louisville General Hospital in 1947. Some of us senior students had been invited to observe an autopsy on a man who had died of peritonitis of unknown causes. It was a peculiar case and had presented a real diagnostic dilemma to the attending staff. While he was being readied for exploratory surgery, complications set in and the patient died before surgery could be set up. Permission for a post mortem was obtained and he was taken to the autopsy room and the procedure started. Upon entering the abdominal cavity it was evident that he had a wide-spread peritonitis. Pus was found throughout the cavity and the peritoneum was angry and inflamed. The next job was to find out what had gone wrong sufficient to produce this lethal condition. A ruptured organ was about all that could have done it. The stomach was exposed but nothing found. The duodenum was found and there was an abscess around the second portion. The abscess had leaked, causing the widespread and uncontrolled damage. Dissection was carried into the abscessed pocket and low and behold the unbelievable was discovered. A toothpick had lodged in the duodenum and had perforated the wall and had given rise to what was to kill the patient.

This patient had a habit of eating and then cleansing his teeth with a toothpick. He then lay down for a nap, leaving the toothpick between his lips. On this occasion he went to sleep before he removed the toothpick. He proceeded to swallow the toothpick and it made its way into the duodenum and got stuck there and finally perforated with rupture. The intestinal juices leaked out and peritonitis ensued, killing the patient. Wow! It is a dangerous world to be sure. This points out several things to think about. 1) Don't lie down and go to sleep with a toothpick in your mouth. 2) If you have a terrible belly ache, get to a doctor soon and don't procrastinate. 3) A toothpick held in one's hand and used for its intended purposes is okay, but swallowed, it is not our friend. 4) We have a saying among doctors to this effect, "If you can swallow it, you can pass it." But obviously there are exceptions and this case was one of them.

—3—
Philadelphia General Hospital

Philadelphia General Hospital was for many years the charity institution for the disadvantaged of Philadelphia. Hundreds of thousands of patients were treated during this time. Hundreds of thousands of interns and residents were trained during this time. It was considered in its day one of the outstanding training centers for young doctors in the United States.

Blood, Sweat, Toil and Tears

As I write tonight, it is 100 degree weather here in Salem, muggy, hot and sweat dripping. But many of us are comfortable with heavenly cool air circulating. Homes, hospitals, jails, funeral homes, office buildings, schools and even farm tractor cabs are blessed with that good stuff.

Not so in 1948 when in July I was a freshman intern in the 3,000-bed Philadelphia General Hospital. The hottest summer anyone could remember, sweat everywhere, no air conditioning save one small unit in the cast room. It was usually occupied by nurses and interns, with Cokes in hand, getting a minute of refreshment.

The fifth floor of the tuberculosis pavilion was my first assignment, seventy-five patients. The hopeless ones were mine. They were dying in the cruel heat wave. There was yet no certain effective treatment for that dreaded killer. Streptomycin, pneumothorax, and thorocoplasty we utilized, but bed rest for months or years was the fate of all if you lived. The dead were taken to the morgue that summer and an autopsy was done on them all. As I recall, to enter that hospital, everyone signed an autopsy permit to be used if necessary. On any given morning at the pathology building, I have seen a dozen bodies being simultaneously dissected searching for the clues of death. What a scene for a green intern! I must have waded through billions of tuberculosis germs that month and I know a million crawled on me but I didn't get my apical tubercular lesion until twenty-six years later. As I lifted the x-ray from the developing tank of my own chest on a routine physical, I saw the apical lesion and I knew what it was. The germ that once killed hundreds of thousands now I had, but, fortunately I didn't lose a day's work, I didn't cough once, and I fully recovered because of the marvelous drugs that we had by that time.

It was "hot as hell" on the medical ward of the famous Tom Durrant, M.D., who was the modern version of the famous and historical grand teacher of them all, Sir William Osler. All the interns yearned for the Durrant service to sit, as it were, at the master's feet. After the dreadful TB ward, I got that marvelous and famous teacher, Dr. Tom Durrant. What a joy and what a delight, but I had to work hard to be his intern.

A funny thing happened on my first day of the Durrant service. The old war horse nurse in charge of the floor who knew more than fifty interns, took me on ward rounds to introduce me to my thirty or more patients. She gave forth with wisdom she had gleaned through her long exposure to the sick and suffering. Timidity and modesty were not characteristics of the old battle ax. We rounded a corridor to a private room, one of the few in the hospital. "Doctor," she said, "this patient is old John who has asthma or thinks he does, but he is nothing more than an old crock who holes in here too often." We walked right into the room and so help me, he was dead. I looked at her and she looked at me. I figured that would cut her down to size. It didn't even faze her. "Well," she said, walking without loss of composure, "even the crocks eventually die and usually not soon enough!" Between that character and the great Durrant service with a flood of pathology day and night, I had a seventy-five mile an hour air-born ride through germs and disease without crashing. But it took blood, sweat, toil and tears. *Blood* to the lab for analysis such as we did in those days and blood transfusions. *Sweat* dripped from my body that month and I had to carry a towel with me to put under my arm to catch the sweat drip as I wrote orders on the carts, (so help me, I am not lying). *Toil* all day long and on call and usually up every other night. There were *tears* for the dying but some died without tears. There was no one there. They were forgotten, the homeless, and the rejected.

For two years I rotated through the wards of Old Blockley, Philadelphia General Hospital, the heaven and the hell for the intern. Pay? Nothing, no dollars, zero. Our pay was experience that we gained from the patients in those corridors where the famous Sir William Osler had taught decades before and whose legacy hopefully some of us would inherit. Today, the hospital is no more. It is history. It exists in the memory of the thousands of residents and interns who cut their medical teeth in that great institution. We cannot forget, although there are some things I would like to forget. Blood, sweat, toil, tears. That was life at Old Blockley and that is life for us all when we struggle toward a goal which we are earnestly and compulsively seeking.

Philadelphia General Hospital — 1948 to 1950

Old Blockley, the affectionate term for Philadelphia General Hospital, had been in business a long time when I started my internship in that massive institution. I would be there for two years, rotating from specialty to specialty and gathering as much information and knowledge as I could. We worked almost every day and half of the night. Our pay was the experience. There was no salary but they did provide a room to sleep in while we were on call and food to keep us going. At the end of the two years we did receive the mighty sum of $60 to help us with our uniform expenses. In as much as I was a top student in Medical School with good references, I had been accepted at three outstanding hospitals for internship. Cook County Hospital in Chicago, Charity Hospital in New Orleans, and Philadelphia General Hospital in Philadelphia were top notch teaching hospitals and I received an invitation to all three. I chose Philadelphia General where I was exposed to 3,000 patients. There was the medical service, the surgical service, tuberculosis, obstetrics, neurosurgery, pediatrics, neurological, psychiatric, oncology, orthopedics, ear, nose and throat, pulmonary, emergency room, syphilis, urology, radiology, pathology, anesthesiology, and metabolic (diabetic coma). There were no intensive care or coronary care units as such in those days. We had no equipment to staff such a place. Disposable material, such as we have today, was nonexistent. We washed and resterilized our surgical gloves, our instruments and our needles. We reused our intravenous sets and tubing as well as our blood donor sets and recipient sets and the accompanying bottles. Syringes and needles were cleaned and resterilized and used again. Plastic, in general, was unknown in the hospital setting and consequently most all equipment and service trays were reused.

The nursing staff was excellent and I learned a tremendous amount by listening to nurses. The resident staff was constantly available to help us. The attending physicians we saw perhaps two times a week for hospital rounds, teaching and general supervision. But the intern was the "doctor." We were given heavy burdens and great responsibility and the resultant esprit de corps was exhilarating. We really felt important and we were. Philadelphia General Hospital was truly the poor man's hospital. Our patients were not used to fancy things and it's a good thing. Most of the beds were on long open wards containing as many as thirty patients per ward. There were no television sets and private phones, no private baths and no private anything. The patients appreciated their care and the doctor's word was law and lawsuits were virtually unknown. Government and third party interference in medical practice was unheard of. Our main stresses were the long hours, the loss of sleep and the responsibilities we bore. Another great stress was the near poverty level of existence that we had to endure. Financial salvation came to me in the form of a working nurse wife who brought home $180 check each month. Out of this we paid $45 for a fourth floor apartment without elevator or air conditioning. We could not afford an automobile. We relied on our feet and public transportation to get about. The walking was good exercise and we didn't need to join a health club. The fourth floor apartment was no problem until Virginia's last trimester of pregnancy when it did become a problem to her.

Virginia worked for the Philadelphia Visiting Nurses Association and enjoyed her experience working with all kinds of people in all kinds of homes. The $180 a month check kept us alive. I was totally immersed in my exhausting work at PGH. Knowledge and experience I soaked up day after day like a dry sponge taking on water. I loved most of it. At times there were squabbles between house staff members and usually we worked them out without a major confrontation. PGH was steeped in medical history and many famous doctors of history had walked the halls and imparted their wisdom to the younger set of docs. Sir William Osler, the grand ole man of medicine from England, graced our halls and lecture rooms at one period in his life and his pictures could be found in various places around the building. Five medical schools had staff members on our visiting staff and a vigorous inservice training program was conducted.

As I recall, patients or their family were asked to sign three papers on admission to the hospital. One was permission to give general care, one was permission to operate if necessary and a third gave consent for an autopsy in case that was appropriate. Wow! A far cry from today when autopsies are rarely done, in small county hospitals at least.

Our meager social life consisted of activity at the Belmont Avenue Baptist Church and the inevitable friendships we formed with couples there have existed to this very day. Virginia took courses at the Philadelphia School of the Bible and I had Bible courses at Wheaton College. Our plans at this point were to be medical missionaries in the Belgian Congo with the American Baptist Foreign Missionary Society. We were poor by today's standards but that didn't matter. We worked very hard and we expected to. Automobiles, stereos, televisions were not part of our lives but we got along quite well without them. We did have each other. I had a marvelous place to train for my chosen field and Virginia enjoyed her work and we had lots of friends at our church. Early on in the internship we were approached by a Navy recruiting officer who gave us some excellent advice. The Korean War was going on and he advised us to join the Navy now and be put on the Navy payroll and we would be allowed to continue our internship and then go into the Navy on active duty following completion. This sounded very good to me and I did it. I got a nice check for the first time in my life and we were on our way to living properly. I bought my first car, a Chevrolet, brand new, for $1,500 after a four-month wait to get it. What luxury! It was basic transportation, no power anything, no radio, no air conditioning, just a car with engine, wheels and doors, but it was beautiful to us. My Navy check made it possible to consider producing our first child and so it wasn't long before Virginia was pregnant and Carol Ann was on her way. She delivered on April 4, 1950, at the Philadelphia Lying In Hospital. I knew that in July I would be getting my orders for my first duty assignment with the Navy and it probably would be good-bye to the family for an unknown period of time. I had finished up the last of June at Philadelphia General Hospital after I had had a marvelous experience and crammed into my brain as much knowledge as possible. How I stood the long hours and the loss of sleep and the unending responsibility is still a mystery. We made some never-to-be-forgotten friends. We were graduates of Philadelphia General Hospital, one of the top teaching hospitals in the United States. I was bursting with pride to be a member of the Old Blockley Ex-Residents Association, which we felt was the marine corps of the medical profession. In the amphitheatre of the General Hospital we were gathered together as interns and residents and staff members for our last session of "grand rounds." It was during this time that we presented our interesting cases and discussed them. A resident presented a paper describing our innovative ideas regarding the use of intravenous potassium to treat diabetic coma cases. We were using large amounts and one of the first institutions to do so. At the conclusion of the paper a visiting professor from Jefferson Medical College responded to the resident and his remark stated that in his view we gave huge amounts of potassium and surely we must have brave doctors at Philadelphia General. Whereupon the resident responded that he agreed that we were a brave lot but that in fact one had to be a brave patient to come into Philadelphia General. I guess it is a good way to finish this paper and describe my sentiments.

■————————————————————————————■

Far Out Tales from Philadelphia General Hospital

I was emergency room doctor at Old Blockley when the city police brought in a "wild man" in handcuffs who was yelling and resisting as best he could. Four cops were too much for him and he lost the fight. They took him in a room and secured him to the table with straps. I started my examination. The city cops in Philadelphia were a savvy and experienced bunch and some of them projected the image of being nothing less than a doctor in uniform. They had made a diagnosis of agitated schizophrenia with this man and urged me to get him over to the psycho ward immediately where he belonged. Although he was presenting an acute and violent agitated state, there was something unusual about this guy that caused me to question the obvious diagnosis. I had just spent a month in the psychiatric unit and while there I had treated several cases of insulin reactions. There was something similar about this man's behavior. I wondered if he could be diabetic. While the cops were out of the room and while he was secured by a belt to the table, I fished out his wallet and sure enough I found him to be diabetic and so I decided to have a little fun. I ordered a syringe of fifty percent glucose from the nurse and then asked the police to come on in. I said, "Boys, before we go to the psycho ward, let's see if this might help the situation." Although they said nothing, I am quite certain by the look in their eyes that they thought I had rocks in my head and was obviously an inexperienced young "shave tail" intern. Nevertheless, they watched with interest. I injected fifty cc's of the glucose into his veins with him struggling, but managed to get it all in. As we were finishing the injection, he suddenly relaxed, opened his eyes, looked around and asked what was going on around here. "Let me out of here," he said. He was alert and coherent but sort of confused and mixed up about what was going on. I told him he was in Philadelphia General Hospital Emergency Room and that the cops had found him in his agitated and unresponsive state and had dragged him into the emergency room with great difficulty. I assured him that he was okay and that all he needed was a good meal. The cops' eyes bugged out and you could have knocked them off with a stick. Those that had hair to scratch did so and they walked away a bit embarrassed but mainly dumbfounded. The little "shave tail" "wet behind the ears" intern shone and loved it.

66

And now let's talk about insulin shock that was at one time a treatment for hopeless schizophrenia. This is a mental disease which was poorly understood in 1948 and still is. Treatment was minimal then. Mostly it was custodial care in a mental or psychiatric hospital provided the patient could not safely function on the outside. Electric shock treatment was available but didn't help a great deal. Medications which do help considerably today were unknown at that time. We treated schizophrenia with insulin, induced coma, and this had been introduced elsewhere and brought to the United States. During my month on the psychiatric ward, I assisted in the treatment of ten such patients and we gave on a regular schedule insulin injections up to 1000 units and deep coma was induced for several hours. A feeding tube was then passed into the stomach and sugar solutions were given to terminate the coma. Usually it did, but on occasion it failed and heroic efforts were taken to save the patient's life. I did observe one death during that month as a result of irreversible coma, but the quality of life of these patients was so bad that it was living hell in reality. Insulin therapy went out the window when drug therapy became available. We still don't know the cause of schizophrenia and we don't have the cure. We can assist the patient to have a much better quality of life now and fewer need to spend their lives in hospitals.

And now I come to the subject of prefrontal lobotomy which was used for hopeless psychiatric patients in those days. The procedure could and often did make a kitty cat out of a roaring lion, so to speak. A wild man could be reduced to a tame patient by this procedure. Such patients were obviously impaired to some degree by the separation of the prefrontal lobes of the brain from the remainder. The patients selected for the procedure were taken to the x-ray room and placed on the table and electric shock treatment was given to the patient and following the convulsion a second shock was delivered and a second seizure followed. After the two seizures, the patient was then anesthetized well enough to do the procedure. A long thin knife-like instrument was inserted into the brain at the base by entering the brain through the space between the upper eyelid and the eyeball. If a desired result was obtained, the patient who was so difficult to manage was calm and placid instead of in his constant mental turmoil resulting in loud, provocative and aggressive behavior.

Electric shock therapy was being used extensively in 1948, and we gave it two days a week on an open ward with perhaps thirty beds, fifteen on each side of the center aisle. We could go from one patient to another and deliver the shock and the convulsion would follow. There was minimal privacy obtained by a portable curtain. We moved from patient to patient giving shock treatments and by the time we reached the last patient he was pretty well in shock from having observed all of the activity ahead of him. But the electric shock treatments did work very well in some cases, especially manic depressive disease and in particular depressive disorders. It worked, it worked, it worked beautifully.

Back to the emergency room. One night when I was on duty there, a very well-dressed lady was brought in because of severe abdominal pain. She was approximately forty-five years old. She had had cramping abdominal pain for several hours and finally gave in to come to the doctor. She consented for the examination and was made ready by the nurse. I went into the room and just as I was coming in I found her twisting and turning and moaning with abdominal pain. In about a minute she quit this and lay perfectly quiet and apparently the pain was gone. When I pulled down the sheets I saw that she was very distended in the abdomen and I thought perhaps we had a case of intestinal obstruction. I took the medical history and began my examination. She had never had anything like this before and the pain was coming intermittently. I put my hands on her abdomen and I couldn't believe what I was feeling. I actually felt something hard and then whatever it was began to move and then it dawned on me that this forty-five-year-old lady who claimed never to have had a pregnancy was not only pregnant, but she was in active and hard labor. Vaginal examination revealed that she was fully dilated and ready for the delivery room. I told the couple what the problem was and of course they could not accept that. She had never conceived before and had assumed she never would. I let the husband feel her abdomen and feel the baby's movements and listen to the heartbeat. He, of course, finally was convinced but I don't think she still was. Nevertheless, we took her up to the obstetrical floor and delivery soon was accomplished. To say that she was amazed and surprised would be the understatement of the year. However, in time when it finally dawned on them that they were parents their joy was overflowing. This seems like a fish tale but so help me it really happened.

I was assigned to the syphilis department for a month. We had syphilis in all degrees of severity, primary, secondary and tertiary. Tertiary syphilis consisted of central nervous system involvement either with the spinal cord or brain or both. It was a horrible killer and the patient often suffered from hopeless psychosis and sometimes total paralysis. We gave bismuth and mapharsen by injection into the hip for sometimes two to three years. At times we gave typhoid fever vaccine to induce very high fevers in cases of brain syphilis in order to try to "cook" the germ in the central nervous system. I was giving hip shots one day to a group of patients going from bed to bed. We were using mapharsen. I had the habit of putting the palm of my hand on the patient's buttocks and then using my other hand to deliver the shot like throwing a dart. This would let it go deep into the muscle but not too deep. On one occasion, I threw the dart and penetrated my hand and pinned it to a lady's butt. Now that really did present a problem. If I pulled it out of my hand I would contaminate my hand with syphilitic blood and I really didn't want to get syphilis. So, I removed the needle from the patient's anatomy and got ahold of one of the maintenance crew members who came up to the ward with a wire cutter and then we cut off the needle that had penetrated the patient and relieved me of the possibility of contamination. I then removed the remainder of the needle from my hand and I hoped all was well and evidently it was. When the word got around the hospital it was the talk of the place for a time although I didn't think it was very funny.

The summer of 1948 was hot beyond description. No air conditioning, even the operating rooms were like bake ovens. During a surgery, one nurse did nothing but wipe the brows of the staff members to keep us from dropping sweat into the wounds. Every now and then if she didn't get to us in time, sweat would drop into the open surgical wound. Flies were chased around the operating room by a nurse with a fly swatter and sometimes we managed to get them killed before they landed in surgical wounds. We were not always successful, however. Elective surgery was delayed and emergencies only were done on the hottest of days.

I was assisting one day with a pneumonectomy. That is the removal of a lung, and we were doing it for cancer. The cancer was near the root of the lung or the hilum, as we call it, and it was a difficult case. After the lung was removed it became obvious that the cancer had penetrated a portion of the pericardium which is a sac around the heart. In order to do the surgery properly, we had to remove that portion of the pericardium in order to give the patient a chance for survival. We did remove a sufficiently large chunk of pericardial sac to accomplish the job but we could not close the wound because to do so we would have snugged the sac too tightly on the beating heart and prevent its adequate functioning and so it was left open. As we concluded the closure of the chest, we moved the patient from the operating room to the stretcher and at this moment he up and died. In those days, we knew nothing about CPR and so when you died, you died. An autopsy was done that afternoon and to our amazement the beating heart had slipped through the hole in the pericardium, got stuck outside and the great vessels were squeezed like a noose around one's neck and effectively cut off the circulation.

I suppose if all the tales were told of Philadelphia General Hospital from its inception to its destruction not too long ago, the libraries of Philadelphia would be full of books. I had done enough, I had experienced enough, and I had had my fill. I wanted to move on and so I did to Uncle Sam's Navy as a medical officer. I wanted to see the world and I did see part of it. I had a ball!

—4—
Salem, Indiana

Virginia

Our paths crossed when Virginia was babysitting for Peggy Sue, daughter of my Aunt Virgie and her husband, Dr. Robert Ellmore, who lived in Virginia's home town of Salem, Indiana. I lived in Louisville, Kentucky, and Virginia lived forty miles away. Nevertheless, we were together occasionally during our high school days. We went to separate colleges and we drifted apart. We saw each other again a few years later when I was a junior in medical school at the University of Louisville and she was home in Salem on vacation from the Yale University School of Nursing. Quite suddenly, we saw one another in a new light and this time we did not part. A year later we were married in the First Christian Church of Salem. For a number of years we lived in New Haven, Connecticut; Philadelphia, Pennsylvania; San Diego, California; Long Beach, California; Louisville, Kentucky; and then in the mountains of Kentucky. We are now living out our lives in the house next door to the church where we were married forty-three years ago. Washington County, Indiana, is the place of our roots and often birds do come home to roost. We live in sight of Virginia's girlhood home and we occupy the 118-year-old house that her grandfather built.

Most doctors' wives have had to "put up with a lot" in order to keep their stability. They have to accept sharing their husband with the world and this is an impossible task for some wives. To Virginia I give high marks for her record. She has "put up" with a lot, has stuck it out with me through thick and thin. She, too, experienced a year of clinical depression after the birth of our first child and a "too soon" pregnancy thereafter. Furthermore, at that time I was aboard a Navy ship expecting to go to Korea. It was a very tough year. There was no medicine for depression and she received no counseling, no nothing. She simply gritted her teeth, went on despite it all, and she recovered. She is tough.

Virginia and I spent twenty years in rural Appalachia where family living was difficult because of transportation problems, distant schools and church, and the living in relative isolation. On occasion she was scrub nurse for me in surgery while we were at Homeplace Hospital. She was also county school nurse for a period of time and visited children in the rural schools of Perry County. Through the years Virginia has worked intermittently in the office of Salem, carrying out the usual chores of office nursing. She has been supportive of church activities and has been available for leadership roles many times. Virginia's mother, Lennie Berkey, has been referred to as the saint of Salem. Virginia, I must confess, looks like her mother, and in many ways is truly her mother's daughter. She is loved and respected by her husband, her children and her community. During my periods of clinical depression she has pushed and shoved and encouraged me to go on when I thought I couldn't. I did go on and I succeeded and surely I share that success with Virginia and without her encouragement I just might not have made it.

Some People I've Known

Wherever one lives for any length of time certain people will stand out and live on in our memory. We somewhat affectionately refer to them as "characters." I am now in my sixteenth year as a physician in this southern Indiana county and have known several who would qualify as "characters."

Bill came to the office with a belly ache and after examination it was clear that he needed a thorough going over in order to make a diagnosis. He reluctantly agreed to go into the hospital. The first thing that happened after his admission was a good scrub down and clean up by the nurse's aide. After the diagnostic workup, old Bill was found to have gallstones and he agreed to surgery. Surgery was eventually carried out and the post operative course was smooth until the fifth day. All the patients who have had their gallstones removed have some of the stones given to them in a bottle sitting on their bedside table. Everyone is usually happy with this arrangement including the doctor who can brag, the patient who can brag about withstanding the ordeal, and the visitors who are curious. On this particular day, old Bill asked for some pain pills. The nurse said she would go and get him some. When the nurse returned to Bill's bed she noticed that the bottle containing the gallstones was empty. The nurse asked him about it. He looked up sort of puzzled and said he had already swallowed his pain pills and why was she bringing him some more. The unlikely, if not impossible, had actually happened and Bill had swallowed his gallstones down, thinking they were pain pills. When he realized what he had done he was real upset about it, not so much that he had swallowed the gallstones, but that he didn't have any more to show off. So we went back to surgery and we found a few gallstones we had saved back and brought them to him and put them in the bottle and he was real happy.

I had been in my Salem office only a few days when Jim came into the waiting room and told my receptionist that he had an urgent situation and that he had to see the doctor immediately. He would not tell the nature of his problem, but he was exceedingly agitated and wild eyed. The girl up front agreed that there must be some sort of emergency and so she came back and informed me as to the situation. I saw him quickly. Old Jim was an alcoholic having withdrawal symptoms at the moment. He told me he needed $25 right away because there were two men out in the car waiting for him and that if he didn't pay them the $25 they would kill him and he begged me for the $25. I thought about that for a while and realized that it might be a true story but he could be in the midst of the DT's or he might simply be trying to bum $25 off of me to get some more whiskey. I told him that I was $40,000 in debt, having just moved to Salem and bought the office and probably needed the money worse than he did. Furthermore, I told him that I was not running a lending institution and told him he better get on his way, whereupon he departed.

Every doctor has a patient or two or more who seems to be sick with one thing or another about fifty percent of the time. They are in and out of the office like they were caught in a revolving door. They appear for themselves, their spouse, their children and their grandchildren. It would seem that they function best and life is most rewarding when there is illness. If the illness is minor, they manage somehow to fan it into flames and make it major. Such a patient's record can be voluminous. There are patients who are sick much of the time for reasons that are obvious and beyond their control. These patients hate every minute of their illness and hate to bother the doctor. These poor sufferers are in no way to be compared to the patients who are ''sick'' all the time and seem to enjoy every minute of it. These ''sick'' people function at their best in an atmosphere of illness. They get attention, and they avoid certain responsibilities. They are at their best when they are able to manage the lives of family members when they are ill.

Johnny was loved by all. He was known by all in the community and was universally respected. He was found to have cancer of the stomach and he didn't have long to live. He accepted his fate with equanimity and without complaint. He was in and out of the hospital several times toward the end. The hospital staff loved him just as all in the community loved him. It was easy to be nice to Johnny. This is in contradistinction to some patients who are so difficult that no one wants to be around them. Johnny's last admission came and he was asked by the nurse if he had any valuables to check into the safe. Johnny fumbled around his things and finally admitted that he had spent all his money and that he had nothing left of any value except maybe his shorts, and come to think of it, considering all of the indignities that a man has to accept during a hospital stay, I do believe old Johnny had a point. A man's shorts are valuable indeed while in the hospital.

Billy came into the office one day with pain and a full feeling in his right ear. He couldn't hear very well, either. I got Billy to lie down on the examination table and I looked into the ear with my trusty otoscope. What I saw was a reddish brown sac-like object completely filling the ear canal. I took an instrument and sort of touched it or poked at it and it seemed to be soft. I poked a little bit harder and something ruptured and dark bloody material came out. To my amazement I discovered that it was a tick full of blood which had embedded itself in Billy's ear. And so I commenced pulling bits and pieces of tick out, piecemeal like, until I got down to the head and then pulled it loose and with it came out a chunk of tissue. When I saw up close what I had done I feared that I might have pulled a portion of the eardrum out and I can tell you it was a moment of subdued panic on the inside of me. I cleaned the ear out as best I could but it was still bleeding and I knew I couldn't do much more. I let him go home and he came back the next day, everything had subsided and I thoroughly cleaned out the ear, and much to my relief, the eardrum was intact and that flesh was a piece of skin from along side the ear canal which would quickly heal.

Sue came to work for me having previously been a hospital nurse. She was tired of the hours at the hospital and wanted to work daytime in a doctor's office because of the convenience

I told her that the hours would be much better, but that very little excitement occurred in the doctor's office compared to the hospital. She understood that and was quite willing to make the switch since she had seen enough excitement at the hospital over the period of years. Anyhow, on her first day of duty at the office, things were going smoothly, when we got a call that Mae was coming in by taxi and that her heart was acting up. A few minutes later, a cab pulled quickly into my carport in back and the cab driver came in at once and suggested I get myself out there immediately. I could tell by the look on his face that he wasn't kidding. I went out and I found Mae slumped over in the back of the taxi. There was no respiration and no pulse. I dragged her out onto the carport floor and started CPR. I did the chest compression while the cab driver did the respiratory activity. She quickly responded and began to breathe spontaneously, her pulse became perceptible and a detectable blood pressure was obtained. The hospital ambulance was called and it quickly got her to the coronary unit at the Washington County Hospital. She did beautifully, recovered from this episode, and is still doing well and it has been perhaps two years. At the end of the day, Sue asked me what sort of a no-excitement day we would have on her next day of duty. It is certainly true and it has been said many times that when a doctor opens his office, he never quite knows what is going to come in the front door and maybe it is a good thing he doesn't.

Gail

Gail, my daughter, backed into this world butt first on April 21, 1954, at Highland Baptist Hospital. Her shoulders were stuck and it was not an easy delivery, according to J. B. Marshall, M.D. Gail was reared in the mountains of Kentucky, went through high school in Hazard and married Mickey

Napier, a Hazard boy, soon after graduation from high school. After Mickey's near fatal accident, they came to live with us in Salem as we nursed Mickey back to health.

Luke, my son-in-law, and I were practicing together when Gail became pregnant and Gail insisted that we take care of her during her pregnancy and delivery. I had not done obstetrics for at least ten years, since my Kentucky experience, but with Luke in Salem to help me, I had already decided to start obstetrical practice. I wasn't terribly thrilled with the idea of taking on my daughter as my first patient after this many years, but she insisted and, so be it, that was the way it was. That turned out to be a bad decision. Gail's pregnancy was uneventful but her delivery was eventful. She did not progress well, the pains were weak and inadequate, and so a Pitocin drip was started which was effective in bringing her labor around to third base, you might say. However, between third and home plate, we got stuck and she simply could not rotate the baby from an occiput transverse position to an occiput anterior and get it on down so that we could get the forceps on and do an extraction. And so the surgeon was called and the operating room was made ready on that particular Sunday morning and at about Sunday school time the incision was made and Michael Andrew Napier was born, healthy, hale and hardy. I assisted at the delivery and Luke took care of the baby. Gail had an uneventful recovery, but I determined that that would be the last of my children that I would attempt to deliver.

After the baby was well established, Gail came to work for her doctor daddy as office manager in 1981. That was a good decision. Gail has functioned extremely well, has done her job expertly and accurately, is well accepted, even loved by the patients and is generally professional with her daddy. I am happy with my decision. I hope she is.

In 1984, once again Gail was pregnant, and this time the pregnancy was complicated. She bled intermittently during the gestational period and a placenta previa centralis was diagnosed by ultrasound. This means that the afterbirth or placenta was positioned at the outlet of the uterus, making it impossible for her to have a normal delivery. A repeat section would be accomplished anyhow, because of her initial caesarean section. The problem was that she bled off and on during this pregnancy and had a very sharp hemorrhage toward the end of the eighth month. She was admitted as an emergency to Clark County Hospital in Jefferson, Indiana, where she remained in bed, resting for the entire month. This was a long and difficult time of course but was necessary. On the appointed day for her caesarean section, she was taken to surgery and the baby delivered without incident. Then the trouble started. The placenta was removed with difficulty and of course was in the lower uterine segment instead of the other where it normally should be placed. There was more bleeding than usual and the uterus failed to clamp down properly. Because of the unavoidable injury to the uterus in removing the placenta and because of the failure of the uterus to contract properly, bleeding continued despite all measures to control it. Furthermore, to make matters even worse, she developed DIC Syndrome, which means that the clotting mechanism is seriously impaired in the body. To deal with this obstetrical nightmare, blood clotting factors called cryoprecipitate are given in order to enable the blood to begin to coagulate properly. Bag after bag was given and unit after unit of blood was given. Gail was conscious throughout this time but was extremely weak and fully aware of the dangers involved. Afternoon and night came and still things were not under control. She continued to bleed. Her vital signs were weak and so was she. By midnight, the doctor let me know that the only hope was an emergency hysterectomy in order to stop the bleeding. In her weakened condition, of course, this would be a hazardous undertaking. I had talked with Gail off and on during these hours but the last talk before the final surgery was one I shall never forget. I simply told Gail that the likelihood of her tolerating the surgery was pretty good but there were no guarantees. I kissed her, had a brief prayer and left. Other family members and pastor John Hart saw her briefly. John was with us all the way. Dr. Mayhue asked me to come into surgery and I reluctantly did so. It is a different ballgame when your own daughter is caught up in the drama.

The anesthesia and the surgery were smooth and she slid through with blood going in both arms. She had fifteen units of blood; in all fifty bags of cryoprecipitate given. Barring another complication Gail would likely live to rear her baby and continue her life.

The wonderful relief and joy that comes with the realization that you have won the battle after staring death in the face is an experience too precious to find words to describe. Thank God. Thank Dr. Mayhue. Thank the anesthetist. Thank the scrub and circulating nurses. Thank the CCU nurses. Thank the Red Cross for the blood and thank the hospital staff in general. Is modern medicine and treament and surgery expensive? Very. But to save the life of your daughter is worth any price that it might require.

■————————————————————————■

I Love This Place, I Love This Place

Tonight I am at the lake house. It is February. The night is cold. A light snow is falling and a wonderful fire is warming me and keeping me company. I love that fire, so cozy, so bright, so cheery. This place is secluded from the world. It is quiet. No television, minimal phone calls. No dogs barking, quiet and peaceful. I do love this place, I do, I do.

I am busy all day seeing a lot of patients and trying to diagnose, treat and relieve suffering, tension and fear. Doctoring is a stressful occupation, just ask any doctor. Yes, we are paid well and maybe we, like others, are paid more than we are worth. Who is to say? Nevertheless, stress is real and it takes its toll. Emotional ills, drug dependency, alcoholism and suicide claim a greater than average number of doctors. Some of us handle our stress in one way and some in another. Some are at the mercy of their stress and attempt to cope in very bad ways.

My coping mechanisms have not been the best, I must confess. Stress has been handled by me by working full throttle. The workaholic, I believe, is simply immersed in work because he wants to be and because his anxiety is actually relieved somewhat by work, work, work. Of course, this brings on more stress and an impossible situation can arise and often does in such an instance.

I have also attempted to cope with stress by being involved with the church and pursuing a Christian lifestyle. My social contacts have been largely through the framework of the church and there I have opportunity to assume leadership and responsible roles.

Getting away from some of the battle helps. The fire and smoke of medical battles I can escape by coming to my lake house. I can't listen to anyone, I don't see anyone. I rarely hear the phone. I don't hear noise, no barking dogs, no cars, no TV, wonderful! Only the cracking of the fire. It is beautiful at this spot, my Garden of Eden. The lake is lovely year around, refreshing in summer, snow and ice in the winter, glorious shores in the fall, and in the spring coming alive with animal and plant life. We who love it here say that if you are fortunate when you die you go to heaven, but if you are really lucky you go to the lake to spend eternity.

■————————————————————————■

Luke

James Douglas Lukins, M.D. is the man I refer to affectionately as "Luke." When I first met him, he was the fiance of my oldest girl, Carol Ann. He was a medical student at Indiana University. He was born in Key West, Florida, reared in Jeffersonville, Indiana, and was a bright student and a good athlete. Carol Ann and Luke got married in June 1973, following his graduation from medical school. They spent several weeks in Europe after that on a holiday and had a ball. Returning to Indianapolis, internship was begun.

Big problems soon arose. Luke's behavior became unusual and he was not the same. He was becoming withdrawn and did not exhibit the expected intimacy toward Carol Ann. He grew a heavy beard which seemed inappropriate. One day Carol noticed some lumps in his neck, despite the beard's cover up and she asked the usual questions. He obviously pushed the questions aside and said they were only sebaceous cysts, entirely harmless. Further, he said he had been to the doctor and had this confirmed. The weeks passed, the cysts became larger, and Carol insisted that he have surgery. He agreed, but simply did not get it done. He continued withdrawn, quiet and his general behavior was different. He was not the same Luke she had married. Finally, Carol Ann insisted he set a date to see the surgeon and so he did, but he didn't go after all. He had another excuse. He had two or three more dates set up, but each time there was an excuse for cancelling. In exasperation, Carol Ann told him that she was going to call his doctor and find out what on earth was going on, whereupon Luke suggested that they sit down and talk the matter over. The story that unfolded was absolutely unbelievable. Luke was caught in the jaws of a profound depression. He had noticed the lumps three months after their marriage. He knew, beyond the shadow of a doubt, that he had the dreaded killer, Hodgkin's Disease, or at least he was almost sure. He decided he was going to die and that if Carol Ann found out about his disease she would abandon him. So he decided not to tell anyone, but to live a life of denial and wait for the killer to run its course. He grew a beard to cover his lumps. He withdrew from intimacy with Carol Ann in order to avoid her discovery of his disease. The "internship" was a fabrication. Rather than go to the hospital, he spent the day here, there, and yonder, just anywhere but the hospital. He had never consulted a doctor at all.

Carol Ann called us on the phone and she could hardly talk for the tears. The unbelievable story rolled out, and so a date was set for Luke to see his oncologist friend, Dr. Bates, in Indianapolis. After examination, Luke proved to be right about one thing. It was Hodgkin's Disease and it was far advanced. Despite this, chemotherapy was still appropriate and could still possibly be very beneficial, even the remote possibility of saving his life, even after this long delay. And so chemotherapy was begun at once, and it began to work immediately. The lumps, which were by this time widespread, began to melt away as if by magic. He felt better, his strength returned, his depression lifted and he started residency at St. Francis Hospital in Indianapolis. He completed his first year of the three in the program and decided to join me in practice rather than continue the entire program. His time might be cut short and he was eager to get started. He trimmed his beard and cut his long hair and he looked great.

To Salem they came in 1978, and we began our practice together. Two peas in a pod could not possibly have been more different. The only thing we had in common was the fact that we were both reasonably intelligent and ambitious, but from thereon we were different. Nevertheless, the partnership worked because we made it work. We rotated our hours in the office and rotated rounds at the hospital. In essence, there were two doctors who covered the same large practice. That was a difficult chore and that was a difficult assignment, especially for two doctors who were so different in personality. Together we were seeing 400 patients a week at the office and eighteen to twenty patients a day at the hospital. We were assisting at surgery and delivering babies. We rotated nights and weekends on call. We were busy, busy, busy. We had a ball. I gave Luke his chemotherapy by intravenous injection and each time a tight tourniquet was placed on his scalp to prevent the chemotherapy from going to his scalp and destroying his hair.

Carol Ann and Luke adjusted well in Salem and the practice flourished. He felt good and optimism carried us along. Douglas Edward Martin Lukins was born in 1980. Another miracle had entered Luke's life after the horror of the revelation of his disease two years before. His disease, by this time, was responding beautifully and he felt good. He enjoyed his practice. They put an addition on their house and their social life flourished.

Luke was intelligent, industrious and had the ability to be frank, forthright and "tell it like it is." He was admired by many nurses for this quality. On occasion, patients were offended by this bluntness. He had little sympathy for the whining, complaining female, or the stubborn male. On one occasion a man became rude and overbearing with Luke and Luke's anger boiled over and he literally chased the man out of the office.

After three years together, Luke left Salem to open his practice in Jeffersonville, Indiana. His health was stable and he felt secure. I think this decision may have come as a result of several factors. In the first place, young doctors working with older doctors present a real problem. Also, being second fiddle can be difficult for a doctor to accept and then, two doctors trying to manage one large practice in an integrated fashion is not easy. It is like a wife married to two husbands; problems are inevitable. Furthermore, Luke's home was Jeffersonville and his desire had always been eventually to be his own man in his own home town and do his own thing. In June 1981, therefore, he opened his office in Jeffersonville with his mother as his receptionist and a nurse to assist him. Things did not go well. The practice was slow in getting started. He came to Salem one day a week in order to help his income and assist me at the same time. He was showing signs, by this time, of fatigue and not feeling as well. In December of 1982, his first major illness descended upon him. A mosquito bite became a rattlesnake bite, so to speak. He caught chicken pox. Normally, chicken pox is no problem to us, but in Luke's case with his immune depressed state, because of his disease and his treatment, he was overwhelmed. The virus caused pancreatitis, pneumonia and extensive eruption. He ended up on a respirator in a critical care unit for several days. This was literally a "hell of an experience." An anti-viral antibiotic given intravenously saved him from certain death. He slowly fought his way back to partial recovery but he was never the same after this. Although he worked part-time, he simply couldn't get his practice off the ground. He spent another horrible week in the critical care unit of Methodist Hospital on a respirator with further complications. He spent his last months in our home in Salem. The last hospitalization was in December 1983, and he came by ambulance back to our home, profoundly weak, discouraged and debilitated. He made it home just in time for Christmas on a wing and a prayer, so to speak. The last Christmas was spent with Luke in bed observing and entering in as best as he could to the festivities. It was a happy time, but mostly a sad time for all of us. The disease and the irradiation had taken their toll on him and his lung function was greatly impaired. Pain was not a major problem, thank God. He was reduced to skin and bones and was on oxygen constantly and in bed most of the time. Television was a godsend to him. He didn't enjoy a lot of company and it was hard for Luke to give and receive love. It always had been. His last day was June 30, 1984. He awoke that morning very short of breath and profoundly weak. He knew his time was getting close. We discussed together whether we would go to the hospital or not. He knew it would mean a respirator again and the experience was literally "hell." He made his decision to ride it out at home, come what may, and so he did. He soon mercifully lapsed into a coma from pulmonary failure and he died peacefully that afternoon. And so at forty, a young doctor was taken from us, a husband and a father. The cruelty of cancer is beyond our ability to describe. Only one who has been through it could make an adequate description of the ordeal, but for them it is too late to do so. Carol Ann remained courageous and faithful and at Luke's side throughout the entire ordeal. She was strong and courageous. We were all proud of her. The funeral was held in Salem, in the First Christian Church and John B. Hart officiated in a loving and appropriate manner. The church house was packed. Friends came from Jeffersonville, Louisville, Indianapolis and many other places.

He was well respected in his profession, had many friends and the tragedy of a young doctor leaving prematurely always evoked sympathy. In preparing the message, John asked me for any input that I might want to add. I gave him a letter that I had written to Luke on his last Christmas. John was impressed by the message in the letter and felt it would be an appropriate addition to the funeral message. He asked my permission to read it in its entirety. Permission was granted, of course, and so as a final testimony to Luke's life, from my own heart, here is my letter to Luke on Christmas 1983, the last one he enjoyed.

To My Dear Son Luke:

I am going to start off this letter by calling you my son, Luke, because in reality, it sort of seems that way. I think both of us can fit into this role without any hesitation and so I am taking that liberty. This is perhaps the most memorable Christmas that I have ever experienced and the reasons are obvious. The fact that you can be with us is gift enough for me, I need no other. As I was going to the hospital the other night, I heard the old familiar refrain of the Christmas song, "I'll be home for Christmas." As I listened to the notes and as I realized you were up there in the Methodist Hospital, a wave of sadness swept over me that was almost overwhelming. At that time, we didn't think you would be home. And so your presence with us is a real gift, and for that we are grateful.

Luke, you know and I know that unless the unexpected miracle occurs, we will not be together for another Christmas, and so on this Christmas I would like to share some thoughts with you while you are here with us. I want to say that I think you have done an amazing job with your life in many ways, living as you have the past ten years, with the knowledge that you have a fatal disease. You have functioned for the most part very well indeed, considering your entire situation. You have been able to provide for your family, you have helped me tremendously and you have been able to help many people. I can't even begin to tell you how many people in the past six months have told me that they have admired you for your intelligence, for your ability, for your forthrightness, for your directness and for your ability to tell it like it is. Of course, in the process, some tender souls have been offended, and this is understandable, but the majority of people with their feet on the ground, good solid citizens, have appreciated more than you can ever imagine, the way that you have conducted your practice. Day after day, here in the office, people have asked me to remember them to you and, of course, I can't remember them all. The entire town seems to be caught up in the drama of your illness from day to day.

There will be a memory that I shall always treasure and never forget and that occurred on two occasions at Methodist Hospital in the Intensive Care Unit. The first time was on, I believe, a Monday night, when you were in extremis, and we weren't sure from hour to hour what would happen. John Hart and I and you were hand in hand, and John prayed. That was a moment of intense emotion and I felt closer to you than I had ever felt before. Then, the second moment occurred approximately four months later when, in Intensive Care again, in the midst of your great suffering, the three of us were once again together for a similar purpose. These moments will linger in my treasure house of memories always.

The nurses at the hospital ask about you daily. You are greatly admired by many because of your abilities, your intelligence, but especially your willingness to be frank, forthright and tell it like it is. The latter characteristic is somewhat rare among doctors, and I think, greatly admired by nurses.

Luke, I am very grateful that my health has held out, and that I have been able to carry on, and it has been a pleasure and a privilege for me to be in a position to help you and Carol during this year of travail and suffering. As I see the strength leaving your body, I am continually grateful for what I have, and I hope to take good care of this body of mine for as long as my days are allotted. Some say it is a disadvantage to have one's children living so very close. I think just the opposite. It has been a marvelous experience for me to have all of you near and for all of us to be of mutual support and help during all life's joys and sorrows.

Little Doug has been a lifesaver to all of us. God bless him and keep him, and I can assure you that he is very precious to me personally. I pledge to you, without reservation, to stand behind him in every way I can. I am profoundly grateful, Luke, for your wife and my daughter, Carol Ann, and the wonderful way that she has held up through difficulty. If I do say so myself, she is a marvelous girl, and I am proud to be her father.

And finally, Luke, I'll end with this note: All of mankind yearns for something better beyond this life. It seems to be the way God has made us. I cannot imagine a God who has made a world of order and complexity such as this one, putting this universal hope within his children, and have it only to be a hoax and a dream. The scriptures are filled full of expectation of things to come beyond this life. All religions point in that direction. The hope of all men look in that direction. I personally believe, not only because of my religious heritage, but because of my common sense, God in his mercy has prepared something better beyond the sufferings of this world. By faith I accept this, and it helps to bear today's burdens.

And so, Luke, my son, it is wonderful to have you home for Christmas. The miracle of your possible recovery seems very far distant, and yet we look and we pray.

Affectionately,
Doc

Salem Visit, December 4, 1988
by Charles Hay, M.D. (1801-1888)
(A paper presented by Dr. Martin at the Stephens Museum, Salem, Indiana)

Good evening dear friends of Salem and Washington County. I am Dr. Charles Hay, father of my famous son, John Hay. John was, as you know, personal secretary to Abraham Lincoln, Secretary of State of the United States, and was instrumental in giving birth to the Panama Canal and the open door policy in China. I practiced medicine and surgery in Salem 158 years ago, arriving here in Salem only fifteen years after Salem was founded. Salem was a town of 400 at that time. Washington County was still largely forest, but farms and farm houses were rapidly being established. The Delaware Indians had lived in the area of Salem but had departed by 1812.

Houses were largely made of wood and they were heated by wood stoves. Light was obtained by lantern and candles. Water we obtained by collecting rain in cisterns. There was no indoor plumbing and toilets were outdoors in privys or latrines. Our food we grew and ate fresh or canned it and preserved it in other ways for later use. We had our own beef, pork and chickens for meat. Our cows gave us milk and milk products. Our women made much of our clothing although some could be purchased in stores. We had our general stores, churches, schools, courthouse, jail, blacksmiths and our mills, such as Spring Mill and Beck's Mill. We had our lawyers, teachers, merchants, farmers, clergy and doctors. We had large families and many children died prematurely.

I was born and reared near Lexington, Kentucky, and was educated at Transylvania College in that city. I spent nine months in study to get my medical degree, just prior to coming to Salem.

You may wonder why I am here for this occasion this afternoon. I wonder myself. I haven't been back to Salem since 1841. I practised in your town for eleven years. I was doctor for the poor for a while and I was there in Salem during the cholera epidemic of 1833. From Salem, I moved my family to Warsaw, Illinois, and remained there until my death. John was three when we moved and I have often wanted to return to Salem for a visit, but I never got this mission carried out in my former life on earth. How is it that I have been able to reach you, you may wonder? John has been present with you on many occasions since he left. I am pleased that you have honored him in so many ways. But I have never been with you. I have gone to several people in the past years trying to get your attention and wanting permission to use their body to come for a visit. I have been here in spirit but you could not see me nor could I really see you and sense your presence as I now can. Finally, only a few weeks ago I came to one of my own colleagues in the medical profession, Dr. Donald Martin, known to most, if not all of you, and I hoped I could get his attention. In as much as I was one of his colleagues and in as much as I attended a Disciple of Christ School, Transylvania University, and in as much as Dr. Martin is an elder in the Disciple of Christ Church, I thought that this might help and it did. He listened to me one night as I found him in his study at the office across the street from the museum. I let him know of my earnest desire to use his body this afternoon and tonight and to visit with you, to have a real visit, so that you could see me and I could see you, and he consented and became excited about the idea and called Willie Harlen and the arrangements were made. So, here I am. I look like Dr. Martin and talk like him, but for the moment Dr. Martin is out there with you in spirit while I occupy his body and visit with you. What I say to you tonight is from me and I am fully responsible for what is said tonight.

Frankly, it is a sheer delight to be with you. You look wonderful to me! I would love to speak and visit with each one of you privately, even to go to your house and get acquainted but alas, time does not permit. I have to be back on the other side by midnight and I have promised Dr. Martin he can be home by then.

I simply can't believe what I am seeing and experiencing here in Salem. When I left Salem the roads were dirt and gravel. The stores were small and simple. The schools were one or two or at the most three rooms. Our transportation was by horseback or buggy. Since being with you I have ridden in your fast automobiles, been to your hospital, gone through your schools and visited your churches and your jail. It is hard to believe that life can be so beautiful as you now have it. But you are all in such a rush! And you have so many older people. You have so many luxuries. Your televisions, your radios, your washing machines, your appliances around your home, your farm equipment, your airplanes, your war machines, and alas, your bombs, your hydrogen bombs. You have the power to destroy everything that your ancestors have so faithfully worked for and built. It is amazing to me that your lives are so complicated. In my day, we had so many children in our homes and many died young. Now you have so many old people but many are living in nursing facilities if you can call that living. I can hardly believe what I am seeing.

And, now let me tell you about the medical profession in 1830, when I arrived in Salem. There were twenty doctors in the county. No hospitals, no clinics, no nursing homes. We doctors visited and cared for our sick within their own homes mainly. Most people in my time didn't consult a doctor unless they were so sick that they couldn't possibly get out of their home. And so we went to them by horseback or by buggy or we walked if it was near. We doctors maintained our offices principally in our homes. Medical school required only nine to twelve months to complete and we had very few textbooks, only one or two. We treated illnesses, attended complicated labor cases and deliveries, repaired the injured as best we could. I did some surgery in the outbuilding behind my home across the way. I sewed up lacerations, set broken bones and occasionally performed amputations. We had no x-ray, no anesthesia and only a few medicines. We did have Laudanum made from the opium poppy similar to your morphine today. We had herb medicine in abundance. We had stimulants, laxatives, emetics or "pukes," purgatives, tonics, ointments. We had no means of fighting infection. We didn't understand even the cause of most diseases. We didn't know anything about germs and bacteria. We used bleeding therapy extensively and sometimes removed one, two or three pints of blood in an attempt to treat many illnesses. With a lancet, we cut a vein in the arm and allowed the blood to flow freely out. It seemed to help many conditions. It relieved pain and discomfort, quieted the restless and put many people into a restful and peaceful state, and as a matter of fact, a number of people were so relieved of their suffering by bleeding, that they went to sleep and sometimes, alas, did not even wake up again. Bleeding patients brought down high fevers, quieted the anxious and restless, relieved pain and we used it extensively.

In 1833, the great cholera epidemic was in full force in Salem. People who became ill on Monday were often dead before the weekend. It was a horrible killer. It had spread over Asia, Europe and was rapidly spreading across America. The illness was characterized by profuse vomiting, persistent diarrhea, profound weakness, high fever and finally dehydration and then often death. We knew not the cause of the disease. We only recognized certain diseases by the symptoms presented and we had no x-ray, no laboratory and no tests to find out what was happening to patients. We did the best we could to help to relieve suffering, to be concerned, to be a help and a friend to our patients.

I was called to the home of John Mitchell, on North Main Street, to see his daughter, Melissa. She was ten years old. We had already lost eighty people in Salem from cholera within two weeks. John Mitchell's older son came for me and I left as soon as I could. Although I often rode horseback, on this occasion, John sent for me and I went with his son in his buggy. I found Melissa very ill indeed with a fever of 105, vomiting repeatedly, having diarrhea uncontrollably. I administered Laudanum for the relief of pain and cramping, gave her an enema of special preparation for cholera and took from her a pint of blood. Her suffering was relieved and she lay motionless and she seemed to be much better. Her fever went down and she slept peacefully. The following day I received the grim news of her death at 4:00 in the morning. Little did I realize then that what I did hastened her death. There were so many dying we had no time for funerals. Coffins were being made as fast as they could be prepared. Three or four were buried every day. Crown Hill Cemetery was used primarily. Of those who died, there were over 100. Half of the town was ill and those who escaped were in a state of panic and fear. The epidemic lasted six to eight weeks and then vanished. Salem was never the same. Many moved away and very few settled here afterwards. I stayed on another eight years but moved to Illinois because of the family and because of the blight upon Salem brought about by the cholera. Salem never recovered while I was there.

Before I leave you, one more story. The grinding mill stone mechanism at Beck's Mill had broken down and urgent repairs were being made. Business was booming and time was of utmost importance. The top grinding stone was lifted up four feet by hoists and the repairman was under it working away. Suddenly the hoist broke and the huge stone came crashing down and caught and crushed the right arm of the repairman from above the elbow to the hand. They wrapped the mangled arm in feed sacks and brought him to me in a wagon. He was in agony and his color was pale. His skin was cold and he was sweating. He obviously had lost much blood. The sacks were soaked in blood. I had him carried to the outbuilding behind the house and placed on the table. I sent for my surgical helpers, six blacksmiths in Salem, who, whenever possible, answered my call for help. As they assembled, we washed and cleaned the extremity and the surgical tools were laid out. Three men on each side of the patient stationed themselves and he was secured by belt restraints to the table lest he break away during the amputation. The entire forearm, hand and elbow were damaged beyond repair and bone exposed and crushed in pieces. The tourniquet was placed high on the arm and the fishmouth incision was made through the skin and fat down to the muscle. There was no shriek of pain, only quiet moaning and beads of perspiration on his face. Next, the muscles were cut through to the bone, above the skin incision. There was minimal bleeding and the tourniquet was holding. Quickly, the bone was sawed in two and the men had to restrain him as he struggled in pain. Next, the arteries were ligated with heavy thread and the tourniquet released. More bleeding was encountered and these bleeders were clamped and ligated with thread. The muscle was closed and the skin edges proximated with heavy cotton thread. The entire procedure took less than fifteen minutes. The fast surgeons in my day were the most popular ones for obvious reasons. The patient was given Laudanum as he required it for pain in the post operative period. The wound healed very well without mortification. He was taken home the following morning. He fully recovered.

I must leave you now and return to the other world. You all sooner or later will be joining me. Let me tell you that the outstanding emotion that all have who come to this land beyond the river is the element of surprise and amazement. It is an altogether different life and one that cannot be adequately described. It is like a family reunion, the place you refer to as heaven. Love, acceptance and mutuality exist. You are loved as you are. It doesn't matter if you are rich or poor, bright or dull, an important person or a nobody, black or white. We are nourished there in part by memories of our life on earth. When our lives have been productive and we have stored up good memories it does help. Yet, on the other hand, those who have suffered the most on earth in a very special way, seem to enjoy heaven in a unique and special way.

I have experienced Salem as it was in the 1830's and now I see it and have experienced it 150 years later. Having lived eighty-one years on earth and 104 years in the afterworld, let me leave you with these words. Allow me to use the words of the Apostle Paul and I quote, "For now we see through a glass darkly, but then face to face. Now I know in part but then shall I know even as also I am known and now abideth faith, hope, and love, but the greatest of these is love."

When you reach the end of life's road, the only thing that really matters is how much of yourself you have given away to your family, your friends and to your fellow man. You can't take anything with you to this place. Only what you have shared of yourself with others really counts. I urge you in the time you have left to tear down fences, accept and even love those who are different from you. Try to bring peace where there is conflict. Bring comfort where there is sorrow and help someone carry a heavy load.

My flight does not depart until midnight and so I will have some time to visit with you. Please come by and speak. And finally, I wish to thank Dr. Martin for the use of his body and his brain in making this visit with you and I want to thank each one of you, my dear Salem friends, for this visit and for taking time to come and share with me a portion of yourself.

Cardiac Arrest in the Pew

Occasionally I have been asked through the years to bring the sermon in church when the minister was absent. This I have always enjoyed, have usually spoken from notes with relative ease, and I think the congregation listened well because I was coming from a different world than the usual man "of the cloth." On the particular Sunday of this awesome event, I had finished my twenty-five minute sermon and we were singing the closing hymn. As is customary in the Disciples of Christ Churches, I was standing facing the congregation as the usual and customary invitation is given to anyone to embrace the Christian way and enter the congregation by way of membership. Suddenly and without warning, one of our church members near the front pew fell forward over the bench in front of her in obvious cardiopulmonary arrest. I quickly went to her, dragged her into the aisle and started CPR. The congregation was dismissed and the ambulance and the EMT's soon arrived. On to the hospital we went, a two-minute run, while still giving CPR. We got her to the emergency room, intubated her, and got her going. She lived three days in the coronary care unit but never did regain consciousness. She actually died in the place where she had worked tirelessly for years and years in leadership roles. The church was her home so to speak and it was her last earthly experience.

How many of us ever give a thought to the place where we will be when we breathe our last? I don't suppose many of us do give this a thought whenever we are in good health. If we are ill and have a diagnosis of death upon us, no doubt we think from time to time where our last moments will be spent. My mother-in-law was found on her couch one day as if peacefully alseep, although it was her last sleep. My father lingered for four years in the local nursing home in a vegetative state before he died. My son-in-law died in our family room where he had lived for many months.

We traditionally have regarded death as our greatest enemy. And so it may be. The tragedy of a child who is killed accidentally, the soldier who dies on the battlefield, the young doctor who succumbs at the threshhold of his career to cancer, the teenager caught in the grips of a depression who finally pulls the trigger. But nevertheless, so often death is our friend. So many aged in our nursing homes live from day to day in a demented state and await the death angel. They are kept alive by all sorts of medical activities which, in my opinion, are inhumane to say the least. I think death will be a friend if I am stricken with incurable cancer and in great pain day after day. I think death would be the friend of the person with end-stage emphysema and kept alive on a respirator. I think death is a friend of the hopeless schizophrenic living huddled in the corner of a mental hospital unable to give or receive the human touch of kindness and fearful of everyone, tormented with hallucinations and delusions. I am sure death has been the friend of the victims of torture through the centuries. To Jesus of Nazareth, dying the death of immeasurable cruelty, death had to be a relief as he uttered, "Father, into thy hands I commend my spirit."

All things have a beginning and an ending. And so if there is birth, there will be death. If there is a cradle, there will be a grave. If there is a start, there will be a finish. I wonder how many people in the western world having lived lives where there was opportunity, with sufficient provisions for the good life, can look back at the twilight of life and feel fulfilled and satisfied with their lives and accomplishments. Would it be a minority? Would it be a majority? I wonder.

Thus far, I feel good about my life and that makes me glad. I have family, friends and good health. I have achieved many of my goals. I have worked with a significant handicap and made the best of it. I have had illumination in a dark world by religious faith and lifestyle. To date, I believe I can truthfully say as did the great Christian missionary, the Apostle Paul, "I have fought a good fight, I have kept the faith," but I have not yet finished the course. I recognize that the game of life is not over till the last whistle. I hope I don't make a fatal mistake enroute from third base to home. All of life has its dangerous times, and the latter part is no exception. I believe that my chances of receiving a trophy at the end of life's race will in a large part depend on how many I have helped along life's road to receive theirs.

■————————————————————■

—5— Here, There and Yonder

USS Delta AR9 1950-1951

My very first experience as a fully-trained medical doctor came after my internship at the Philadelphia General Hospital. I was a commissioned medical officer in the United States Navy. I had joined the Navy, voluntarily, during my internship and was commissioned a lieutenant junior grade and was allowed to complete my training at the Philadelphia General Hospital. I was on full pay, on active duty and assigned to the hospital. I was still in civilian clothes. What a fantastic deal! Having existed on zero salary as an intern, to suddenly be the recipient of a monthly check was financial heaven! After the internship, my first orders directed me to report to the chief of staff at the US Naval Hospital, Philadelphia, Pennsylvania, and I spent four months there working in the orthopedic outpatient department. It seems I saw a thousand sore backs a day and I gave the same speech over and over again like a broken record. To distinguish between a malingerer and a truly painful back has always presented a problem for the conscientious military doctor. For some hard nosed docs it was no big deal. If a guy could manage to walk into the office, complaining of his back, then he was sent back to duty. If he was carried in, he might possibly be given some consideration. Next patient, please!

After four months of looking at backs, I got my orders to report to the commanding officer of the USS Delta AR9. This was an auxiliary ship, a repair ship, and was in the moth ball fleet, tucked away in preservation after World War II. The Korean conflict was raging and the United States was back at war. Ships were recommissioned, military installations were re-opened, and reserve officers and men were brought back into active duty again, and many of them had been exposed to the horrors and deprivations of World War II. It took us six months to get that ship squared away and ship shape and operating smoothly. The officers lived and ate above deck, the crew below deck. The chief petty officers were forward below deck to themselves. The medical department was adequate: treatment rooms, operating room, a ward for inpatients with two-tiered bunks for beds attached to the bulkheads (walls). There was my office, the chief pharmacist mate's office, and the pharmacy. I had ten men under my supervision and command. No females in those days were aboard ship.

There being no chaplain aboard the Delta gave some of us officers and men an idea. We formed a group of those interested in religious matters and I became the leader and hence the chaplain. And so, for a year, we had "divine services" aboard the ship and I brought a sermon and led the worship. One of the men played the hand organ and we sang from books which had been stowed away after World War II. We had a communion set, an altar, and on occasion, we celebrated the Lord's Supper. The print shop prepared a bulletin for us each Sunday for services. The word got around the ship that if you went on sick call, all Doc Martin would do for you was to pray. I must confess some of those birds needed prayers more than pills for sure.

In January 1951, the ship left Philadelphia, cruised to Norfolk Naval Base, and anchored out in the bay. Burr! The cold blasts of wind cut across those decks unmercifully during the month. Going ashore on liberty meant a small boat ride from the ship to shore. One day a coxswain on the captain's gig (boat) fell overboard into the icy waters of Norfolk Bay. To the sick bay he came and he was dried off and allowed to stay with us a brief spell until he could get over his exposure problems. He received the old Navy tradition, a two ounce bottle of brandy from the brandy locker to warm him up. He quickly recovered and went back on duty. From here on the story is unbelievable, but so help me, I am telling it as it was. Two weeks later, the same guy was dragged to the sick bay again, soaked from head to toe having fallen overboard again. We went through the same routine and he got his brandy and he departed. A short while later, yes, it's true, the same coxswain was brought into the sick bay area having suffered again from exposure when he fell headlong into the water. But I was ashore this time and wasn't available and the brandy locker was locked up and I had the key. And so the pharmacist mate scratched his head and wondered what he might give him in the place of brandy. He decided elixir of terpin hydrate with codeine would be an excellent medicine to warm him up, this being a standard cough syrup, and when it went down, it really lit you up. And so he gave him two ounces of elixir of terpin hydrate with codeine the same as he would brandy and forgot that the usual dose of this drug was only one teaspoon. Did he get sick or did he get sick? He vomited up his socks, but he recovered. He managed not to fall overboard anymore. That was the last episode.

On one of our monthly three-day cruises out to sea in order to shoot guns and target practice, a funny thing happened. A sailor came into the sick bay and he had acute appendicitis. I told the captain that we would have to either operate at sea or go back to shore and transfer him to the Naval hospital at Norfolk for surgery. The captain asked me if I could do it. I said, "Yes, I could do it, but it wouldn't be easy considering all things under the circumstances." To my great relief, the captain decided to head back to shore and spare me the difficulties and perplexities of trying to get ready to do an operation under the circumstances that were before me. On the way back to shore, the sailor told me that he was a Christian Scientist and that he thought that doctors were not all that necessary. And then he asked me more questions about acute appendicitis. "What would happen if I didn't have an operation?" he asked. And I told him that he might get well with natural healing processes, but that more likely he would have an abscess and perforation followed by peritonitis and death, and with that he looked up at me and said, "Doc, I have never been a very good Christian Scientist, so let's get on to the hospital." That was a big relief to me. I wasn't prepared to have a major argument with this boy.

Before the ship got underway for Korea we had our final inspection by the commodore of the fleet. Captain Harrison and he were going about the ship with their entourage, observing the drills and inspecting the sailors and officers, watching the gunnery drills, and things seemed to be ship shape and all was going well. But then it happened. "Man overboard," a sailor yelled out. The dummy was sighted on the port side aft (back side of the ship) and general quarters were called, all taking their respective stations about the ship. The lifeboat coxswains got on board their boat, and it was expeditiously lowered on the davits to the water. The engine was started and the lifeboat took off properly to retrieve the man overboard (dummy). All of a sudden, to our horror, the boat was rapidly filling with water and started to sink. The coxswain turned the boat around and sluggishly it made its way back to the ship and it was hooked into the ropes quickly and lifted out of the water before it sank. The boys had forgotten one small item. They didn't replace the two stoppers in the ship's hull and they came very close, as a result, to creating an embarrassing situation for the ship. Stoppers are seemingly like a lot of things in life. They are useless items, apparently, until at a critical time and then indispensable. Sometimes our lives are like that. We go along with a day-by-day routine, sometimes drudgery, and experience a feeling that the world could get along very well without us. Suddenly the time comes for us to quickly fill a void in someone's life and perchance save a soul. If one has not had the experience, he is missing a great deal.

In February 1951, we left the cold, cold winds of Norfolk Bay and arrived two weeks later in the warm sunshine of San Diego, California. Thanks to the engineer and men who constructed that marvel of its day, the Panama Canal. Special gratitude to the men who died of yellow fever in the process of the building and special thanks to the doctors who solved the medical riddle, found the cause of the disease and took the steps to prevent it. The canal experience was unique. The amazing engineering wonders we beheld! The beautiful tropical scenery. The operators who safely guided the ship through, with the hull of the ship almost scraping the walls but not quite, the precision of the locks in raising and lowering the ship at the proper time. It took all day and I wouldn't have missed the experience for the world. There was the weekend in Panama City and the people were friendly and eager to serve the sailors. And that simply is another demonstration of what life is all about. Selecting and enjoying what is good and avoiding the contamination that could spoil or destroy us.

Arriving in mid-winter in beautiful balmy San Diego, from frosty and amost frigid Norfolk, was a wonderful experience to be sure. From ice and snow to blooming flowers. From cold winds to balmy breezes, from the drabness of the Norfolk winter to the gorgeous colors of the San Diego landscape. Ah, San Diego, where else could you cut grass in July at noon using an old push lawn mower without even working up a sweat!

The Delta docked at Pier 1 San Diego Naval Base, and there we sat with ships along side, all undergoing repairs that our crew was prepared to handle. I held sick call every morning for all the ships but there was no great challenge and I had time on my hands. A sailor from the deck force came to the sick bay one day and asked if he could be circumcised and I said, "You bet, lie down." I was thrilled to do anything. He was so proud of his job that he went out three or four days later from the sick bay and the word got around. Within two weeks, I had circumcised a dozen or more sailors from the deck division. Each spent two or three days recuperating in the sick bay afterwards. They were simply too sore to swab the decks right at first. They laid around and were waited on and got out of duty. That became a popular item. One day Captain Harrison sent for me. I reported to his state room topside. "What the hell are you up to?" barked he. "Do all these men you are disabling for a time really need to be operated on?" "Well, Sir," said I, "I am not sure they did, but I was happy to do it and if they wanted it, it gave me something to do." "Well, whatever you think you are accomplishing, doctor, you stop it at once or else you will have this ship half disabled at one time or another if you continue." At this point I had done my last circumcision aboard the Delta.

The successful operation of a Navy ship depends upon each sailor doing his job and each officer leading effectively. Whether it is a fighting ship or a support ship, it is the same and this, of course, illustrates a point in life that is fundamental. If the coxswain fails to put in the stoppers of the lifeboat, bad things would happen and did. If the navigator makes a miscalculation, the ship may go aground or collision may occur. This principle is basic to all of life. Responsibility and privilege go hand in hand. The captain and officers bear heavy responsibility and accordingly are given appropriate privileges — the fancier uniform, the better living quarters, the salute, the pay. To prepare for an officer's responsibility may be long and tedious in terms of school and experience. A mistake at a high level of command can bring disaster to the ship, a correct judgment at a critical time can bring glory.

And so it is in all of life. Combine talent, motivation, determination, persistence despite mistakes, correction of errors, going on when the going is rough, keeping the goal in sight, yielding to no temptation to quit the struggle, and success can follow. Of course, good luck and good health can make for success or failure depending on what happens.

My ship in life was launched sixty-five years ago in Louisville, Kentucky. I would say it has been more of a support ship than a fighting ship, more like the Delta AR9. I have been in repair work all my life. It has on the whole been a good voyage thus far. The ship has gone through some very rough waters, but it has made it through and come out with battle scars, but basically sturdy and sea worthy. I anticipate joyfully the rest of the voyage. The ship's log will contain many experiences along the high seas and the distillate of wisdom gained by many encounters. The hull is scarred and it shows signs of wear and tear. But the engine room works efficiently and the communication system is fully operative and the stateroom passage ways and ladders (stairs) are in good repair. As my ship gets closer to the port of destination, the voyage is exciting, if not thrilling. I hope to arrive, still in command of my ship, still enjoying the voyage to the limit; learning, adjusting, discovering, experiencing all the way to port. One of the greatest thrills of the voyage consists of cruising with other ships along the journey. To exchange, to interact, to give and to receive, what a joy! You pass many ships along life's seas; most of them you forget, some of them you remember, and still fewer will profoundly leave their strong influence and memory. I am blessed with life at this moment. I have had bad times but this makes the present time all the better. To give of oneself in love and devotion and receive the rewards in return, provides the best that life can offer.

■———————————————————————■

Trials Along the Appalachian Trail

Working night and day at Homeplace Clinic and Hospitals was fun, rewarding, exhausting, and at times, frightening. I was month after month, year after year, elbow deep in blood and knee deep in illness and suffering. It constantly took commitment, dedication and willingness to work hard. To do it, one had to love it and I did. But I longed for a new experience to shift gears for a while. I had heard of the Appalachian Trail (A.T.), a footpath through the mountains extending over 2,000 miles from Springer Mountain, Georgia, to Mt. Katahdin in Maine. I wanted to learn more. Backpacking along this path was becoming popular and one could take day trips, week trips, or go all the way through one season, providing there were five or six months available with nothing else to do. I eagerly read more about the trail and corresponded with one experienced Appalachian Trail backpacker. I was enticed. It called me, and I was ready for the challenge. There were five of us who wanted to go. There was my son, Don, along with Sam, our hospital orderly, his son and a neighbor boy. We each collected our hiking gear and made our plans. We each had a backpack, sleeping bag, special food, a tiny one-and-a-half pound stove, canteen, eating and cooking gear, rain gear, a minimum of toilet articles, and a camera. The trip would extend from Klingman's Dome in the Smoky Mountain National Park to Fontana Dam, a thirty-five mile trip. We would take three days.

Perhaps the most traveled portion of the 2,000 mile footpath was along the seventy mile ridge in the Smokey Mountain National Park. We would do one-half of it. There were trail shelters along the way approximately five miles apart. There one could spend the night and enjoy the company of other backpackers and we would arrive tired and exhausted and hungry. Those backpackers of us over forty were ready to quit in the late afternoon, believe you me! The shelter was crude but adequate. Open in the front, a lean-to type shelter, and each provided bunks in two tiers for our sleeping bags. Each housed eight to twelve people. A spring was usually nearby for our needs and a pit toilet available.

Our trip was to be in June and hopefully the weather would be ideal although frequent rains could be expected. Cold nights and early mornings were followed by warm, sunshiny afternoons, excellent for hiking. The trail from Klingman's Dome to Fontana was moderately difficult. Up and down all the way. Mountaintops and ravines, forests of spruce and pine along with yellow birch along the ridges and plenty of hard woods in the lower sections. Wildflowers and ground cover were in abundance. There was the wonderful aroma of the woods and vegetation. Mountain streams splashing in all their glory. Clear, pure water, one could get a safe drink anytime. Flowering trees and shrubs, wild grapes, huckleberries, service berries, ginseng. Birds, game, deer and bear. I never did see a snake.

We started our journey on a Sunday morning from the Dome. The five of us were outfitted for hiking with packs in place and spirits high. We carried approximately thirty-five pounds on our backs. Sam and I were about forty-five years of age and not in the best of shape. The boys were twelve to fourteen and sturdy. We had a hard time keeping up with them. I had the guide book of the Appalachian Trail in my pocket and it contained a detailed description of the trail. Distances were noted, trail descriptions were there, location of springs, trail shelters, dangers and beauty spots were identified. A white blaze was painted on trees at fairly close intervals and so you knew by the mark you were on the A.T. (Appalachian Trail). It was a comforting sign when you were in doubt as to your location from time to time. It was foggy and misty and rain was threatening as we departed and locked up my Ford station wagon in the parking lot of Klingman's Dome. We quickly found the trail and off we went down the mountain headed for Siler's Bald, about an eight-hour journey. It took us twelve hours, however, because we made a wrong turn very quickly and we went two miles south instead of going west. I was uneasy about our direction, but I didn't tell the gang until we reached a spot that indicated that we were definitely off the trail. At this point I suggested we sit down, each lunch, and then I broke the bad news. Just then it started to rain and just then I cut my right thumb on a sharp edge of a sausage can. A trip to the friendly local emergency room would present a few problems, so I did the best I could with my trusty band-aids. Here we were two hours away from our point of departure. We had descended all the way from the Dome to this grassy bald and were sitting there in the rain, rain gear in place, eating whatever was easiest in a rain storm. My cut thumb didn't feel very good and my crumbling reputation as a leader and guide didn't feel very comfortable either. Our jovial laughter and hilarity en route to this lonely, unwelcome spot on the wrong trail was replaced by a considerable degree of silence and grim remarks. Would we reach Siler's Bald before dark? The street lights out there were not very bright. Up, up, up we trudged back to Klingman's Dome and there we were back to square one five hours after departure and we had gone essentially nowhere on our thirty-five mile journey. We found the right trail and began the hike that would put us at our destination at Siler's Bald just at the edge of dark and as we arrived it started to rain and I mean it poured. The two trail shelters at Siler's Bald were already full of scouts from Jacksonville, Florida. Girl Scouts filled one and Boy Scouts filled the other. All the bunk space was gone. But they kindly improvised and three of us spent the night in the girls' shelter sleeping on the ground but out of the rain. Two of us stayed the night in the other shelter with the boys. We slept under their bunks and occupied a dirty crawl space along with cobwebs, spiders, mice and no telling what else. Every time the guy above us moved, dust particles of who knows what filtered down on our face and head which projected out of our sleeping bags. Three sleeping pills and six hours later, I awakened and crawled out wiping the night droppings from my face and hair and after staggering about a time, I finally stabilized and went down to the spring. Face and hands were washed in the cold water, teeth were brushed, hair combed a bit and back to the shelter for breakfast. Instant oats, instant coffee, dried fruit, bread and Canadian bacon fried on our trusty stoves made a good meal. Breakfast was over, our sleeping bags rolled up and secured to the pack, pans washed and stowed, and we were ready for the trail. We found out as we were leaving that the brown bears had come in and out all night in the girls' shelter and caused a great deal of havoc. Their packs were hung on the rafters out of reach of the bears, but they could smell them anyhow. Their curiosity brought them to the edge of the shelters and from time to time they walked in a little piece. The girls would scream out in panic when someone spotted the bears and this scenario was replayed all night long. My sleeping capsules got me through the night but no one in the girls' shelter was that lucky. Their leader, a scouter of sixty-five years, told me that this could be his very last scout trip. He said by the time the trip was over, if it continued the way it started, someone would have to carry him off the mountain because he wasn't going to get any rest. Whereupon I reached in my pack and gave him something to save his life. I gave him eight Tuinal sleeping pills to make sure he made it through the rest of the journey. He said if he lived through it he would give me the credit. I smiled and winked and waved good-bye to the sleepless scouts and their grey-headed disgruntled scout master.

Hiking was perfect that morning as we headed west along the ridge of the mountains, the border between North Carolina and Tennessee. The trail was well worn but it could be dangerous with stones and roots exposed waiting for the careless hiker to stumble. The forest was mainly spruce and pine and hemlock along with yellow and white birch. Wildflowers were in evidence, all kinds, delicate, beautiful and plentiful. Birds were singing, the forest was fragrant, and there were ground squirrels, grey squirrels, butterflies, beautiful skies, gorgeous views of the mountain ranges when we came to a clearing. This was God's land. This was our land. We would struggle for a couple of hours up a mountain path and reach the summit and there was a clearing with wild azaleas, rhododendron and mountain laurel everywhere. A breathtaking view of the mountains and valleys and above, the glorious clouds and sky and that place, that holy ground, that magnificent scene, was all ours. We worked for it and there was no one else there to share this majestic scene, transfixed, speechless, awestruck. What a

107

land! What a glory! This was our land, our America. I thought of the song, "O Beautiful for Spacious Skies." The harmony out there. Nature in all its glory and magnificence. Oh, that men and women, boys and girls of all nations could exist in beauty and harmony such as we were beholding.

Now we must press on toward our destination where we would have a shelter for the night. We hiked mainly in the shade of the forest. Periodically we would traverse a bald spot and walk in the sunlight for a time and then back into the forest. But always on the ridge of the mountain. Usually at noon we would stop at a trail shelter and there we would find spring water, a privy and other comforts such as guys and gals from distant places doing what we were doing. And so we tale-swapped and made friends and looked each other over. We would stretch out for a brief rest, gaze up at the sky, look at the hawks and the birds soaring overhead, listen to the forest sounds and enjoy the smell of the wood smoke.

It was time to move on, clean up, and our packs were made ready. We said good-bye to our newly-formed and never-to-be-seen-again friends. We shared together for a moment in our lives, fellow travelers, lots in common, instant friendship, no time or reason to fight. How good it was to exchange, learn about your new friends, receive them, appreciate them and love them (most of them) instantly and then leave them. This scene we experienced for three days at noon and night around the campfire at our trail shelters. Life can be good, life can be beautiful, people can be good, people can be beautiful. And so the Appalachian Train got into my blood and I will never forget those days. The second day out we climbed Thunderhead Mountain and it was a doozy, with steep ascent. It was raining, really pouring. The trail was like a mountain stream with water rushing down. Our feet were soaked and our rain gear was in place. It was rough going. Up, up, up we climbed and as we neared the summit, tired, sweating, panting, aching, the rain suddenly stopped and the sunshine came out in all its glory and we were on top of the world. Again, the marvelous mountain ranges! In all directions we could look without any obstruction. A plane passed overhead. It was so close we could see the pilot and we were up about six thousand feet at the time. That lovely scene, that magnificent scene was all ours and we need not share it with anyone. The fat, rich, lazy crowds in Gatlinburg, getting fatter by the minute, munching chocolates and ice cream did not participate in our well deserved joy, no way. Backpackers can feel very righteous and smug at times like this. Don't think we can't. And it was a good feeling. We worked for it. We sweated for it and we earned it. And so this illustrates a point about life that we are all aware of. You enjoy especially the things in life that cost you something, that you struggle for, that you gave of yourself for, that you committed yourself to. It may be a degree, a diploma or a trophy. Perhaps the grandest prize in life is a new found friend that you have cultivated, given yourself for and one with whom you can share, cry with them, laugh with them and love them.

On the third day out, we made our way up the last mountain, Shuckstack. There was a fire tower lookout there and we climbed to the very top. There we could see in all directions again and, once again, we were thrilled to be alive, to see God's glory, to breathe the fresh air. Then after our last meal together at the foot of the tower we started the last descent to Fontana Dam. We switched back and forth along a magnificent trail. The spruce and pine and birch gave way to the invasion of the hardwoods, hickory, oak and beech trees. The mountain streams cascading down the mountain sides were spectacular. We often stopped, scooped up the delicious, pure water, and cooled our hot engines. About this time my feet started aching but we were only about half way down the mountain and the longer we went, the worse it got. I stopped and dropped my pack and pulled off my boots and socks and my fears were confirmed — Achilles tendonitis. Swollen, hot, tender heel cords. Ouch! Could I get off the mountain? Suddenly, that became a real live issue. I ate aspirin three and four at a time repeatedly. I rested, I grunted, I groaned. But on we went and pretty soon my walking became so peculiar that

109

the guys were taking notice and making some uncomplimentary remarks. I did my best to hide my pain. I couldn't do it. It hurt badly but I struggled on. This pack became heavier and my ankles and heel cords were like coals of fire in my boots. I walked stiff legged, flexing and extending my feet as little as possible. I walked like a guy going through six inches of mud but I got off the mountain by gritting my teeth and determination and a sack full of aspirin. Thank goodness I brought the Bayer bottle. So help me, I would still be on Shuckstack Mountain were it not for that most useful of all drugs. Across the dam we went and found Sam's car that we had left in the Village parking lot. En route to Klingman's Dome to pick up my station wagon that we had left three days earlier, we had tire trouble and the spare was flat. A couple of hours later and after calming down from our utter frustration, we arrived at Klingman's Dome parking lot to get the wagon. What took three days on foot took about one hour to travel by auto.

And so we opened our packs, made our last drink of Tang and had a toast to our victory celebration. I was a mess but a happy mess, unshaven, stinking from body odor, with my heel cords absolutely on fire. Although every step was an agony, otherwise, I felt so good about what we had done. The trip started badly when we got lost in the rain and ended badly for me with my affliction. But all in all, it was a marvelous learning experience, the introduction of what was to become a big thing in my life for the next ten years. It started the wheels turning for my youngest son, Rick, who fell in love with the trail after his first trip. Ten years later, Rick became a two-thousand-miler as he stood with upraised arms in glory on the summit of Mt. Katahdin in Maine. Five months before he began his walk at Springer Mountain, Georgia, and continued until he finished. Through rain and sunshine, through mountains and valleys, suffering from diarrhea, aching muscles and lonesomeness, he made it. My introduction of the backpacking experience to my son paid off, as I joined him and together we climbed the last mountain, rejoicing in his victory.

And so this is a part of life. How grand to introduce a child, a friend, a colleague, to something you have experienced with joy and see them enter into your world. And then, to see them go above and beyond your accomplishments and enter into their own glory, that is the payoff.

To be a role model for someone you love and to see part of you in their life, provides an unparalleled joy and to see a part of that person in you completes the picture. It is the icing on the cake. It is what life is all about. It makes it worth the living.

■————————————————————————————■

I Walked Where Jesus Walked

I didn't want to go to Israel. Virginia, my wife of thirty-four years, did. She wouldn't accept "no" for an answer from her workaholic husband. Her persistence paid off. I finally agreed to the trip to get her off my back. We went to the city to get a passport. We had to have a photograph made. The photo shop was closing. I said, "Forget it. I am not coming back." But the photographer said he would take us even though it was past closing time. We got the photo and the trip was saved. Louisville to New York, New York to Rome, Rome to Tel Aviv. No problem. November 1981, shirt sleeve weather, nice. Tel Aviv, a city only a few years old, was vigorous with its youth. The Israelis say if you want to play go to Tel Aviv, if you want to work go to Haifa, if you want to worship go to Jerusalem.

Israel, no bigger than New Jersey, a troubled land, an amazing place, a land of Jews and Arabs, a land precious to Christians, Moslems and Jews, is called the Holy Land. But paradoxically, it is perhaps one of the unholiest lands of modern day. It is the scene of constant struggle betwee warring factions, both claiming their right to possess the land. When one visits the area, you must accept the fact that terrorist activity, rioting, and general unrest may be part of your experience.

111

Our accommodations in Jerusalem were good. We could drink the water out of the spigot safely there. In any other area, we were admonished to drink bottled water (at considerable cost) and we did. The hotel in Tiberias on the Sea of Galilee was excellent. Transportation of our group of eighteen was by air conditioned bus with a PA system for tour descriptions and discussions by our guide, Ziggy Klapp. This man was intelligent, pleasant, was well versed in history, geography and politics. He did his best to explain the situation from the Jewish point of view and we were impressed.

One is struck by the military presence everywhere you go. The landscape is devoid of trees in so many places and so one can stand on the Mount of Olives and see all of Jerusalem without obstruction and this is true almost anywhere in Israel. It is a dry land, and save for the Jordan River and the Sea of Galilee, it would be altogether a different place. The Sea and the Jordan provide a marvelous supply of water for the thirsty arid land. At one time in history, Israel had more trees and vegetation than they do today, but tree planting is bringing a change in the barren landscape.

A visitor to Israel is struck by the vigor of the people and their determination to persevere in a hostile environment. There is a spirit of patriotism, of national pride, of willingness to serve the state that is remarkable by American standards. A spirit of harmony and cooperation is evident as one visits the communes known as kibbutzim. Here people live together, work together, and share many things and enjoy a good life. Israelis and Americans are on the same wavelength, so to speak, whereas there is a vast difference between Arabs and Americans.

One of the real problems a Christian visitor to Israel has is the commercialism that pervades all of Israel. One is taken to a site of an event in the life of Jesus and as he stands there lost in thought trying to get into the atmosphere of reverence and worship, someone thrusts an article for sale in your face and says abruptly, "This for you, only one Amelican dolla." This scenario is replayed over and over again and everywhere commercialism is eating away at one's attempt to be in a mood of contemplation and worship. Actually, the second largest industry in Israel is tourism.

Another problem is the matter of authenticity. So often in describing events that occurred in Jesus' day, the guide will say, "tradition says that it happened here." However, we know that it is only tradition and no one knows for sure. There are very few places where it can be said with certainty, "This is the spot." One of those places is Jacob's Well. Through the centuries there has been deposited fifteen feet of sand and silt around the well. It becomes necessary to descend these fifteen feet underground in order to get to the chamber where the original well opening was to be found. One can descend those steps, go into the chamber, and the water will be drawn up by a bucket and one can drink from the same well that Jesus drank from when the Samaritan woman gave him the water at his request. Another place of authenticity, a place where Jesus walked for sure, is to be found outside of the house of Caiaphas, the high priest of Jerusalem. The steps have recently been discovered by archaeologists and one can ascend and descend on the same steps that Jesus walked in the long ago. A third place of certainty is the synagogue of Capernaum. The actual stone floor of the synagogue has been unearthed and one can actually stand and walk where Jesus stood. Here he announced to his own people that he was the Messiah of God and was rejected.

As one approaches the Sea of Galilee from the high western slope, suddenly the Sea comes into view in its entire length and breadth; it is a beautiful sight for certain, like a jewel in the desert. To realize that this is where Jesus spent a good part of his teaching ministry, that he saw the same sights that you are seeing, provides one with an entirely new experience.

To look in awe at Calvary or Golgotha, one does see immediately a skull in the hillside and it is easy to believe that this spot may well have been the actual site of the crucifixion. The dome of the rock Moslem Mosque is beautiful to behold and stands at the actual site of the temple of Jesus' day.

113

Within the dome is the actual rock where sacrifices in the Jewish temple were performed.

Israel is a dry, thirsty land. Water is precious; it is not wasted. Israel is a rocky land for certain. It is said that when God passed out rocks throughout the earth, he stumbled and fell in Israel and lost the entire load right here. Those of us who have been in Israel can easily understand why Arabs throw rocks at Israelis. Rocks are to be found any place you reach down.

The high rock fortress called Masada in the south is a spectacle to behold. The knowledge that a thousand Jews committed suicide on that spot rather than surrender to Romans is awesome to think about. Israelis going into the army proudly stand on top of Masada for the ceremony of induction into the armed forces. Throughout the land of Israel one sees the pride of the people and the determination to persevere despite all obstacles.

To walk through the Oasis of Jericho is a singular experience. In the midst of desert is this lusciously fertile area alive because of the artesian well bringing in life-giving water to this thirsty land. All manner of fruit and vegetables are available there. Palm trees, bananas and citrus grow in abundance. The countryside around, by contrast, is rock, dusty, sandy and barren.

The Dead Sea nearby is like nothing else in this world. The water feels like oil. People float in the salty water. The mineral content is valuable to the Israelis. Nothing is alive in the Dead Sea, hence the name. Nearby on the northwest shore of the Dead Sea is Qumran, where the famous Dead Sea scrolls were found.

Leaving Israel one has many thoughts. First and foremost, it is a land of contrast.

1. There are miles of desert but also acres of fertile land because of irrigation from the Jordan River.

2. Israelis are much like us but the Arabs are entirely different.

3. Israel is a land of intense religious belief but also a land of unparalleled hate.

4. Israel contains ancient structures preserved for our interest and study and yet it contains the most modern evidence of technology and progress.

Israel is a land of unforgettable memories for the Christian and for the Jew and for the Moslem. Israel is a land of opportunity and presents a challenge for hatred to thaw out and melt into a sea of cooperation and acceptance between Arab and Jew. If Israel and the Arabs can solve their problem, what a marvelous example to the world community. It would be a role model indeed for all of mankind.

If the intensity of hate can turn into the beauty and joy of love and acceptance, we would have heaven on earth. Jesus talked about this a lot, come to think about it. He spoke 2,000 years ago about loving one's enemies. My Arab friend, my Jewish neighbor, why not try the Jesus way? He said it would work and we know it is the truth; there lies a glorious opportunity.

Berea

Berea, Kentucky, and all that goes with it is "Mecca" to those of mountain culture and tradition. This weekend of mid-May, my wife and I went back again to see the beauty of the foothills of the Appalachians. We went to Boone Tavern where we were treated like a king and queen and where we dined in the elegance that only Boone Tavern dining room can provide. My office girls gave us a gift certificate for Christmas and the Berea trip was the result. A great gift, a great trip! Forty-two years ago in September, we arrived at Boone Tavern to spend the first night of our honeymoon trip. I am not sure that we have spent a night there since, till now. It is a lovely place in every sense of the word and you are made to feel at home, and the welcome mat is out for sure. The hotel is furnished with furniture exquisitely-made at the college, and the building, although showing signs of age, is maintained beautifully. The food is great and the service leaves absolutely nothing to desire. You eat perhaps more than you need and you are the object of attention as the boys and girls of the college make your dining experience a delight.

The sales room of the college is irresistible and one can spend a pot of money real fast if he doesn't look out. Beautiful handmade black walnut and cherry drop leaf tables you may have for a few thousand dollars. Five to seven thousand dollars will buy you a secretary that would make any homemaker drool. Wood carvings and pottery abound. You name it — they've got it when it comes to crafts.

Basically, Berea has not changed in the past forty-two years since our previous visit. The Berea flavor is there — the beauty, the charm, even the elegance. But we have changed. Our bodies show it, our mind set, no doubt, too, shows it. Forty-two years ago we hit the ball and were en route to first base. Now we are on third base and heading for home. I can appreciate Berea more than I did years ago — why? Oh, for one reason, I have been to lots and lots of other places since then. I realize now that there is only one Berea. It is special. I have met lots of people in the past four decades and I realize that Berea people are special. I was privileged to come to know Francis Hutchins, beloved president of Berea College for many years. He was on the Board of Trustees who operated Homeplace Hospital where I spent perhaps the best twenty years of my life. My children enjoyed the spring Folk Dancing Festival at Berea year after year during our mountain sojourn. Neighbor children became students at Berea and told us of their experience. Yes, Berea was and is the "Mecca" for those who love ·the culture and the traditions of the southern Appalachians. I count myself an adopted son of the Appalachian Mountains and I still, at times, get homesick for "my people." A trip to Berea surely does help that sickness.

Andy of Andersonville

Andy was my great grandfather, Andrew Cauble, one of twelve children born to Adam and Polly Cauble of Washington County, Indiana. Andersonville was the most infamous of the Civil War prisons located in southwestern Georgia. Andy gave a few months of his life as a prisoner of war in Andersonville and only this week I set foot on the very spot where perhaps grandpa had trudged many, many times during those days of unbelievable hell. One third of the 45,000 Union prisoners of Andersonville died, and are buried side by side in a huge common trench as a grave site. They died like flies, of disease, starvation, wounds and execution. A hell hole in America, yes. The Civil War claimed 500,000 dead of the three million who fought. When a nation fights itself, it is the bloodiest of all fights; when a church fights it often is the cruelest of all social combats.

I saw Andersonville prison's stockade area. There it was, a huge green field, quiet, peaceful, birds singing, tranquil, the brook in the valley flowing clear pure water, markers where the gates were located, where the stockade wall was, and where the dead line was, monuments commemorating the agony of 125 years ago. In my mind's eye I went back to 1864, and there was the stockade, the thousands of diseased, injured, malnourished, forlorn, hopeless and helpless Union soldiers, crowded together under bits and pieces of canvas, hoping against hope that someday they might be delivered from that "God awful" nightmare. Nothing to do, eating a morsel of food, usually, hopefully once a day, that was unfit for a dog scrounging food in a back alley. Sanitation was so bad that the stench would stretch for two miles in any direction depending on how the wind was blowing. Drinking water was from a creek, by our standards, not fit for cattle.

The stockade wall was of pine logs twenty feet tall and on platforms all around the stockade were the stationed guards with loaded muskets ready to fire. The dead line was about ten feet from the stockade wall and any one who touched the line for any reason was shot dead without warning.

The dead were picked up each morning and carried to the dead house and then taken to the cemetery where they were buried in the common grave. Their clothing was eagerly scavenged for use of the living. In the heat of August of 1864, the stream of water was almost dried up, for there had been no rain for weeks. Death was perhaps imminent for the entire prison population. Suddenly at the worst of the drought, a storm came up and lightning struck in the midst of the camp and a spring of clear, wonderful water burst forth from the earth and the prisoners were saved. They say it was a miracle. I saw that spring today as clear water gushed forth and it has been flowing all these years. A monument is there depicting the miracle for the dying of Andersonville. I wonder if Andy drank from that spring and I suspect he did. I figure that every prisoner did, taking his turn. Andy made it through his prison sentence and then the war was over and the gates were swung open. He made it back to Indiana to the farm where his wife lived. She had long given him up for dead. He saw her at a distance out in the field working. He walked slowly up to her, ragged, filthy, skin and bones, bearded. She didn't immediately recognize him until he called her name. Then she knew the miracle of miracles had happened. I am here today because of that miracle. How many of us owe our existence perhaps to some miracle? How many of us are indebted to the events which we perhaps know nothing about? We Americans are indebted to hundreds and thousands of men and women living and dead who went through hell that we might enjoy the miracle of America.

Cape Hatteras — Hello and Good-bye

In the 1960's, camping out was coming on strong and still is going strong, for that matter. Finances demanded that we take modest vacations and camping out seemed to be the way to go. We asked the usual questions of friends and relatives about what we needed, where to go, etc. etc. So we decided to join the throng and bought basic camping equipment, nothing fancy. We were advised that Cape Hatteras presented a real challenge and offered some excitement. So we elected to take Hatteras on as our first camping experience. That turned out to be a bad decision.

We loaded up our Comet station wagon with tents, sleeping bags, cooking gear and all the rest, and headed east to the outer banks of North Carolina. The Comet was a small station wagon to start with and we had the audacity, or perhaps the stupidity, to fill it with two adults, four children and all the camping gear for ten days on the road. The wagon was draggin' for sure.

Hatteras was interesting, different, windy, sunny, sandy, and finally, the scene of a destructive storm. Four children came to the quick conclusion that mom and dad had made a real bad mistake when they elected Hatteras to make their maiden camping experience. Interesting? Yes. There was a long and wide sandy beach with no trees for shade and nothing to obstruct the wind whatsoever. It filled up soon for the weekend with various and sundry types of camping arrangements. We noted first off that most parties arrived in R.V.'s — sturdy and strong — able to withstand the wiles of Hatteras. Those who pitched tents were well prepared. Sturdy tents with long ropes and stakes driven in by mallets. The stakes were at least three feet in length and what did we have? We were sadly and ill prepared for the place as I looked out with dismay and saw what others came along with. Small tents we had, with not over a ten inch stake and they were flimsy at best. But we had no choice. Either put up with what we had and hope for the best or beat a hasty retreat. We decided to risk it and that was a bad mistake as it turned out.

The days were extremely hot and there was no shade. The wind was brisk and constant. Sand was everywhere. It was in our eyes, hair and food. The first two nights were no big problem. The third night I was awakened by a noise that sounded like something I never heard before. The canopy of our tent was flapping in the strong wind violently. I got up, went outside and knew we were in for it. Before long we were in the midst of the full fury of a Hatteras storm and both our tents came down. We got into the station wagon for protection until morning. Then on Sunday morning we surveyed the damage. Everything we had was soaked. We broke camp (it was already broke and soaked) and headed for the laundromat. Here we spent the morning drying out all our gear, clothing, sleeping bags and the rest. I guess the Lord forgave us for not going to church that Sunday; he sent the storm, we didn't ask for it.

We headed then for Myrtle Beach, South Carolina, and upon arriving it was obvious that we had made a good decision. The beach was beautiful and the shade trees were wonderful and the wind brakes from the storm were evident. We made camp and enjoyed a wonderful week. It was like the Garden of Eden. No sand in the food, face and sleeping bags; good shade, no storms. Quiet and peaceful.

This story illustrates a lot of truth about life. 1. Don't try to climb Mount Everest before you have climbed the Indiana Knobs. 2. If and when you decide to take on a formidable challenge, go prepared with good equipment. If you want rest then go to Myrtle Beach. If you want a challenge, go to Hatteras!

Long Beach to Louisville 1952

My tour of duty in the United States Navy was over and I, along with Virginia and two children ages two and one, was heading to Louisville, Kentucky, where I would start my surgical residency at the Veterans Hospital. It was July. It was hot, very hot! Wheat harvest time. No air conditioning. Chevrolet car, basic transportation only. It took four days to cross the country. No interstates. We had to go through all the cities, towns and villages. It was so hot that the air streaming in the open windows was like a blast furnace and after a while it became intolerable and we would have to close up the windows. Then it became unbearably stuffy and we had to open up the windows again but for only a short time. We couldn't stand the windows open and we couldn't stand them closed. We carried water in a big thermos. Virginia was busy passing water from one person to the other. By the time she made the rounds with water, she started another round. We were drinking almost continuously and sweating up a storm. We were like wilted lilies and feeling terrible. Nausea, weakness, and abdominal cramping followed. It finally dawned on me that we were suffering from low salt syndrome. It was the same condition that the sailors suffered when they were in the engine room of the USS Delta and they neglected to take their salt tablets. At my next opportunity I bought a package of salt tablets and we started in on them. Wow! What a difference. Within an hour we were all perked up. The wilted lilies took on life again and we quit drinking all that water. Amazing! I had preached about low salt conditions to the sailors below decks, but neglected myself and my family. Finally, the message got through and I was truly a believer.

We had another problem. The traffic was terrible. There were many two lane roads and no interstates and only a few cities were bypassed. No use to be in a hurry for sure. And then we had another problem. The hotel rooms were taken up by the wheat threshers. Wheat was being harvested all over the midwest and the west and the threshers had occupied most of the available motel beds. It was get anything you could if you could. One night we looked from six to ten before we found a place. Finally, we obtained a room with only one bed, the best we could do. Virginia and I slept on the floor. It was hot, very hot. No breeze. No air conditioning but we made it through. We arrived in Louisville in one piece. Today, we could go in a beautiful car on interstates bypassing the cities. There would be air conditioned comfort, no low salt problems, and we would have pop in the cooler. Motels and fast foods would be in abundance and available to us. The good ole days did have their problems.

―――――――――――――――――――――――――――――

Pekin, Indiana — Heaven on Earth!

To eight-year-old Donnie Boy, Pekin was absolutely, positively, the greatest place this side of heaven. Why? Because that is where grandma and grandpa Cauble lived and they loved their first-born grandchild, Donnie, with all their heart, soul and body and he loved them. Donnie Boy lived in Louisville with his mom and dad, Merle and Earl Martin, along with sister Merlene, and they all went to Borden and Pekin on weekends in their Willis Knight, a four-door automobile. Basic transportation. No air conditioner, no radio, a lap robe to keep you warm in the winter.

Dad Martin was a school teacher at DuPont Manual High School and mom kept house. That was no small task in the days of washing all day one day and ironing all day a second day, scrubbing and polishing, canning, mending, darning and shoveling coal in the furnace and removing the ashes daily. Come Friday afternoon and the Martin family was Borden bound. That night we ate with grandpa Martin in Borden, where he was affectionately referred to as Uncle Dick. He had been widowed eight years and Miss Ida kept house for him. The house was only yards from the Monon Railroad tracks and when the passenger train went through non-stop, it was a glorious sight to behold and a thunderous noise to hear. The windows rattled and the house shook. There was the well and the pump, the cellar house, the wood and coal shed, the two-holer at the end of the path, the garden and the chicken lot and the chicken house.

Donnie could hardly wait until Saturday morning in time to go to Pekin. So little for a boy to do in Borden and so much excitement and things to do in Pekin. As we left, dad would give grandpa Martin some money for expenses and grandpa accepted it with shame and bowed head. The bank failure in the depression days wiped out all of his savings from his farm sale and there was no social security whatsoever. Each family cared for their own as best they could. The poor house lodged the infirm and the elderly who had no family or no funds.

Then on to Pekin, glorious Pekin. The flour mill, the new ten-room, modern hen house with automatic watering troughs, and semi-automatic feeders, the hatchery, the broiler houses, the barn, grandma and grandpa's house, Uncle Murray and his family.

I loved Pekin because I was adored in Pekin. I was smothered in love. The excitement of it all, the machinery and the flour mill, the marvels of the hatchery, the big trucks with their huge loads of Purina feed. How I loved to ride in the truck bed on top of the load of feed as the truck sped along. I loved the feel of the wind whistling through my hair as down the gravel roads we went, throwing a cloud of dust in all directions. How I loved to race through the flour mill and watch the machinery as the wheat was processed into twenty-four pound sacks of White Rock Flour. To see the chicks taken from the hatching trays after twenty-one days in incubation was a mystery to behold. And there was Pete Hurst in the old barber shop downtown Pekin where we would wait for two hours on a Saturday night for a haircut. Religious fervor and religious certainty prevailed in many churches. There was fellowship and brotherhood and, in addition, there was ugly separation and division. There were the post millennialists and the pre-millennialists, depending on how one viewed the Biblical prophecy. There were the four cuppers and the one cuppers depending on how one interpreted the understanding of apostolic practice of communion in the early church. It was family against family as religious warfare was waged. I listened to grandma tell about how awful the scene was when many of the pre-millennialists were thrown out of the church by the post-millennialists.

Oh, those early morning breakfasts with beef steak, gravy, biscuits and honey! The round table with the glass top in the big kitchen I shall never forget! The back enclosed porch with the gorgeous begonias, bougainvilleas, ferns and lemon and orange trees. Grandpa was tall, had one blind eye but was a successful businessman and was loving and kind to everybody. Grandma was short but mighty, fiery and certain of her convictions was she. Her forefinger pointed straight at me and to many others as she told us how it was in no uncertain terms. There was Aunt Laurie, grandmother's sister, who did her work, baked her pies and loved the grandchildren.

The greatest of all days were the Sundays when many would gather at the dinner table after church around 1:00 o'clock. A huge dining table, loaded with fried chicken, mashed potatoes and gravy, green beans, corn on the cob, tomatoes, yeast rolls and butter and fruit cup for dessert with angel food cake, iced tea and coffee. The house would be filled with family. People of all ages and sizes. Lots of noise. Lots of story telling. Lots of yelling from the kids and lots of admonitions from the parents. There were grandma and grandpa, the children, the in-laws, the grandchildren, the nieces and nephews and cousins. Grandma and grandpa were known as Omar and Lillie by the town of Pekin. There were five children. 1. Merle Martin married to Earl, school teacher and later principal in the Louisville school system. 2. Wallace, preacher and pastor in Louisville, married to Mary. 3. Murray, businessman, assisting grandpa Cauble with the business, the flour mills, the laying hens, the hatchery, the feed mills, the lumber and building supply warehouse with extensions in downtown Pekin and Martinsburg. Grandpa was contractor with farmers throughout the region to supply recently hatched chickens and supplies to grow them into broilers for the market. Murray was married to Florence. 4. Virgie, married to Dr. Robert Ellmore, dentist in Salem. 5. Shirley, married to Floyd Call, executive secretary of the Florida Bankers Association.

At Christmas or Thanksgiving, some or all of the clan would gather and sing and laugh and play and eat — especially eat! Grandpa was generous, especially at Christmas time. Ten dollar bills filled the Christmas tree — one for each person. In 1931, that was a lot of money. Ah, family, how wonderful when there was love. How dreadful when there was jealousy and hate. The Cauble clan mostly loved, thank God.

What a fantastic change since those days in 1931, fifty-seven years ago. Driving from Louisville to Pekin in 1931 was over winding roads in automobiles without heaters or air conditioners and adorned with tires that might go flat. The countryside was generally quite different from today. The houses were humble, many of them. The lawns were small and grass was cut by a push type unpowered mower. Flowers were few. In general, many were poor by 1988 standards. Those were days of depression and many houses and farms and the countryside in general looked unkept. What a contrast to today's large, beautiful, manicured lawns, lovely shrubs, flower gardens and beautiful homes.

And the schools, wow, what a change? From little to big, from standard to deluxe, from pencils to computers, from reading, writing and arithmetic to great ball teams and beautiful cheerleaders. The kids walked to school for exercise and now they are transported in buses and they get their exercise in beautiful gymnasiums. The kids in those days were afraid of authority figures and respected them on the whole. Nowaways, it is a different ballgame all together. Old Doc Green in Pekin was something else by today's standards. A kindly and compassionate man to be sure. Doc was a friend and he was loved. He did what he could with what he had. Today, the medical scene, like all else, bears little resemblance to Doc Green's office. Hospitals, helicopters, computers, pacemakers, open heart surgery, diagnostic and therapeutic measures unheard of by 1931 standards.

As today, many people went to church in Pekin in 1931. But as today, sectarianism abounded and each group tended to believe that it had a special pipeline to the throne of God and many people acted accordingly. Catholics, generally, were considered beyond hope or so it seemed to Donnie Boy. Some churches regarded every other Protestant denomination as objects of missionary activity. There were the pre- and the post-millennialist groups and generally they did not exactly love each other. Family was often divided against family and the conversation at the Cauble dinner table indicated evidence of bitterness and resentment existing in the community because of religious strife.

And there was Bierly's store with everything for sale from cow feed to cracker barrels. And the sages of knowledge sitting out front, spitting tobacco juice, and watching the trains go by and swapping tales. Now the supermarkets with their tempting and gorgeous displays of food from all over the world await our fat pocketbooks and as a result, the lean, poor, farm families of the thirties are now pot-bellied and their cholesterols are off the board.

In the thirties, every little town had a flour mill. Grandpa Cauble had one at Pekin and one in Salem. Now they are all gone and Pillsbury, Ballard and other conglomerates have taken over. The flour mills are gone, the country stores are gone and the family farms are going.

The rural hospitals are in a state of transformation. In my judgment, sooner or later most of them will cease being acute hospitals and become triage centers. They will be emergency centers, and send hospital patients to the medical centers. They will continue to have clinics for many of the medical specialties and provide long-term care. Home nursing will continue to expand. Eventually, a form of total government control of medical practice will likely follow.

Today, Pekin is not the Pekin of my boyhood and you wouldn't expect it to be. It was heaven to me then but now it is simply a little town near to Salem which I pass through en route to Louisville and have to slow down. Pekin is Amaray, Fourth of July celebrations, stores, bank, churches, Dr. Carty's office, the homes. There are a lot of poor ones and there are some more affluent. But Pekin is a place of happy memories because of grandma and grandpa Cauble. There was excitement in those days. There I was loved. There I was a king and there were family gatherings and I was baptized by Uncle Murray in Blue River down by the mill.

But yet, in another sense, Pekin is the place it always was. There are the people and there are the things that people make and produce. There is love and there is hate. There are the righteous and there are the self righteous. There are stable families and there are dependent families. There are good people and there are the bad people. There are the upright folks and there are the crooked ones. There are the loving, the accepting, the helping. There are the conniving, the selfish, and the parasites. And so in ways, life is ever changing and yet it is always the same.

Pekin, no doubt, looks to the future with hope. Doubtless, Pekinites and mankind in general, hope for peace and brotherhood in the world with enough for all who will work and opportunity for those who want it, help for those who need help. A society where there is reasonable opportunity and freedom and yet a society that accepts responsibility for the less fortunate and the handicapped and the born losers. To me this is the essence of a kind of community that most of us want, for which we who are so motivated will strive with our commitment, our energies, our hopes, and our prayers.

—6—
Personalities

Everett Dean

Last night in Salem, Indiana, a testimonial dinner was given in the honor of one of its greatest citizens, Everett Dean, who by all accounts, is recognized to be in a club of men where there are few members. Outstanding basketball player at Salem High School, Indiana University, outstanding coach, winner of NCAA tournaments. He has truly been the coach of coaches. But there have been lots of great ball players and there have been lots of great coaches. The uniqueness of Everett Dean lies in his character, his caring for people, his kind spirit, his lifestyle. As we ate together last night, 300 strong plus many guests, as we heard players and coaches give testimony to the life of Everett Dean, it was crystal clear that the focus was upon his outstanding character, compassionate and loving spirit, and ability to motivate men. We see ''success'' obtained by the knife in the back, by devious means, or by foul play. Not so with Everett Dean. He made the grade by being a gentleman, a friend, and an encourager.

Person after person testified to the fact that Everett Dean had been their role model. As I thought about that, I realized afresh and anew my own responsibility to my friends, my loved ones, my patients and my constituency. As I continue to go along life's road, if I make a stupid mistake, how many people will I let down? How many look to me for guidance and see me as a role model? And so I came away from the dinner last night with a new and fresh determination to say "no" to any temptation that might lead me to disaster. I came away convinced that the life of Everett Dean is a life I want to follow, and to emulate. General Robert E. Lee was asked at the close of the war if he wished to send a message to one of his fellow officers who had spent much time with him and who was his very close friend. His reply to that person was, "deny yourself, learn to say no when you know it is the best." I think Everett Dean operated that way. I would like to do the same. But the temptations to break the good rules in life sometimes overwhelm us and we mess up. Last night I believe many of us received a shot in the arm to vaccinate us against the enemy who would destroy us. The gentleman coach, Everett Dean, instilled in his men the principles of hard work, discipline, denial for the sake of glory. He is still doing his job. Last night he became my coach in a fresh way. I have the honor of being his private physician. Last night he became my doctor. I love that man.

Neva Grimes

Today I pulled out of my files a folder containing poems and mementoes from this aged lady, a patient of mine a few years ago at the local nursing home. For several years I visited with her each week and she has since departed and gone to her reward. At the time she was virtually blind but managed with a large illuminated magnifying lens to write and to read a little. She was in her nineties, but was clear as a bell mentally. She was widowed and lonely. She seemed to especially appreciate my visits, and so I made it a point of always going to see her on my weekly trips to the nursing facility. I did not afford this luxury to any other patient with this degree of regularity. There developed between us an unusual bond of respect, admiration and affection. She wrote poetry and some of her poems were to me personally and told of her love and appreciation.

She also wrote poetry about nature, her childhood, about her predicament of age, blindness and loneliness. I grew to appreciate her in a special way. A relationship developed that was a mutual source of joy and gave to each other what we both needed and what humanity needs, namely love, acceptance, and time. When I failed to show up at the usual time because of a conflict in my schedule, she really missed it and told me so. So did I, but not so intensely, because my life was so full and her life was so empty.

This relationship is an example of what I think life is all about. And that is, human relationships are number one. It is just that simple. Good relations, good life; bad relations, bad life. I can say without hesitation that my greatest joys in life have come from friendship, closeness to a select few, and love on occasion.

As a human being, as a physician, I have come to the conclusion as many have, that people are crying for friendship, closeness, affirmation and love. And so often we miss opportunities to give and receive these elements so much needed and wanted. I think many have come to realize that to get love and attention, you usually must give it first. The loving person is the one who is loved.

Jesus talked about loving our enemies. That indeed is almost impossible for most of us. It is simply the natural thing to hate your enemy. Recall the events through the ages that bear that out, and witness the clashes of today, culture against culture, black against white, Jew against Arab, not to mention the clashes at home and in the neighborhood. I don't have any formula to bring instant success in this arena of life. But I can make a few comments. I think it is far easier for some to love, forget and forgive than others simply because that is their basic personality. It is in their genes. Secondly, I believe that some are better at forgiveness than others because they have been forgiven and have been loved and treated well in life. And then, finally, I believe it is possible to adjust our hate relations and transform them into a more tolerant attitude by trying to understand where our enemies are coming from. But we must want to do this if we are to succeed. If we really want to continue hating, then there is no hope.

My observation is that there are few out there who can expect to achieve Jesus' high standard when he said to love your enemies and have compassion on those who spitefully use you. When one attempts to do this, it is not only hard work, it is not only against the grain, but many solid citizens will call you a fool for the attempt. We have gone to the moon and back, but to love one another is still a goal we have not fully realized and perhaps never will.

■———————————————————■

Black Suits and Buggies

I have nothing but admiration for the Amish people in our community. Are they different from the mainstream of Americans? You bet your life they are! They pay their bills, they carry out instructions, they come to the doctor only when sick, their children sit quietly and behave, they work hard, they don't accept food stamps, medicare and social security and on and on and on I could go describing their unusual social behavior. Yes, they are different all right. They do conform to one another in the Amish community but not to mainstream America. The Amish are polite, they are quiet, they mind their own business. Although I would not find their lifestyle to be attractive to me personally, I know their way is to them a good way, and it is a good way, a very good way. Their lives are rigid obviously, but many thrive in that sort of environment. It relieves one often the agony of decision. The structured life is for many the good life and the good life is a blessing to society for sure. If a doctor goes into an examination room where the usual American family (consisting of husband and wife and say three children) is located and waiting, the noise and confusion in that room during the waiting period will likely have been obvious to all. But go into a room where an Amish family has been waiting, and all is orderly and quiet.

One Amish man came in not too long ago with a nasty power saw cut on a finger. He was a candidate for the hand surgeons. He refused to go and implored me to do the best I could. I didn't want to at all, but I saw he had no intention of going to the city. So I fixed the finger as best a country doctor could. After he left, something happened that I had never observed in my office before. He stopped in the full waiting room and publicly thanked the people for their patience with him during his emergency. He had held everybody up another half hour. We were already behind when he came in. He then went over to the counter and paid his bill in full and left the building. I don't ever expect to have this happen again in my office. Yes, I love the Amish. I think there will be lots of buggies and black suits in heaven.

━━━━━━━━━━━━━━━━━━━━━━━━━━━━━

Tom

Tom came in the back door of my office one day as was his customary habit when he was drinking. He wanted help. He was trying to quit his drinking again and he was shaking. He wanted something, anything, to calm him down. He was in misery and was struggling. On this particular July day, he was standing in one of the exam rooms waiting for me and he had an open wine bottle in his right hip pocket. He leaned over too far and spilled some of the precious cargo down the air conditioning duct and we were blessed with the aroma of the fermented fruit of the vine for two days.

This illustrates one fact about the alcoholic scene. Funny things do happen and maybe that helps society bear the terrible burden of this dreadful addiction. The horror of it generally exceeds the humor, obviously. About this I suspect all of us agree. But then when you begin to make other statements about alcoholism, come to conclusions, make suggestions, we begin to go our separate ways. Recovered alcoholics have certain ideas. Counselors, psychiatrists and social workers have certain ideas about the subject. Wives and children of alcoholics have certain ideas and finally John Doe public has certain ideas. On some things we would all agree, such as, "Wouldn't it be a grand world if alcoholic drinks could be consumed only to a point and if that were exceeded, vomiting would automatically ensue." Seriously, we would all likely agree that America wants the freedom to make alcohol a part of the current scene. We would all agree that excessive and uncontrolled drinking is a curse. And we would likely all agree that to have the freedom to drink and at the same time achieve the necessary discipline is not going to happen. The problem will not likely be solved any way soon. There are many approaches to this blight, but the problem remains and the challenge is ever before us. AA's are doing their thing (and it is tremendous) detox centers do their thing, counselors and psychiatrists do their thing, spouses, friends, neighbors of alcoholics do their thing. Slogans, admonitions, threats, bumper stickers, articles in magazines and newspapers concerning the alcoholic problem flourish. Despite all of this, the alcoholic demon is still at large, hale and hardy, and gobbling up our youth and significant numbers in all of society.

Years ago it was fashionable to believe that alcoholics simply suffered from a character disorder or a behavioral disorder and were nothing but sinners. More recently it has become fashionable to consider this a disease over which the patient has little or no control. My own feeling is that probably both

134

extreme views are wrong. I do think that alcoholics have some control over their condition and cannot abandon all responsibility, like a victim of appendicitis would say that he could do nothing about his disease. It is my firm conviction that although alcoholics have a severe handicap over which they have only partial control, they must be held responsible for their actions. They can if they will commit themselves to the twelve step program. I think the same can be said of people who suffer various emotional illnesses. Often such people are not totally at the mercy of their disease but can exert some influence on the eventual outcome by discipline, determination, courage and an unyielding spirit to failure.

All doctors have to deal with alcoholism in one way or another. I have had my share of problems in that regard and have had my prejudices for sure. Neither I nor any member of my family have been afflicted with this disease and therefore I am less sympathetic. Getting up at 2:00 in the morning with a foot of snow on the ground and zero weather to take care of an alcoholic who owes me a great big bill has not been my idea of a marvelous way to practice medicine. As a matter of fact, my prejudice under such circumstances has often complicated matters in as much as my attitude toward the victim has not been good. One night as I was making a call such as I described, I made a decision and things have been better ever since. I looked upon this particular man cut up and bleeding, uncooperative, nasty, foul, in a new way. I tried to see him as the son of a mother and father who were very much concerned and who loved him. It could have been my son, but it wasn't. I decided right there and then to take a different attitude and I think I have achieved it. It has been easier ever since. And so I believe that an attitude on all of our parts which does not condone, but which contains compassion and understanding is far better. Indeed, it would take an almost overwhelming spirit of understanding and generosity to feel accepting of an alcoholic who had killed my child during one of his binges. I do not have the answer to this monumental problem, nor does anyone. The causes are multiple and the purpose of this paper does not include a discussion of causes. I do feel that we are seriously lacking in the will to deal with this problem in terms of punishment for the offender. I think we have made it much too easy in this country and although there is some progress in this regard, we have a long way to go. It is one thing for a person to hurt himself and to shorten his days by alcoholism. It is quite another thing to kill another person because of it.

■————————————————————————————■

Pearl and Clark

What a pair! Mother and son. Pearl was a widow. Clark had Down's Syndrome and was a life saver to Pearl as well as a burden. He was able to function well enough to understand simple things. He went to the post office, to the grocery and the pharmacy. He could safely negotiate the traffic. He was attentive to his mother and she to him. It was really a remarkable, if not beautiful, relationship. For medical problems, Pearl usually called me to her house, for she was weak and frail in body, but mentally, she was a rock. Rock of Gibralter, that is! She was intelligent, resourceful, headstrong, determined and usually got her way. One morning my phone rang about 2:00 and it was Pearl. "What's the matter, Pearl?" I asked sleepily. "Dr. Martin, I want you to come over right away, I need you." "What's the problem, Pearl?" "Doctor, I simply fell out of bed, but I am not hurt. I am too weak to get off the floor and into bed. Clark can't help me, he is not strong enough." And that was true! "Pearl," I said, "Why can't you ask a neighbor to help you, I am worn out." "Doctor, I didn't want to bother my neighbor." So what could I do but go over to her house and put her back into bed. Fortunately, she didn't live too far away. That is a pretty good example of the way Pearl operated. She knew what she wanted, when she wanted it, and made the necessary arrangements to get the job done.

I knew the time was coming when Pearl would have to surrender her independence and come to the nursing home along with Clark. I knew it would be a difficult adjustment. Well, the time came and the move was made. But the period of adjustment never ended. Most patients after an initial period of rebellion and turbulence, hostility and anger, finally get into gear with the facility and things cool off. Not so with Pearl. She was angry and upset every time I went into her room. She was used to being in the driver's seat and now she was taking orders and it was bad, bad, bad, bad. Clark didn't seem to mind the adjustment and he didn't even visit his mother all that much. This made matters worse for Pearl. In one fell swoop she lost her reason to live and lost her independence. To take care of Clark was her one joy and reason for existence. Now he was no longer her charge for he belonged to the nursing home. And Pearl fought the rules and regulations like a tiger and never did relent or give an inch. Toward the end she gradually became demented to the point that she could be more easily led and managed. Amazing but true. One of her last rational requests to me was regarding Clark. "Dr. Martin, promise me that you will take good care of Clark." I did. Clark lived on another five years or so before he died in his late fifties or early sixties.

We usually admire and respect people of independence, intelligence and resolve. Pearl was such a person. But in the nursing home setting, that very quality which made her shine, made her almost impossible to deal with. She simply could not or would not shift gears. Some of us with strong characteristics of behavior such as Pearl will face the same dilemma if we should find our last days in a nursing home. It is a tremendous advantage if we have the insight, the will and the resolve to shift gears at various stages in our life when we need to. We need direction. We need goals. We need acceleration. We need brakes. We need fuel and we need power. How nice when we have all we need for life's challenges and the ability to synchronize our energies and our talents purposefully and smoothly. How great it is to realize our ambition, our goal.

How satisfying to arrive without a major breakdown, but if we do break down and get fixed, even if it is more than once, it is still grand to arrive in home port, the voyage over, the task completed and enjoy the rewards that are at hand.

Dave

It was raining and I was driving to Scottsburg en route to Louisville. A young man was hitchhiking. I looked at him and decided to break my usual and customary rule, and I picked him up. I introduced myself and gave him my hand. His name was Dave. He looked at me and said, "Doc, am I ever glad to see you. I haven't seen you for ten years. You sent me to Louisville when I had a brain hemorrhage and I had surgery. They said I was real lucky. I have been okay ever since. They said I had an aneurysm on the brain. Doc, you saved my life — you sent me to a great hospital and the right doctor." We talked on for a while and it kept on raining. He said he was a carpenter and was doing well. He said he blew up his car engine the other night showing off in front of some girls down by the car wash in Salem. He said he found himself another engine and was on his way to Little York to a friend's garage where he would install the engine himself. So I took him on to Little York and let him out and resumed my trip. That experience really made my day. I looked up Dave's records when I returned to the office and sure enough I had sent him to Louisville, about ten years previously. I had suspected a brain aneurysm which was leaking. This was confirmed and he did have surgery and he was doing fine. He was a grateful boy. A life had been saved. As I have said so many times before, that is the bottom line of what being a doctor is all about.

This event illustrates a point in life that good news often is contained and not much is said. Consequently, I hadn't received any news about this boy and somehow or other the usual letter from the surgeon didn't come. I am not sure why. Maybe he returned to another physician and that physician got the record. But just suppose I had missed the diagnosis and maybe sent this boy home instead of to the hospital. As all of us know who have lived long enough, good news doesn't have the travel qualities of bad news. Let the preacher's daughter graduate as valedictorian of her class and a few people take note and some may even be envious. But let the preacher's daughter get pregnant and the news is all over town and the county almost before she misses her first period. We all recognize this tendency on the part of most of us — namely, we pass on delicious morsels of someone's embarrassing misfortune, but not always do we talk about, at length, someone's trophy. This is the way it is and human nature is not likely to change any way soon. There are a few people out there who are glorious exceptions to this rule. They simply don't talk about anyone if they cannot say something decent about them and then there are those who rarely say anything good about anybody, and if they do, it is always negative. No good to belabor the psychology of all of this, I think it is pretty obvious why these things are done.

I think people of good will and those who are positive about their fellow man can be found in all walks of life. The church has a grand and obvious opportunity to carry out Christ's command in this arena of living but sad to say, the church fails badly many times. Sins of the flesh will cause the church to rise up with righteous indignation promptly. The sins of character assassination over the coffee cups are regularly committed and no one bothers to rebuke. It is a small wonder that the church finds itself often losing its power and influence — this is simply one of many reasons. I do not claim any trophies for perfect behavior either. But in recent years I have learned one thing. It is so much fun to send a person a note of congratulation about a success or an honor when that person least expects it.

J. S. Bell

J. S. Bell is a retired "missionary Baptist" preacher. If his name was mentioned about anywhere in his home county to a person over fifty, I suspect he would reckon that he knew him. Certainly everyone in that age bracket in Hindman, Kentucky, would know him, and just about everyone up the hollers would, too. For many years he was pastor of the First Baptist Church, and he also was the power behind the formation of satellite Sunday schools and mission churches in Knott County. He was perpetual motion. Funerals, weddings, teaching, preaching, seeking the down and outers and pleading with alcoholics to mend their ways. He and his wife and four children lived up Tadpole Holler on the edge of town. In that part of the world there simply wasn't any expanse of flat land and consequently about everyone lived up a holler. Those who lived in the town lived very close to the road and the creek.

J. S. Bell was a man of action, commitment and compassion. I loved that man, I still do. I long to see him on our annual visits to Hindman. When I returned to the church where I served as deacon and Sunday school teacher for fifteen years, I am loved, hugged and made to feel like a king. Mountain people are like that. When you are liked, you are loved.

After I had been in the church only a year or two, J. S. felt he needed to give the church a chance to do their thing without him and perhaps it would be good for them for him to move on. He virtually gave birth to the church and had mothered it along for several years. He thought they needed to be cut loose from his apron strings, so to speak. So he accepted a call to a church in Champaign, Illinois. With much sorrow and tears by pastor and people, good-byes were said and Brother Bell and his family departed. The church didn't get over it. Brother Bell didn't get over it, either. Everybody was depressed. I visited Brother Bell at the Illinois church and he was obviously in a state of clinical depression and so it turned out — well, you guessed it — he came back to Hindman amid tears of joy this time. He continued his ministry many more years in Hindman.

Brother Bell usually was gentle and not given to aggressive pushiness. But he was persistent in going after what he was after. I recall and everybody in Hindman recalls the momentous day when an alcoholic husband and wife yielded to Brother Bell's pleading and walked the aisle of the Baptist church, embraced the Christian way, never to take another drink.

In his early ministry, his only foray into the political scene took place. The dry and wet forces were lined up for battle in the little town and the politicking got hot and heavy. Matter of fact, to be too outspoken for the drys could be flat out dangerous. Brother Bell didn't flinch. He thrust himself into the fight with the drys and they won hands down. His family worried about his safety. But no one took a shot at him. I think about everybody admired his youthful courage.

Brother Bell was a powerful preacher and sometimes he exceeded the time limit in the pulpit. At the close of his sermon he would give the customary invitation to accept the Christian way and request church membership. And at this time, on many occasions, he would launch into a sermon that was emotional and tear jerking at times. I have seen his eyes wet on many an occasion as he yearned and pleaded with his people to break away from whatever was holding them back from coming into the church family. He cared for and he loved the people.

If you go to Hindman today, the old church is only a shell. Fire destroyed it. A new church stands on a shelf carved out of the mountains across the road. An unbelievably lovely structure for a mountain town where people work for a living and no one is very rich. I was there for the dedication a year ago. The church was filled. Preachers were all over the place. There was a two-hour service. It was unbelievable what was accomplished there by people with limited means. This was food stamp country, Medicaid country and country where federal subsidies poured in year after year. At this service there was singing and rejoicing and there were tears. It seemed to me that I was experiencing a preview of heaven on that never to be forgotten Sunday. There were old friends, many of my former patients were there, and all of these people I loved and they loved me. To me, this is the essence of the good life. This is what life is really all about, and were it not for this sort of thing, to me life would be very dreary and without significant purpose.

Denzil Barker, M.D.

Hindman, Kentucky, is a little town in the Eastern Kentucky coal country on Troublesome Creek in Knott County. It has played a significant role in my life. This mountain town isn't big, isn't fancy, isn't much of anything noteworthy, but to me, it was the home of friends and patients, the location of my church (Hindman First Baptist), and the scene of Denzil Barker's doctoring. Soon after the family arrived at Homeplace, we found a church where we felt at home and among the leaders in the congregation was Dr. Barker. We met, we got acquainted, we liked each other. Our family clicked. It was the beginning of a grand friendship that has stood the test of time. We were both country doctors, had similar ideas and goals, agreed on religious matters, and simply liked to be together. Friendship of this sort is a marvelous thing. It is not always found in this world. You can't buy it, you can't advertise for it, you simply discover it. I had graduated from medical school seven years before. I had been in Waterbury, Connecticut, several months interning, spent two years in Philadelphia General Hospital interning, was a medical officer in the United States Navy two years, and had done a two-year surgical residency in Louisville, before going to Eastern Kentucky. During this time I had worked with scores of doctors, had been friendly with many people in and out of medical circles, but it was in the little town of Hindman that I met a man who has occupied a place in my heart such as few have. We trusted each other completely and referred medical cases back and forth. We knew that the other would always attempt to do the best for the patient.

This relationship illustrates the point that one of life's greatest joys comes through intimate friendship. This relationship is always built on trust, mutual interests, common ideals and simply having a good time together.

Dr. Barker was born and reared in Knott County, Kentucky, the son of a coal miner. He was a bright and hardworking boy and was able to get into graduate school because of Alice Lloyd College's preparation and sponsorship. He made it through the University of Kentucky and Tulane Medical School. He gave his professional life to the people of Knott County by simply being a darn good doctor, being available, and living the life of service. Thirty-five years have passed since I first knew this man. We have worked toward a common goal. We have reared our families and we have kept in touch. A diamond I found in coal country when I found Denzil Barker.

George Drushal

This man I dearly loved and his memory lingers on and I shall never forget him. Why? Well, I will tell you. It was because of his courage, commitment to a task, and love for the mountain people. Brother George came to Lost Creek, Kentucky (Breathitt County), many years ago. He came for two reasons. He realized the need for education and for religious training for the mountain children. Educational and religious opportunities were hampered because of the rugged terrain and travel problems. Many people in those days lived at the end of nowhere. To get an education under those circumstances was almost impossible for some. As a result, boarding schools became a part of the educational scene in the Eastern Kentucky hill country. They were operated by Christian people of various faiths and denominations. In some places they were independent of any religious groups but simply represented the effort of individuals or groups whose main thrust was education. Examples of this type of school could be found at the Hindman Settlement School in Hindman, Kentucky and the Pine Mountain School to the west.

When Brother George came to the mouth of Lost Creek at its junction with Troublesome Creek, he saw some flat bottom land where a school could be developed. Bottomland was and is a precious commodity. The rugged mountains occupied by far most of the terrain. He made his initial move toward the formation of Lost Creek Christian School and was met with opposition and even violence initially. This can easily be understood. To have our deficiencies and needs pointed out to us and by a stranger is not easy to take. Brother George weathered the storm and the school became a reality and has continued through the years to play a significant role in education and religious training. Children who lived in relative isolation could come to Lost Creek School and live there and receive what was offered to them. As a result they were equipped to put their talents to use.

In his later years, Brother George was my patient at Homeplace Clinic. He was one of many missionaries in the area who found Homeplace to be their much appreciated headquarters for medical care.

Why did I like Brother George so much? First of all, he liked me and trusted me completely. He was a man of God, a man of principle, a man of commitment. He saw a need for a boarding school with Christian teaching and he met that need. He prevailed despite vigorous opposition to him at the outset and he saw it through. He influenced and enriched the lives of hundreds of youth. He was a charming person who loved people. I will not forget Brother George.

Willie Dawahare

Willie was a friend to about everybody who knew him. He was instant warmth, like getting close to a stove on a winter day. He would give you his shirt, not off his back, but off his store shelf. You see, Willie was owner of Dawahare's Men's Store in Hazard, Kentucky. He was mayor of the town. I think he liked about everybody and about everybody liked him. No kidding, about every time I went in his store, he gave me some item of merchandise that I could use. He liked to see people happy and he was instant success in making happiness. He pushed and shoved on the good projects around town. He was active in his church congregation.

Not long before Willie told me about the intensity of his symptoms (I was not his doctor), I had been to the Lexington Clinic where a doctor by the name of Sonnes gave us an electrifying lecture about coronary arteriography. He showed us on film (video tape) how he had learned to pass a catheter into the heart by way of the artery in the arm. He then learned to inject dye into the coronary arteries and demonstrate for the first time in medical history, the appearance of diseased arteries. He found out what the problem was and introduced into the medical world for the first time, a technique which was to make medical history and break through to pave the way for open heart surgery. Furthermore, we were told about a brand new technique of bypassing the obstructed coronary arteries by suturing a vessel around the diseased arteries and creating a new blood supply for the heart muscle. We doctors were sitting on the edge of our seats. No one was asleep that day. Unbelievable. Astounding! And so I told Willie about this new procedure done only at the Cleveland Clinic. That is, open heart surgery and coronary bypass surgery using leg veins for the bypassed vessels. I suggested he give this serious consideration. He thought about it a while and said that he was afraid to risk it. I could understand that. However, six months later Willie got up the nerve, went to Cleveland, had his surgery and was a new man. I mean he was on top of the world. He could run from one end of his store to the other. He was so happy and joyous that he went up and down the streets of Hazard telling people about his resurrection experience and praising God and the Cleveland Clinic. I had never seen such a happy man. He wanted to live life to its fullest and whereas he was on death row, so to speak, now he had a full pardon. He simply couldn't contain himself, he was so high.

He told me he went to Cleveland scared spitless. But the Clinic knew how to deal with that anxiety situation. He was exposed right off to the men and women who were convalescing from surgery and were feeling great. They allayed much of his fear and he went more relaxed into the operating room as a result. That was at least twenty-five years ago. At that time Cleveland was the only place in the United States where coronary surgery was done. Now it is done in every major city in the country. Thousands of patients have this done annually.

One of the largest referral centers for heart surgery in the United States now is the St. Vincent's Hospital in Indianapolis, Indiana. Last summer I had an opportunity to observe heart surgery and angioplasty (balloon procedure for opening closed arteries) in that institution. My wife was a patient in that hospital and after her condition was stabilized, I had an opportunity to learn about the surgical techniques right up close. It was an experience of a lifetime for this country doctor to see this dramatic and amazing surgery being carried out in a mass production assembly line manner. And yet the patients were tenderly and efficiently looked after and felt at home in that busy hospital.

I was invited to join Dr. Don Cristell on the appointed morning to observe a procedure. The procedure had been started when I arrived, the patient was asleep, the chest was opened by a split in the breast bone, and the heart exposed. The veins had been harvested (removed) from the left leg and were ready for suturing as bypasses around the blocked coronary artery. The heart lung machine was operating and the blood was detoured so that it would not flow through the patient's heart or lungs. The machine was pumping for the heart and breathing for the lungs. The surgeon identified the diseased arteries and explained what he intended to do. The beating heart was stopped by injecting a solution into the heart chamber. Then the bypassed veins (three of them) were sutured into place, carrying a new supply of blood to the heart muscle. After all were in place the heart was injected with another solution and it started beating again. The rhythm of the beat was not right, a shock to the heart was given, and this corrected the faulty beat. When all was well and things were working and the bypasses were functioning, the patient was taken off the heart lung machine and circulation restored to the heart and lungs of the patient. All was well. The monitors indicated success. The wounds were closed. Wire sutures were used to hold the sternum together. During the procedure music was playing and the atmosphere was relatively relaxed. Another life was extended. Hundreds of operations like this are done in that hospital every year and thousands throughout the world.

When I was in medical school, only very simple procedures could be done on the heart. When my father was a young man only a minimum of an elective surgery was done. When my great grandfather was a boy, there was no anesthesia and surgery was reserved only for life or death situations.

Progress, yes, yes, yes! Where do we go from here? Who knows? One thing is for sure, we have to learn how to live together or else there won't be any doctors or any patients or any surgery. Surely if our brains can figure out open heart surgery techniques, we can learn to live and let live. We will live together or we will die together. I believe we will live.

Mickey Napier

Mickey is my son-in-law, married to my third child, Gail. He was born and bred in Hazard, Kentucky, in the heart of the mountains and in coal country. Mickey and Gail were sweethearts all the way through high school and then married soon after graduation. Mickey had a near miss with the death angel in 1976. He worked for a coal mine and his job was to weigh coal trucks filled with "black gold." One afternoon at Mickey's weighing station he got into 7,000 volts of electricity when he tried to do a job which required him to use an aluminum ladder to get on top of the weight building. The electricity surged through his body and he was found lying unconscious on the ground. He was taken to Appalachian Regional Hospital, Hazard, Kentucky, and then transferred to St. Joseph's Hospital in Lexington, Kentucky. He remained in ICU for days and was in the hospital for weeks. He had extensive damage to his skull and scalp and to his legs and arms, hands and feet. After he was stabilized from the immediate threat to his life, he underwent multiple operations on his hands and scalp and skull to restore function and to give coverage where the tissue was destroyed. The burned skull was replaced with a plastic cap and the burned skin was replaced with skin taken from his abdomen to his arm and then to his scalp. This involved a long and painful experience for sure. He spent three years at our house where he was nursed back to health. He had physical therapy for months and gradually he went on to maximum improvement. His intellect and emotions were preserved without harm. He walks with an unusual and somewhat unbalanced gait. His hands are damaged but useful, the scalp and skull have been restored by multiple procedures. He is very lucky. Most people in his situation do not recover but lie in their graves.

Mickey was a fighter in Hazard High School, on the football team and on the baseball team. He was highly competitive and always gave his best effort on the athletic field. He exhibited this same fighting spirit in the hospital and during his long road back to productivity.

Mickey receives a monthly check from the settlement of the liability suit against the responsible party for his accident. The coal company, unknown to all, had allowed an electrical line to remain hot that was assumed to be cold and Mickey inadvertently got into it. Mickey could sit down the rest of his life and live off his disability income check. He elected not to do this but he saw an opportunity for him to be productive. Today he owns and operates Napier Auto Sales in Salem, Indiana. He is a successful businessman despite his significant handicaps. I think he is admired by the community for his grit and guts. I admire him. He is a good salesman. He coaches in Little League. He is not a complainer. He is not a quitter. He will give the game of life his best effort till the clock runs out.

Ole Jim

It was a nice mid-May morning in Berea, Kentucky, and it had rained the night before. The grounds of the Craftsmen's Fair were a bit damp, but straw had been put down and walking was acceptable. Craftsmen from all over Kentucky had gathered for their spring fair and we were enjoying the displays of every conceivable kind of artistry and craftsmanship. As we approached the area, a twelve horsepower engine was running, kerosene powered, and was operating a grinder, putting out corn meal for all who liked homemade cornbread. The sounds and rhythm of the engine, the exhaust puffing away, the flywheel turning, and the corn grinding all together produced a harmony of sounds that were nostalgic and enchanting. Sure, I bought some corn meal and my faithful wife has already made some corn sticks. Good, good, yum!

As we moved along from booth to booth, we marveled at the display of talent. Pottery, wood carving, quilting, paintings, photographs, home crafted jewelry, hand woven dresses and so on. And then we came along where Ole Jim was making shake shingles out of red oak blocks of wood. It looked so easy. He had a splitting axe of special width and design and he expertly and effortlessly split off thin pieces of wood from this chunk of red oak and lo and behold, there was another shingle for the stack. It seemed so easy but I am sure it was not. It represented years of repetitive strokes which resulted in a masterpiece shingle. He had done this, I'm sure, for years and he did it so well. I asked him how business was and he said it was plum good about all the time. I asked if he could keep up with the demand and he said he hardly could. I wondered if he had any help so that he could be more efficient. He said he didn't have no help at all. To quote Jim, he said, "It is hard to get anyone to work where there is any work to be done." I laughed out loud and whipped out my notebook and wrote down those words. They are classic and a lot of truth is in them for sure. We all know that. Actually, he was saying that he could not afford to pay the kind of wages that people would demand when there was a fair amount of work to be done. He obviously likes his work, was justly proud of his product and enjoyed having people stop by and watch his expertise. He was country, real country, mountain country, and was proud of it. And I was proud of him, too. I think he was the greatest. My kind of guy. He had a talent and he worked at it. He made a living at it and he was a useful citizen.

Oh, the joy of work, the blessings of work. How great it is to make a living doing something you enjoy. What a trial it is to have to work at a job you detest. I am sure that a number of the artists and craftsmen in the display area made a living at jobs they didn't especially like. Their joy came with their hobby. Their real joy came to them as they worked with their hands and made beautiful and useful things that people would buy and cherish. Each of the items in that vast collection of artistry on display in some way reveals something of the artist. The things we make tell about us. The poems we write, the stories we tell, the messages we leave, all of this is a partial revelation of who we really are. I have practiced medicine and surgery for over forty years and now I am writing. You get to know me that way. The things I say, the way I say them, and the stories I tell you, give a glimpse and sometimes a good look at me. I want you to know me, maybe that is one reason I am taking time from this fleeting life of mine to write. And I'd enjoy knowing you too, my reader. Knowing each other, sharing our lives, hopes and aspirations, this is the essence of the good life. Herein lies the hope for humanity, too. I want to come to know you as you share with me. This is living, and you know what, you don't have to have any credentials to come to visit with me. I'll let you be you — no matter who you are and I'll listen to you. And guess what, I might actually learn something that I need to know.

———————————————————

David Stewart, M.D.

On this Kentucky Derby Eve, 1989, I went to the hospital to see my dear friend and colleague, David Stewart, M.D. He is a patient now. His doctoring days likely are over. He knows what it is to be on the other side of the fence. He knows that it is better to be a doctor than a patient regardless of the stress and hazards of doctoring. A "no visitors" sign was posted on the door. He is getting chemotherapy. His days are numbered. He knows that. So does his doctor wife, Martha. My coming was announced to them by the nurse and I went in for a brief moment. David was reclining in bed, a smile on his face, and he said with sincerity, "Don, I intend to get out of this hospital if my immune system will just get back into

151

into gear.'' He asked about Virginia, ''Where is she?'' I told him she had to go to a meeting and was unable to come. He seemed disappointed. I told him I had just received news of his decline. I told him that I loved him, I admired him, and I do, I do! He has cancer in the bones, very painful. He gets morphine by intravenous drip. What a blessing at a time of agony. The hospital was clean, the staff efficient, and he was in a private room. Flowers were at the window.

David beat the monster of cancer thirty-five years ago when it grew in his colon. He came home at once from Africa where he was a missionary doctor. Surgery cured him. He has had thirty-five good years. I first knew David in medical school, the University of Louisville, in 1945. We both planned to be missionary doctors and so had things in common. David proceeded to Africa in due time and started up a brand new medical work out in the bush with World War II Army surplus medical and surgical gear that he obtained for a song. He was a real pioneer, unafraid, confident, caring, dedicated. In all, he spent two terms of service in Africa, and then returned to the United States to enter Psychiatry Residency. He has practiced his specialty with success and distinction ever since in Louisville, Kentucky. About ten years ago, David reduced his practice drastically as he tenderly cared for his wife, Laura, who died of cancer. Following his marriage to Martha, medical missionary widow, they together continued to give themselves to people in many ways.

David has coordinated the efforts to bring about overseas CME for scores of missionary doctors. Sessions have been held in Kenya and Malaysia each year and David has put the whole package together. His entire life has been built on the principle of service to others and he has been a happy man, a confident man, a successful person, and one who someday will receive along with many others the glorious honor and reception which Jesus spoke about in a parable one day as he was teaching. He said of the faithful servant, ''Well done thou good and faithful servant. Enter into the glory of the Lord.'' I think it will be this way with David. I know it will.

It has been said that the only thing we take with us at death is what we have given away. I think many of us would agree with that. As I look back on my own life, I would have to say, "Yes, this has been true for me." Giving twenty years of my life in a medically impoverished area I shall never regret. I did not accumulate property, stocks, nor did I have any savings at the end of the twenty years. I did receive so very much in terms of satisfaction, doing the thing I had to do, doing the thing I wanted to do, and doing the thing I loved to do. Despite the stress, the long sleepless nights, the agonies of mistakes and failure on occasion, these were joyful and glorious days for the most part. When I am able to help someone out of a sick bed, when I can help someone who is depressed and perhaps suicidal, when I receive the love that comes in various ways as a result of these efforts, then life is really worth living, then I am fulfilled. I know David has felt the same way in his years of giving to others. We both started out thinking this would be true. And now after years of living, we know this is true.

Earl and Merle

Were it not for these two, I would not be. I had nothing to do with my arrival in this world and no choice in the selection of genes that make me what I am. For that matter, mom and dad had no choice in the gene code that would produce their firstborn. I was delivered breech by a family practitioner in the home in west Louisville. Amazing what nature and a country doctor can do if you put your knives down and let nature take its course. A primip breech today would mean automatic caesarean section, no questions asked.

Dad was a history teacher at Male and Manual High Schools in Louisville, and later was principal in various junior high schools. Mom didn't work outside the home, as was true of most housewives in those days. She worked like a dog in the home, however. The usual chores of the housework took much more muscle and time sixty years ago than they do today. In addition, mom made many of our clothes, she cooked all the meals from scratch, she canned in season, mended, stitched and entertained. Mom and dad supplemented their income by renting out rooms in our family home. We bought a car about every eight to ten years. We took inexpensive vacations when we did take them. Depression days were on and a nickel would buy an ice cream. My sister and I were reared in an atmosphere of authority figures. You minded your parents, you went to church and Sunday School, you said your prayers, you obeyed your teacher and a policeman commanded your utmost attention and respect. Not much wrong with all of this for sure.

Dad was afflicted with colitis or what is now known as irritable bowel syndrome. As a result, he spent a lot of time and money doctoring. His illness took its toll on his life, his disposition, and of course, on those around him. At school he won high honors and respect for his ability. At home, when he let down, there were at times problems. His irritability got in the way of relationships. He didn't relate to children very well. When I became a young adult, he did much better and when I brought home the academic honors, an excellent relationship developed between us which remained constant to the end.

Mom was a workaholic, highly motivated, talented and an achiever. Her religious faith has been number one in her life from her youth on to the present day. At eighty-nine she is alert, independent and gives a large portion of her modest income to the church and religious organizations.

Any ability I have to express myself in word or pen has probably come from dad. From mom came my workaholism and achievement orientation. It is easier for me to love than to hate or to be indifferent to people. This comes from mom's father, grandpa Cauble.

These Men Left Their Mark on Me

1. **Charlie** — Charlie McMahon was my "bosom buddy" from my earliest memory until 1948 when tragedy caught up with him and he died of a ruptured cerebral aneurysm (brain hemorrhage). For twenty-five years we were as close as David and Jonathan in the Bible. We played together, argued together, but never fought except in games and athletics. We lived in Audubon Park, one of Louisville, Kentucky's finest subdivisions. It was a beautiful place for kids. We were the same age. His parents were inactive Catholics and his father was a realtor. My folks, at that time, were members of the non-instrumental Church of Christ, my father a school teacher. Charlie went to church with us and became active. We were brought up in the depression days and I well remember its effect on society. We went through grade school together at Prestonia and then he went to Male High School and I went to Manual. We competed for top grades and we competed in athletics and it was good. We were inseparable. I went to Wheaton College in Illinois, and Charlie went to Indiana University at Bloomington. I was a pre-medical student and he went to business school. Charlie was drafted during World War II and went to the Army, but was discharged early because of a deformed hip as a result of a childhood illness which left him with a slight limp. He was able to return to school and get his degree. He went to work in a bank in Washington, Indiana. I was able to do my pre-medical education and medical education in six years instead of eight because of war time acceleration. I married Virgina in 1947, and Charlie was in my wedding. Charlie fell in love and was engaged and the

wedding date was set. I was interning at Waterbury Hospital in Waterbury, Connecticut, and I was scrubbing to do my first abdominal operation with staff assistance. It was a ruptured peptic ulcer case. An emergency telephone call came to me and I broke scrub and answered the phone. It was my father. Charlie was dead. Cerebral hemorrhage. I went on and did my surgery and then had to make a difficult decision. Virginia's parents had just arrived by train from Indiana to attend her graduation from Yale School of Nursing. To leave for Louisville, to be with Charlie's family, would mean abandoning Virginia during her graduation and missing the visit of her family. Also, to go to Louisville by plane would be very expensive and I had no money. I made the decision not to go. It turned out to be a bad decision. I don't think Charlie's parents ever forgave me. I learned a lesson. To show comfort and concern at such a time really demands one's presence regardless of the cost or inconvenience. Charlie's death was tragic. An only child, a brilliant boy, a good boy ready to assume a new responsibility, engaged to be married, he was headed for greatness until the ruptured blood vessel took him down.

2. **Grandpa Cauble** — Omar Leroy Cauble was the greatest to his grandson, Donnie Boy. He was everything a grandpa ought to be — loving, fun, generous and good. He was a busy businessman with lots on his mind, but he always had time for me. He loved me and I knew he did and he showed it. I was his first grandchild, very special. Grandpa was a man of God and it showed by a loving and generous spirit. He was kind to his employees and he was loved and respected in the community.

3. **Keith Cameron, M.D.** — I first met Keith in 1954 when I went to visit Homeplace Hospital. He was forty years old, an Englishman and former missionary doctor in China. He had come to the states after the Communists took over in China. He had married an American missionary and they elected to come to the United States rather than to return to

156

England. I was fascinated by this man and made my decision to go to Homeplace and help him with the medical and surgical work. For twenty years we were together through thick and thin. He was bright, very polite and had great knowledge of classical music, mechanics, and as a person he was kind and considerate. He was a student of the scriptures and was an able teacher. Actually, he was a genius at mechanics and was known world-wide for his expertise with "Mechano," the English equivalent of an American erector set. He had intended to live his life in China as a member of the China Inland Mission. For ten years he practiced medicine and surgery in a hospital in the interior of China. He spent the rest of his career in the mountains of Kentucky, practicing in an area where at the time few were willing to go. I shall always be grateful for his friendship, his companionship and his kindness. He was a role model to me and one of the reasons why I spent twenty years in the Kentucky mountains.

4. **John Hart, D.Min.** — John arrived in Salem with his family in sub-zero weather and lots of snow on the ground. He came as the new pastor of the First Christian Church and was my neighbor, my pastor, and my friend for nine years. John could be called a liberal by the standards of many of the church members and he managed to alienate a number of members who were of the conservative, fundamental persuasion. He was accepted by the Disciple loyalists. John's wife, Judy, came to work for me in my office and still is a faithful and loyal worker. John was with us as we went through the trauma and trying times with Luke, my son-in-law who died at the age of forty of Hodgkin's Disease. He was with us in the near death experience of my daughter, Gail. I not only appreciated his ministry at First Christian Church, but he became my friend, my good friend. John possessed a sensitivity that made his ministry special in times of suffering and death. His funeral services were relevant and appropriate to a remarkable degree.

5. **Albert AiLun, M.D.** — I was reading the "Burma Surgeon" by Gordon Seagrave years ago at a time when I was

planning to go overseas as a missionary doctor. Seagrave had written a marvelous account of his life in Burma where he accomplished a tremendous amount of work. He built a hospital and a nurses' training school and a thriving medical establishment was launched. His fame as a surgeon spread far and wide. He took special interest in a young man, Albert AiLun, and was able to assist him in getting his medical training. AiLun was able to come to America and spend a year at various teaching centers to obtain further training. I met AiLun at Greenlake, Wisconsin, at the American Baptist Foreign Mission Society Conference Week. He was a delightful person and our friendship grew and flourished immediately. He was a committed Christian and took his faith seriously and worked at it. I asked him if he could spend his Christmas with us in the Kentucky mountains. He accepted the invitation with enthusiasm. We had several delightful days together. After practicing several years in Burma he had a fatal coronary attack. His influence was felt by many people, both in America and in Burma. He was a man of many talents but the best thing I can say of him is this — to know him was to love him.

6. **William Barclay** — I know this man because of his words in print. I did not get to meet him personally while he lived. He was in Scotland and I was in America. This man is known by hundreds and thousands because of the printed word. Pastor, teacher, theologian and author, this man will go down as one of the church's greatest communicators. At a time when my personal religious faith was being put to the test, at a time when I was struggling and growing, William Barclay came to my rescue and presented the faith the way that made sense and had a ring of authenticity. He saved me literally from "throwing out the baby with the bathwater." I am going through his commentary of the New Testament day by day and it is sheer delight to get his insight and understanding. The scriptures have come alive for me as never before because of this man. He is to me the modern Apostle Paul. We speak of inspiration

of scriptures and have our own ideas of what this means. For me, the writings of William Barclay are unique and they speak to me in a very special way.

Part Two:
This I Believe

—1—
Nerves, Worry & Emotional Ills

A Trip to Hell Three Times

It has always been an interesting thing to me as a physician to notice that there are certain diseases that patients tend to be proud of and other diseases of which they are ashamed. Some diseases are okay; some are not okay. We love to tell in detail about our surgical experiences, our open heart surgery especially, and other surgeries of long and tedious nature that we have withstood and come out victorious. But I never hear anybody talk about, in public at least, their experiences in a mental hospital or their experiences with the psychiatrist. Somehow, we regard illnesses of the emotions and mind as an embarrassment, but diseases of the body acceptable. Although we have made great strides and progress in recent years in coming to a better understanding of emotional illness, we still have a long way to go. In Colonial days, people with mental illnesses were regarded as witches and were sometimes executed or at least badly treated and often in public. Later on, we recognized people with such maladies as sick and put them in institutions when it became apparent that they were either dangerous to themselves or others. And with derision we refer to such places as crazy houses or nut houses, and the jokes concerning such have laced our literature over and over again. Somehow we have tended to regard emotional illness as a weakness or a character disorder or something to be ashamed of, whereas we accept appendicitis and pneumonia and heart disease without question and without shame. As medical science learns and understands more about emotional and mental illness, then we will gradually come to the place where we will regard it without stigma, without shame and in the same way as we regard any other illness. It is my feeling that this will be some distance in the future, however. There is still the feeling lingering that our emotional ills could be cured or prevented by ourselves, whereas we need help with appendicitis or pneumonia. This is especially true with men when they become depressed or anxious and are poorly functioning. They resist, often, seeing a physician. They claim they can solve their own problem and so they go to the bar, and instead of solving their problem, they make a problem that is ten times as bad. Women find it less difficult to admit their need for help in this area, and will much more often go to the doctor for appropriate therapy.

The doctor who has suffered a particular illness or disease is much more apt to be empathetic with patients who are likewise suffering, and so this is true with me. I have suffered recurring depression through my life and am in a position to make some appropriate and timely comments about the subject. Depression is a family-oriented and related condition like so many other diseases. Numerous members of my family have been so afflicted and it is indeed a genetic related disorder. We see cancer running in families, heart disease in families, high blood pressure in families, and so do we see alcoholism in families, we see schizophrenia in families and certainly depression. I would like to relate my experience with depression with emphasis on three hospitalizations that have been required for my treatment and restoration to functioning.

Actually, during my entire life, I have been afflicted with this disorder, and even in my childhood, adolescence, high school and college days, I can recall times when my functioning was impaired due to depressive episodes. At the time I had no idea what the trouble was, I simply gritted my teeth and did my best. My first major episode of non-functioning with depression came during my second year as a surgical resident at the Veterans Hospital, Louisville, Kentucky. I was on the urology service and things were going well. The illness came on subtly and gradually and was characterized by a period of increasing self-doubt about my ability as a physician, along with difficulty in sleeping, accompanied by increasing anxiety over what was happening to me; followed by difficulty in concentration, making decisions, with resultant bewilderment. My slow descent into this depression was over a period of perhaps a month and it gradually grew worse to the point that I had to seek help. I simply was unable to function sufficiently to carry out my responsibilities as a surgical resident. I visited our hospital psychiatrist who listened patiently to me and after a session he said to me, "Well, Don, you are either schizophrenic or depressed and I am not quite sure which." My anxiety level after that statement hit an all time high and I went out of that office confused, bewildered, angry and quickly became totally non-functional. Psychiatric units of General Hospitals were just beginning to flourish and this was a far better setting for treating emotional and mental illness than the State Hospitals were equipped to do for short-term illnesses that could be treated appropriately and quickly. And so I admitted myself to the Norton Hospital Psychiatric Unit in Louisville, Kentucky, where I remained for approximately four weeks. I went in with great fear and trembling and shame. The stigma of emotional illness was almost intolerable. Had I gone in for appendicitis, there would have been no problem. To go in for depression or whatever was a major problem.

There was an attempt on the part of some of the patients and their families to even lie about the true nature of the illness and thus try to hide the shame. In my case, I made it perfectly clear right from the start what my trouble was and I tried to be up front and clear cut about the problem. That was a wise decision. It has always served me well and I have been respected accordingly. If you are ashamed of your plight, then others tend to be ashamed with you. If you are not, then they are not.

The year was 1953, and the hospital was located at Third and Oak Street in Louisville at that time. A relatively new wing, it was well equipped, and furnished to do its job. As I recall, there was space for approximately forty patients. I was in a room with three other men. We soon became friends and shared our problems. Quickly, my condition was diagnosed as a depressive reaction and not schizophrenia. There was absolutely not a shred of evidence for that disease and how the first psychiatrist could even imagine such a thing is beyond my understanding. I know one thing. He really shook me up. A doctor has an awesome responsibility in his communication to his patient. He can reassure or he can make matters worse, just as a slip of the scalpel by the surgeon can bring a disaster to the patient, so a wrong word or wrong phrase or wrong explanation can bring disaster to the patient. There were no medicines available for depression in 1953. Depression is a disease which will run its course and everyone will recover in due time. I did recover in four weeks. Relieved and released, I went back to work fully restored but shaken. To be aware of one's vulnerability is a painful experience, one that influences all aspects of one's life.

Virginia and I were headed for Africa and had been commissioned by the American Baptist Foreign Missionary Society to go to the Belgian Congo (Zaire). This would involve a year of French study and a year of tropical medicine study in Brussels, Belgium, beforehand. Before my depression, I faced all this without flinching. Afterwards, I flinched real big! As a matter of fact, I resigned the commission with great regret in as much as I felt the need to prove myself before attempting such a venture. Our supporting churches were upset and disappointed but the American Baptist Foreign Society Board was understanding.

For the next sixteen years I functioned well as physician, surgeon, obstetrician, gynecologist, psychiatrist, and had "hands on" responsibility in about every medical and surgical specialty at Homeplace Clinic and Hospital. In this isolated and rural mountain setting, it was doctor, patient, and God on the team. Through thick and thin we went. Up to my elbows in blood and knee deep in disease and suffering night and day. Life for me abruptly changed in the summer of 1969, when I left my first love, my place in the sun, to practice in Pekin and Salem, Indiana. I simply failed to make the adjustment to an entirely new practice and way of life. The ugly darkness settled again, the self doubt, the early morning awakening, the loss of appetite and zest for living. My decision-making process was a mess and my concentration was lousy and I felt like I was walking through mud in my mind. I longed to return to the place of security where I felt fulfilled. I went back to work at Homeplace, having settled in, but alas, I could not function. So to the hospital I went again, this time Our Lady of Peace in Louisville, Kentucky, for another three-week stay. Only this time the marvelous tricyclic anti-depressant, Tofranil, did the job after a week of top dose, 300 mg. daily. I emerged from my depression suddenly it seemed, and for a brief time I was high. But who wouldn't be? After the flames of hell, the cool breezes sure do feel good! Back to work and fully restored I went.

For eighteen more years, I functioned well, working night and day bearing all sorts of burdens. There were some times at which I was mild to moderately depressed but I managed to keep going. In the summer of 1987, after years of solo practice in Salem, Indiana, working night and day with too heavy a load, I once again fell headlong into the dark passageway of depression. One day at noon I left the office not to return for eight weeks. This time I took my medicine and therapy at Highland Baptist Hospital in Louisville. The unit at

Highland Baptist was well run. The personnel excellent and the food was good. A young Catholic priest was chaplain and he was very special to me. The love of Christ oozed out of his pores, so to speak, and I poured out my heart to him. I shall never forget that young man. He was a saint to me.

I am told that the likelihood of the fourth depression after three is ninety percent. That is not a comforting thought to say the least. All was well again, however, until six months ago when once again I knew I was in trouble, but I was back to the killing work routine of night and day burdens once again. And so, I finally got the message, I think God was screaming at me, and so I blew the whistle, gave up the hospital practice and limited my energies to the office. I obtained the new drug, Prozac, and it has proven to be everything Eli Lilly said it would be. It was effective and the side effects are minimal. It has been a "hell of a trip," but I can see the promised land. I am sixty-five years old and I feel like I am forty. I have adequate rest. I am writing my memoirs.

TB or Not TB

The number of patients presenting psychosomatic complaints is significant and the primary physician must be alert and in tune with this condition. Psychosomatic symptoms refer to symptoms that are felt in the body but the origin or cause is in the emotions. Take this for an example. You are walking in the woods and reach down to pick up a rock and you suddenly see a coiled up rattlesnake ready to strike. You pull back, your heart races, and you are breathing fast and the next thing you know, you are a hundred yards away from the snake. Psychosomatics indicate that your body is functioning properly and that there is no disease there but the problem is in the realm of emotional stress. There are numerous examples of this. The headaches that accompany a stressful day at work, the diarrhea which may accompany a forthcoming examination, and the tensions in the body that prevent sleep from facing an examination are all examples of what we are talking about. And then there is the recurring cramping abdominal pain when the boss confronts you, the vague and persistent discomforts in various parts of the body when one fears that he has cancer are well known to many.

Patients are often reluctant to even entertain the possibility that a symptom of theirs is psychosomatic. To even bring it up incurs the extreme displeasure if not the wrath of some patients. It is okay to have heart disease, appendicitis, arthritis, or whatever-else-it is but "doctor, surely you don't think this is in my head do you?" The problem is that patients believe you are implying that their symptoms are imaginary if you start talking about symptoms having an emotional origin or framework. And they know better, they know darn well that "it is not in my head." The physician will make a determined effort to explain that the pain is real, only its cause is different, but some patients simply will not accept your explanation, their minds are closed. They will run off to another doctor who may offer them a more satisfactory explanation for their illness or go off to some witch doctor of some variety and get his treatment for whatever the diagnosis is given and spend a lot of money. As a result of this very prevalent tendency, many doctors grow weary of patients with emotional ills and psychosomatic problems and simply give the impression that they do not welcome them and the patients, of course, soon get the message and check out.

Having personally suffered depression on more than one occasion, I am able to relate to patients with emotional problems. On occasion I tell patients of a personal experience to explain psychosomatics. When I was a freshman in college

I was under stress and my appetite was not up to par. I lost some weight. A doctor had once told me that I might eventually get tuberculosis some day because I had a positive tuberculin test on one occasion and also some enlarged cervical lymph nodes. I never forgot what he said and worried about it. And so during this time of stress at college, I developed vague aches in my chest and developed a cough and soon I realized that the TB germ had caught up with me. Then things really got bad. My lungs ached, I lost more weight, and I knew I had to go to a doctor sooner or later but put it off. The word came for all freshmen to report to the gymnasium for routine chest x-rays. Wow! That was it. Only a matter of time and I would be out of college and in a tuberculosis sanitorium. The x-ray was taken and a week later the report came out that I was entirely negative. Wow! What a relief. The aching stopped, coughing too, I gained my weight back and I felt fine. This was a perfect example of psychosomatic illness which I had personally developed and could understand. It helps patients when I tell them this story. If one focuses his attention on any part of his body long enough, it will soon begin to bother him. To demonstrate I suggest the following. Close your eyes for five minutes and think of nothing but your eyeballs. Before the time is up they will be burning and aching and very uncomfortable. And so as patients we become excessively concerned and perhaps phobic about certain parts of our body and this aggravates matters because of our constant dwelling on that part of our anatomy.

There are a number of patients who have psychosomatic ills and simply cling to them as a life-long process. Some females are apt to be of this type for it is the only way they can get attention from the family. This alleged illness serves some other useful purpose perhaps. Some patients may adapt this sort of illness simply as a means of escape from certain responsibilities. Some women may remain ill in order to avoid sexual intimacy for one of several reasons. Children can go this route in order to skip school on occasions. Psychosomatic symptoms are not deliberately developed but they come unconsciously to the patient as manifestations of another problem. To deliberately be sick is to be a malingerer and that is not what I am talking about here.

I believe that it is particularly in the realm of psychosomatic illness where techniques of healing of a certain kind may be especially significant and helpful. I believe that Christian Science offers a technique of healing that is quite useful when one is dealing especially with a psychosomatic illness. I am quite certain, too, that the so-called faith healers who bring about "miraculous" healing are often dealing in the realm of psychosomatic illness. It is well known that psychosomatic illness can be helped if not eliminated by various techniques such as counseling, understanding, education, acceptance, faith, biofeedback and the list goes on. Even with many organic illnesses that perhaps are even incurable, our quality of life can be vastly improved by acceptance, fortitude, courage and making the most of the opportunity and time we have left. Concentrating on what we have left rather than on what we have lost does help a lot as one bears his illness and burdens.

And so our response to illness and suffering presents an opportunity to demonstrate strength, patience, acceptance. Some of the outstanding persons in my memory are those individuals who have done just that. I do hope and pray that when my turn comes to face a terminal illness I can demonstrate strength, patience, acceptance; although one never knows until he has arrived at that point.

Helen

Helen was diagnosed as having manic depressive illness. During the manic phase she was roaring around 100 miles an hour so to speak. She was singing, whistling, talking incessantly and you couldn't shut her up. She would drive you crazy.

It was like being on a hilarious drunk twenty-four hours a day, seven days a week. If she was not brought to the hospital, she could go on and on until she literally dropped in her tracks from sheer exhaustion. Usually, she was brought to the hospital and admitted. If it was summer and the windows were open, she would continue her hilarity and she could be heard at Hollywood and by passersby alongside the hospital. We had no drugs to cope with such a problem. Lithium or Thorazine, used so effectively today, were unknown at that time, but we did have a treatment that worked — electric shock therapy, now referred to as ECT or electroconvulsive therapy. The patient was taken to the shock room and placed supine on the table. Attendants were stationed on either side of the patient to hold him or her during the convulsion. Electrodes were placed on the temples, after paste was applied, to contact the current. The shock was delivered and immediately the muscles of the entire body went into a violent contraction. The breath was held until the patient turned blue. Then the rhythmic jerking of all the muscles started and continued for a few seconds. The patient gradually ceased the jerking and deep breathing was restored as the oxygen deficit was overcome and normal color returned to the face. If you have ever seen a patient with an epileptic fit, you have seen a shock treatment. The modern ECT is more humane. The patient is put to sleep with an intravenous injection and the muscles are paralyzed with the drug and a shock is delivered. There is no jerking whatsoever. The patient awakens as if from a natural sleep, no strain, no pain — easy.

And so Helen received a series of shock treatments over a two-week period and normal behavior was restored. The humming bird became a canary bird, the wild woman became a tamed lady, the disturber of the peace became the model citizen. She went home and lived a normal life for a while. But the manic spell would return inevitably and another cycle of shock treatments would be given. She got literally hundreds of treatments during the years and one would have thought her brain would have been fried to a crisp. But after each series of treatments she seemed to be fully restored. Today, thank God, thank the researchers, thank the drug companies, we have Lithium which can be given on a daily basis over a long period and largely prevents the recurrence of that dreadful behavior. What causes all of this? We know not. We do know there is a family tendency for this. Is it a bad gene? Could it be due to a chemical imbalance? It could be. The answers will eventually come. I have seen Helen go into a depression phase of her illness in which she was the opposite of her manic self. During this time she could hardly move, could hardly get out of bed, wouldn't eat and slept fitfully. She was tired all the time, would cry and cry and cry and have the look of death upon her face. Suicide was an ever present concern during these periods. And so, once again, she would come in for shock and after a series she would emerge her old self, once again restored to good ole Helen, sweet Helen, affectionate and doing her duty, enjoying life and being a model citizen. Wow! And to think we used to regard such people as witches or demon-possessed. They would be mistreated terribly and at times even burned at the stake. We have come a long way, thank God, thank doctors, thank researchers, thank patients willing to receive new and untried treatments.

Today, we still have a long way to go in regards to our treatment and attitudes about behavioral diseases or mental illness or whatever you wish to call it. It is great to have had open heart surgery. We are proud! We rip open our shirts on the courthouse steps to boast about our experience, our bravery, our restoration of health and vigor, but did you ever see a guy brag about the number of shock treatments he had to take? Oh no! It is okay to have coronary heart disease, it is still not okay to have a chemical imbalance or an emotional illness. It is rather regarded as a personal imperfection, a weakness or character defect or whatever. My prediction is that eventually mental illness will be better understood just as coronary disease, pneumonia, or appendicitis is understood and it will be okay then to have mental illness and recover the same as it is okay to have appendicitis and recover. I long for that day. I know the need there is for understanding and acceptance.

■───────────────────■

What I Have Learned From Patients

1. The doctor has an advantage in observing people and coming to know them as they really are. Often when patients come to see me, they are in a vulnerable position, and often are more apt to be stripped of their veneer than under other circumstances. Patients come to doctors for various reasons. They come because they feel bad and something is not right and they want help. They come because they are in pain. They come because they are afraid. They come because they are nervous and upset and their functioning is impaired. Some come because their spouse insists on their coming and in order to make peace in the family, they come. Of course, the grand exception to all of this is the very occasional patient who is an imposter and who comes in wanting usually an addictive substance and paints a picture that will appeal to the doctor and sometimes successfully gets from him what he or she is after.

2. I have found, generally speaking, that women are more apt to complain and men tend to be stubborn. Women are regarded still in our society as the "weaker sex." I mean that it is acceptable and appropriate for women to express their needs, express their fears, and admit their role of dependency. We live in a society today which still insists that men should not cry, that men should be strong, that men should not show their down side and that men should be independent and at all costs bear their burdens and be uncomplaining. This

174

exception, therefore, leaves many men to be stubborn and unyielding regarding visits to the doctor and particularly in the realm of emotional disorder. A nervous woman will come to the doctor much quicker than the nervous man. The upset male is more apt to go to the local bar to seek anxiety relief and discuss his problems with the bartender than he is to go to his physician. Consequently, he often makes matters far worse under those circumstances.

3. What do patients want from the doctor? I think first of all, patients want the doctor to listen and to listen carefully. I think patients want doctors to be interested in them personally and to be friendly and accepting. I think patients in general want doctors to appear and act professionally and treat them with respect and dignity. Patients want doctors to be honest and straightforward and especially not to take advantage of them in any way. There are a few patients that I have seen, and all doctors see, who expect doctors to treat them as an exception to all the rules and to give them special attention. In other words, they expect too much and often the impossible. Patients want a physician who is intelligent, decisive and knows what he is doing. Patients generally will gravitate to the doctor who is friendly, personable, loving and accepting. The highly skilled physician who may have serious limitations with his personality, is inclined to be cold and detached, will have difficulty in building an adequate practice, particularly if he is a family physician. In other words, a patient will select the warm and friendly doctor who has intellectual and professional limitations over the brilliant physician who is cold and withdrawn.

4. I have classified by my observations dying patients into three categories: There are those who simply pull everyone down as they go down — they complain, they moan, they groan, nothing is good. Everything is bad, and there is an aura of gloom and despair about them much of the time. Sometimes I hate to even go into the room where such a person is

being treated because it is so difficult. Then there are patients who literally lift you up as they go down. There are a few in this category. It is a joy to go to see them although there is pain connected with it. They look on the bright side. They lift you up and they minister to your needs even during their hours of suffering and anticipated death. It is a joy to go into the room of such a patient and you never forget them. They are giving until the very end. The great majority of people are somewhere in between these two extremes. They neither particularly lift you or particularly drag you down during their dying process. They are good solid citizens, reasonably appreciative for what you do and bear their burdens without too much complaint and face the inevitable with reasonable courage and acceptance.

5. Patients generally expect doctors to take the active role in the healing process and most are unwilling to exert necessary discipline in order to assist in their healing process. To put it simply, when the doctor suggests they quit smoking in order to get over a prolonged bronchitis, they simply are unwilling to do that. They want the doctor to get the proper medicine and to make appropriate suggestions, but they themselves are unwilling to change their lifestyle. This same observation is also made in the obese patient who wants a magic pill rather than to undergo the discipline of dieting. This same process is observed with the drug dependent person or the alcohol dependent person who wants the doctor to take the active role in bringing about a change. It takes a tremendous degree of motivation for the patient to become an active participant in the healing process and few seem to possess it. I noticed this in both patients in the mountains where often lifestyles were loose and disorganized, and also in patients in southern Indiana where life was much more organized and structured. To effect a change in lifestyle and to exert great discipline in order to bring about a healing result requires effort that most patients are unwilling to exert. To the younger doctor, this is a terrible frustration and disappointment. The older physician

tends to take this in his stride, do his best, let the chips fall, park the ambulance, so to speak, and wait for the inevitable crash.

6. Because we live in a society which regards physical illness as acceptable and emotional or nervous illness as generally unacceptable, the doctor has to be especially sensitive and alert in order to identify emotional illness when the patient presents his list of complaints. It is true, in my opinion, that many patients in a family practice present emotional illness which they have not recognized, and if they have, very reluctantly admit to it. In order for the physician to separate emotional illness from organic or physical illness and approach the therapy appropriately, it requires a great deal of knowledge, of ability, of experience and sensitivity to properly do the job. It is not easy and some physicians are far more skilled at this than others. First of all, it requires that the physician be accepting of the patient who presents with emotional illness. Some physicians find this dificult. When they suspect the patient is emotionally ill or neurotic, they make it very clear in their attitude that they would wish the patient to move on and, of course, they ultimately do. Some doctors regard themselves as doctors of the body. When it comes to maladies associated with the emotions or mind, they become uneasy, defensive and resentful. They get a clear signal from the doctor, such as "why don't you get out of this office, you don't belong here." This attitude, I am afraid, is present with more than a few physicians and as a result, helps to foster the prevailing view among the general public that emotional illness is unacceptable, is bad, and is something to be ashamed of. There are a number of reasons why doctors adopt this attitude and it is understandable. First of all, patients with emotional disorders often take extra time from the doctor. Secondly, this is a difficult field in which to work and clear cut therapy does not often bring immediate relief such as a course of antibiotics curing an infection. Thirdly, patients, at least some of them with this sort of disorder, can be difficult and can be selfish and can be frustratingly slow in making improvement. And finally, there

are patients who, it would appear, are only comfortable in this world when they are ill or sick and seeking the attention of other people such as family, friends and physicians. These patients, obviously, will never be well and these patients present an almost intolerable burden to many physicians. Every caring and sensitive and patient physician will have a number of patients who fall into this category. He does what he can. He tries to bring temporary relief, attempts to be supportive, and in the last analysis, he must simply "put up with the situation" and try to be a friend to the patient anyhow. Any attempts that he may make to radically alter the picture are usually met with failure.

7. If the doctor-patient relationship is solid and good, I have found that patients will put up with a lot of inconvenience in order to maintain that relationship. My patients will often wait for me for long periods of time when I am running behind in my schedule and often this is the case. They don't like it but they accept it and usually when I finally come into the room after a long and tedious wait, they are so glad to see me and that the time has come, they forget the frustration and don't say anything about it. Fortunately, the majority of the patients do not expect me to be God and make no mistakes. Most patients will accept the fact that I am human and that I have my good days when I knock a home run or get on base every time, and then I have my bad days when I occasionally strike out. A doctor is not a computer which almost by magic arrives at a diagnosis quickly and brings about a cure effectively. He is a human being, capable of brilliance and capable of mistakes. And, of course, when the mistake is made in regards to you, it can bring turmoil and grief. Most of the doctor's loyal patients will put up with a lot of inconvenience because of the doctor's problems in his personal life. For instance, the alcoholic physician will be away from his practice perhaps a month at a time, periodically, and when he returns his patients return, accept the situation and do not forsake him. I have been amazed how often I have found this to be true. Often the alcoholic physician, when he is functioning, is brilliant,

is capable, is warm, is friendly, is accepting and is a real fine person and for this reason, patients are loyal. On the contrary, the brilliant physician who is chronically irritable, short tempered, cold, detached and who perhaps is trying to be a family physician, is going to have a serious problem in making a living. The doctor whose personal life has been turbulent, who has been in and out of various marriages, and whose behavior may at times have been scandalous, still has the loyalty of many, if not most, of his patients, provided that his relationship with them is acceptable, proper, and if the patient receives from the doctor what he or she expects.

What I Have Left Is What Counts

There are a lot of cliches and old wives' sayings out there that we are all familiar with and certainly all of us have found them to contain a lot of truth. The one that is my subject in this paper has to do with the losses in our lives and how we react. Surely this topic is of interest to all of us because we have experienced losses repeatedly, small ones, medium ones and large ones. No one is exempt. Loss is a usual and universal experience. As I grow older and have benefited from maturity and experience, I am more convinced than ever that our losses are better accepted when we concentrate on what we have left rather than cry over what we have lost.

I must confront patients day after day with bad news as I tell them about their medical problem. I do think that some are enabled to accept the news better when I explain that things could be worse. If they should happen to have diabetes and I so inform then, then I likely will tell them that diabetes may be bad enough, but at least it is not as bad as cancer, leprosy or AIDS. Looking forward to open heart surgery is surely frightening, but it is not as bad as opening the skull for a brain tumor for instance and on and on we could go with these comparisons. "Yes, your baby is dead, my friend, but your wife is alive and you can look forward to another day." Thinking about our losses in this way can and does enable us to bear them better and does make a difference.

To lose one's earthly possessions by fire is devastating, but if the family is saved, it makes all the difference in the world. When our car is totalled out, we are upset for sure, but if life and limb are intact, then the car can be replaced. Most of us have marital problems from time to time and are unhappy and frustrated because of it, but when I think of the horrendous problems that other couples are having, then mine don't seem so bad. If the steak is tough, I am apt to keep my mouth shut when I remember that the starved of Ethiopia would eat shoe leather if they could find any.

Our children can bring us joy immeasurable or can take us to the pit of hell. If and when I begin to feel sorry for myself because of a child's failure or trauma, I accept it much better when I realize that it could be far worse. We worry if a child has an emotional problem and has to enter into counseling, but we can be glad he is not in a psychiatric hospital. It is upsetting if a child is convicted of tax cheating by the IRS, but it in no way compares to languishing on death row in a state prison.

Most doctors have some problems in the smooth operation of their office, even me. But one of my employees has not embezzled fifty thousand dollars and for that I am profoundly grateful. Although my profit expense ratio is not good according to the standards of most offices, I am making more money than I really need, so I don't worry about it. Although patients dirty my parking lot and walk through my shrubbery, no one has broken out my front windows and for that I am grateful. Although the IRS digs deep into my pockets, I would rather pay the U.S. government than the government of the Soviet Union. I could go on and on in counting my blessings rather than cursing my tribulations.

Solo Flight

I was the new young doctor at Homeplace and was trying to get adjusted and spread my wings. Adjustment periods are often difficult and many of us approach the new with caution and uncertainty. I have admired those who sailed into the new and difficult with apparent ease and courage. I have had enough insecurity all my life so that I prepared well in advance for any challenge. After a month at Homeplace, Dr. Cameron, my associate, took off for a much deserved and overdue vacation. As usual, I tensed up knowing that I would have the full load of a rapidly building practice in an isolated community where in any crisis situation, it was doctor, patient, and God, nobody else. No consultants, no fancy equipment, not even a telephone. Medicine, surgery, obstetrics, orthopedics, pediatrics, I had it all. It was twenty-four hours a day, seven days a week, and no let up. Dr. Cameron took off and I took hold. I had twenty beds in the hospital. There were an average of thirty deliveries a month. Emergency surgery such as I felt I could handle, was a possibility during any hour of the day or night. The nearest medical center was three-and-one-half hours away over very rough terrain and winding roads, so my decision to handle a problem at Homeplace, or send it on was not always easy. There is an old saying among surgeons, "When in doubt, cut it out." But in my case, it was, "When in doubt, send it out." But then you had another consideration, could the patient stand the trip? If I were "over my head" I could sometimes get a surgeon from Hazard to come out and assist me. I hadn't been a week into my solo flight at Homeplace when a lady came in, seven-and-a-half months pregnant and bleeding vaginally, heavy, too. I had no choice but to go to surgery. She had most likely a placenta previa. I did the caesarean section under local anesthesia in order to give the baby the best chance. I knew it would be premature and the delivery would be hazardous. There was no pediatrician, of course, to call; I had to take care of that problem, too. Was I uptight about this? I sure was. To surgery we went. The operation went fine. The baby was tiny, but in good condition. We kept the baby about six weeks and then it went home in good condition. All of us find out in facing scary things, the best way to handle them is to grit your teeth and go for it, nerves and all. I made it through Keith's vacation just fine and it was the best thing that could have happened. It gave me what I needed so much. Confidence! We all have to learn that experiences like this are essential to building strength and confidence.

−2−
Religious Matters And All That

Making a Dollar out of Twenty-five Cents

Of the many things I have learned about the American people with whom I have associated during my professional life, I have noticed two things that are so characteristic of all of us. One is that we will almost risk our life in order to park a few feet closer to our point of destination. We will spend time trying to find a place closer so that we will have less distance to walk and at the same time we join a health club to get exercise. A bit ridiculous, don't you think? The other thing that I have noticed about Americans is that we all have a tendency to try to make a dollar's worth of truth out of twenty-five cents' worth. I see this in so many phases of life. Particularly, I have noticed this in matters of religion and philosophy, in general. We come to some knowledge of truth and seemingly want to make it the entire truth for everybody at all times. The fundamentalist in every religious sect, in particular, demonstrates this point. The Moslem fundamentalist believes he has all the truth and so does the Buddhist. The Christian, of course, believes he has all the truth; the Orthodox Jew rejects Christianity and continues to look for the Messiah. Then when we look at the Christian religion, we see it divided into two camps, the Roman Catholic and the Protestant. Catholics believe they possess most or all of the truth. The Protestants are broken down into innumerable groups, many, if not most, of which somehow feel they possess all of the truth.

As I see it, after years of observing people, and after years of being busily engaged in Protestant churches, it is my conviction that each and every splinter group has taken a portion of truth and has attempted to make it all the truth. Why do we do this? For one thing, we have only partial exposure to total truth and consequently come out with conflicting anwers. As a Christian, I am convinced that Jesus of Nazareth introduced a lifestyle that gives meaning and joy to life, but I am quite willing to listen and learn from other religious groups. I can learn from them and they can learn from me.

This same tendency to make total truth out of partial truth is seen in matters of political persuasion, race relations and social issues in general. All of us have a limited world view and only possess a fragment of total truth, and yet in our arrogance we act as if we are right and anyone who disagrees with us is obviously wrong. Fundamentalists in Protestant Christianity certainly will scoff at the doctrine of papal infallibility, but they do not hesitate to assert that their understanding is absolutely correct and thus they lay claim to infallibility. All of us are simply products of our environment and our inheritance and thus we come up with our beliefs and our own individual understanding. An Englishman in London will view race relations one way and an Englishman in South Africa will not see it the same way. A doctor sees the malpractice crisis one way, and a lawyer sees it quite differently. The teacher of a "bad kid" at school has one view and the parent may likely have a different idea as to why things have gone wrong.

As I have matured, I see a lot more gray than I do black and white, and I am referring to life in general and not just the hair on my head. I think the person who grows becomes less sure of a lot of things and more certain of others. As a young doctor, I was "cock sure" about a lot of things. I am not so certain anymore.

Which brings up the subject of the arrogance and God complex of so many physicians and surgeons. We are indeed a privileged and highly educated and experienced profession but we, too, have a tendency to make total truth out of limited knowledge, in my way of thinking. Many of us have a tendency to listen only partially to conflicting ideas and opinions. We tend to regard as witchcraft any knowledge that is outside the boundaries of approved medical science. Many of us belittle chiropractic, health food and vitamin freaks, acupuncture, and any other knowledge that we do not understand or bother to investigate. As my dad used to say, "it is easy to be down on what we are not up on."

It is surely a human trait to believe that we possess special insight and that our particular religious group has a private line to God's throne and consequently we have the scoop on matters of piety and morals. It is surely tempting to inflate our egos by thinking that our view of scripture and our view of the church, our concept of religion, our understanding of reality is the way it is and that those who disagree are either ignorant or in league with the devil.

I am not sure if God our father cries or laughs about all of this. I guess he must react about the way parents do as they observe their children growing up. Some children remain kids all their life and that brings grief and remorse. Some children grow up and become adults and change their attitudes and become wise and mature and this makes parents proud and happy. Maybe, just maybe, it is this way with God, too.

■———————————————————■

One World or No World

I am well aware of the view of many that believe that peace in the world can never be achieved, that there will always be conflict, and the survival of the fittest is the rule of nature never to be altered. Surely as one recalls history, this concept has always proven to be true. The reasons are multiple and well known. There are many things that separate us, religion, political concepts, color, language, our possessions or lack of them, customs, culture, and on and on.

If there is any hope, and I believe there is, then it has to come by way of discussion, interaction, and a mind set that begins to de-emphasize patriotism and begins to think in terms of "our world" rather than "our nation." I am confident that many people think this to be true, but the problem that is obvious is how to achieve this. Can it be done? I think it can. Civil wars have ended and the nation has been healed. We have seen this over and over again. Labor and management have fought it out and peace has come. Organizations have been torn apart and healing has come. The path to peace has always been difficult. It is easier and more fulfilling sometimes to fight. But now we can't afford the luxury of fighting unless we are ready to say good-bye to humanity. I don't think we are ready for that.

So what do we do? Things are already happening that give reason to hope. Russia and the U.S.A. are pursuing a course of negotiations and togetherness as perhaps never before. Marvelous! Nations are collaborating in scientific research and this obviously helps to weave the common thread. The conquest of AIDS may very well depend on the efforts of many nations working together to defeat the common enemy. There is nothing to unite people more than fighting a common enemy, whether it be AIDS, earthquakes, floods or fire.

And now I would like to discuss a subject that is controversial, I mean really. Mainly, it is a touchy subject to the seriously religious people of the world. Knowing I shall take a position that will be highly unpopular with the most committed religious people, and considering myself a person of piety and religious commitment, I don't especially relish the thoughts of launching out into the deep and stirring up trouble and making people angry and unhappy. My nature is not to do this, but rather I like being liked, I like being loved. Well, for better or for worse, here goes.

Religion can bring about the most blessed unity or the most devastating hatred. The history of the world has included some of the bloodiest of all wars because of religious differences. We cannot forget the Crusades and the devastation they brought about. The Inquisition witnesses to murder in God's name. The horrible war between rival religious factions of Iran and Iraq testify to this concept. One could go on and on and on in citing examples of the horrors brought about by religious differences. A church family has serious differences and the church is split and the families leave and communication and friendship is forever ended. The struggles between Catholics, Protestants and Jews is remembered with heartache and embarrassment.

Is there any answer to this? It seems to me that it is essential that we work toward the goal of religious tolerance and peace if ever we are to have "one world." If the people who claim to be in fellowship with God cannot demonstrate peace, is there any hope for the world? If we do not set the example, then who will?

I am a Christian and firmly believe the Christian way contains eternal truth. I think we Christian Americans have a grand and glorious opportunity to live and demonstrate the Christ lifestyle to the world and in so doing, promote brotherhood and peace in a unique way. We do not need to belittle people of other faiths. We simply need to live as Jesus lived, that is sufficient. Religions do not need to compete. We can complement. How about a religious service on occasion with Jews, Moslems, Christians, Buddhists and others all together. The brotherhood of man and the fatherhood of God could thus be promoted in a unique way. Religion could then be a vehicle for world brotherhood instead of another area of conflict and bloody separation. None of us need to give up our religion, our citizenship, our culture, our possessions. What we need to give up is our insistence that our way, our belief, our culture is the only one.

The world today reminds me of the human body. For the body to function, there must be cooperation among the organ systems, each one doing its job. As long as disease is controlled, this is the case. If cancer invades the body, suddenly things get out of control. The cancer cells don't obey the rules and go wild. The body reacts and tries to kill the cancer cells. Often the cancer wins and the wild cells cripple the remainder of the body. So with the world, if there is cooperation instead of wild and uncontrolled competition, there is hope. Cooperation demands discussion, openness and a spirit in which we learn from each other.

How Can They Do It?

Having observed "men of the cloth" all my life, having gone to church since I was a month old, and having lived next door to the minister of our congregation for fifteen years, having worked closely, even intimately, with more than one pastor, I must confess that I don't see how they stand it and keep their sanity. Being a minister is not a "heaven of a job." In my judgment, it is a "hell of a job" too often. A retired pastor once said to my wife, "when I was pastor, it seemed like all I did was put bottles in babies mouths to keep them happy." I am sure that this is a bit exaggerated, but it points out a truth. "Tip toe through the tithers" is another cliche to think about in this regard. What I am trying to say is that we church members can be pretty rough on our ministers. We expect them to be morally impeccable, preach a good sermon Sunday after Sunday, attend every committee meeting known to mankind, keep peace among the church members, keep the money coming in, teach us the scriptures, visit our sick, and don't ever make anybody mad. We put him in a no-win situation and expect him to "part the Red Sea" as did God for the children of Israel. Furthermore, the minister must preach the right doctrine to suit us and not necessarily our neighbor. His doctrine must conform to our expectations. Furthermore, he must be funny if we like jokes, or be serious if we don't. He must be loyal to the denominational leadership if we approve of its structure or he must be a rebel if we disapprove of the hierarchy. If we believe that the world is beyond hope, then he must preach salvation of souls and let the world go to hell. If we believe the world is worth saving and can be improved, then we insist the preacher direct his fire in that direction.

No wonder the Roman Catholic priests are restive and unhappy. The priest, even with all his dedication, still is a human being and in need of love, intimacy and companionship, and yet Rome says no marriage, no family. How do they do it? Some don't and others are going to quit and fewer are going to seminary. Yes, it takes a grand and holy calling to serve humanity. Humanity put Jesus on the cross and it seems to me that we are still doing that to many of our pastors and priests.

Good Religion and Bad Religion

Primarily, I am going to restrict my remarks to the Christian religion for a number of reasons. I am a Christian and know something of what I am talking about. I think I have earned the right to speak. I am not a Moslem and have limited knowledge of that faith. The same can be said for all the other religions in the world and my understanding is likewise limited. So often we are prone to be down on what we are not up on. I refuse the temptation to be critical of other religions not only because my exposure to those faiths is minimal, but because we Christians have our own share of inconsistencies, failures, narrow mindedness and fanaticisms.

My credentials for speaking as a Christian, I lay before you. Having been born in Louisville, Kentucky, U.S.A., I was, by birth, apt to be a Christian. Reared in a family where religious faith was taken seriously and being reared in the twenties and thirties when it was not fashionable to rebel, I dutifully made my commitment to Christ and the Church at age eight and was duly baptized in Blue River in Pekin, Indiana. The non-instrumental Church of Christ, which embraced premillennialism (beliefs in certain prophetic doctrines) was the church of my boyhood. I "preached" my first sermon when I was a high school junior at the Highland Church of Christ in Louisville. I have been exposed to and been a part of the evangelical non-liturgical churches. These have included, in addition to the Church of Christ, the evangelical fundamental interdenominational churches, the American and Southern Baptist Churches and the Christian Church (Disciples of Christ). I have taught Sunday School, functioned as Elder for the last thirty-five years in the church and generally been a leader and a pusher. I have given dutifully and, I might add, joyfully ten to fifteen percent of my income to the church and charitable causes. The big three in my life has consisted of family, profession and faith (religion).

In my spiritual journey I have made changes and for this reason some would say that I have abandoned the faith and have become a modernist. Some would say happily that I have grown spiritually, and could relate to my position quite well. There came a time in my religious life when I simply could not accept Christianity as I had been led to understand it and at the same time be true to my convictions about reality as I had experienced it. Something had to give. It did. I am so happy that it did. I have come to terms with what appeared to be inconsistencies with my previous beliefs and understanding and life as I had observed it and experienced it.

I am spirituially fed and am at home so to speak in a religious atmosphere of freedom, openness and acceptance. I like it when I am loved as I am and not conditionally because of my doctrines, beliefs and attitude. On the other hand, I know perfectly well that this atmosphere is not for all by any means. There are those who desperately need black and white in their religion and no grays. Biblical literalists or inerrantists have a message for these people, while the main line denominations often do not. And so we gravitate to the fellowship where our needs are met and where we are "fed" so to speak, and that is okay. I believe there is bad religion when we spend more time sending spiritual bombs on each other and clubbing each other with the Cross of Christ than we do in fighting injustice, racism, and sin in general. We Christians can sometimes become experts in criticism of one another and superstars at waging spiritual warfare.

The Catholics have something to tell us about authority and conformity and taking orders. The Mormons have a lot to tell us about family support and the good life, conviction and the missionary spirit. The Charismatics can and do infuse joy and emotion into corporate worship. The Episcopalians can tell us about reverence in the house of God. The fundamentalist demonstrates often knowledge and love of scriptures and setting a high priority for serving the Church and recruiting for the faith. Liberals demonstrate more often than not, acceptance, understanding and promote the ecumenical spirit better than any others.

I think a religion is good when it produces good men and women. How else are we to judge? If it produces people who are cantankerous, judgmental and pharisaical, then I say it is bad religion. In this world of suffering, grief and tragedy, I believe we need more love, more joy, more acceptance, more understanding, more support and less condemnation. Didn't Jesus say that he came not to condemn the world, but that the world might be saved?

Experts

In gray areas of knowledge and life, that is, in areas where knowledge is incomplete and no one really knows the answers, in these situations the world is teeming with experts. I have noticed this in so many phases of life. In the medical world it is certainly true. In areas of disease where we know little, experts are to be found on every street corner and will be thrilled to give the gospel of truth on the subject. Take arthritis, for example. There are hundreds of wonderful treatments out there because we simply don't have the scientific answers. In terminal cancer when medical science has been exhausted, there are experts in cancer therapy waiting to take your last dollar as you grasp for a straw. The truth is, such people are experts in extracting your dollar, that's all.

In religion and philosophical matters the door is wide open for any and all to become experts in their pronouncements and often the experts have little or no tolerance for those who differ. The man who has all the answers is one who has had very little exposure to things as they really are, as I see it. I have found that in my own experience as I have grown and matured, I have mellowed out and am inclined to listen more and to talk less. I still find it too easy to talk, and at times, a bit hard to listen, I must confess.

I have no problem with people of conviction and commitment. I think it is fulfilling and energizing to have it together and be off and running. But I do find it hard to accept the person who after he arrives at his convictions and commitments, closes his ears and mind lest his world view be upset by different facts or ideas.

We don't argue much about the world being round. We have settled that issue. But we argue plenty about homosexuality. The facts about the world are in but they are not all in about gender orientation. Let us hold tentative conclusions and convictions in areas where the facts are not all in and where the jury is still out.

Resurrection

It is Easter time again as Christians all over the globe gather on the appointed Sunday to celebrate the resurrection of Jesus of Nazareth. It has been almost twenty centuries since the event and one can't help but wonder if mankind will survive another twenty centuries. It is indeed a blessing to have a knowledge of the past, but not an ability to look into the future. To see into tomorrow would enable us to better plan our lives in some ways, but the problems created by that would be overwhelming. We would, of course, focus on the disasters and pain ahead and be unable to see the good things. And so it is best that we cannot see tomorrow.

The will to live is basic in all of us. The exception to this is seen when we are old, lonely, in pain and depressed. I will make rounds this morning at the local nursing home. There are some there who would be ready to make their journey and cross over Jordan. Another exception is the person, youth or older, who becomes deeply depressed for various reasons, sees no way out, and believes death is preferable, and then puts the pistol to his head and pulls the trigger. Yes, the will to live is firmly implanted in all of us who enjoy some degree of health and who are not deeply depressed to the point of suicide.

This will to live is seen in the religious conviction of resurrection hope that is basic to most religions. To Christians, of course, Easter Sunday is the day of days when we focus on life after death and think in terms of eternal life. Moslems certainly have an understanding of life after death and the concept propels them often to enter into martyrdom. The Japanese and other Orientals believe in reincarnation and this provides hope when one approaches death. The American Indian had his happy hunting ground. And we could go on with examples of resurrection hope.

The will to live is implanted very deeply in the human species. Life has to become unbearable with pain, loss or hopelessness before we opt to die. I am wondering if each and every newborn baby could have a preview of his entire life in a flash, if he would decide to go on with his life or not. I asked my eighty-nine-year-old mother recently if she would like to re-live her life and perhaps do things differently. Whereupon she held her hand high and said, "Never, no never!"

The reality of life after death is withheld from us the same as the fetus knows nothing of life after birth. We wonder about it, speculate about it, hear sermons about it, but no one knows. I suspect there will be the element of surprise and amazement when morning comes after the sunset of life. I believe that the concept of eternal life is valid. Not only do I accept this as a Christian, but also it makes sense. Why should our creator put this hope in all of us if, in fact, it did not exist? And also there is to consider, that about the time that a man has the experience and wisdom to be ready to live, he is then ready to die. Surely, there must be something else.

After sunset there is sunrise, after gestation there is birth, after winter there is spring, after the egg there is the chick, after our bodies decay, our influence, ideas, contributions, children and grandchildren live on. Is it too much to imagine that personality survives? Whatever follows death I am sure it will be right. The God who thought all this up in the first place will have the right ending. The author who wrote the best seller, is going to end the story in a magnificent way, I feel certain.

Easter 1989

Another Easter has come and gone. A great time of the year for sure. Family time. Twenty of us gathered at my daughter's for a good old time of visiting, loving, catching up, eating and rejoicing. Springtime, the beautiful weather, spring flowers, garden and yard work, hope and resurrection. Christian churches across the land with bigger crowds than usual. Colorful clothes, pretty hats, beautiful women. Surely a joyous time of hope and optimism. Victory over death. Victory over evil.

Most of us stand in awe as we seriously consider the implications of the resurrection of Jesus. But what has this to do with modern man, we may ask? Some may say, "I could care less about the resurrection and being resurrected. The life I had was enough, I don't want any more." Some would actually find the continued existence of certain individuals, classes, colors, to be undesirable. Some would vote "no" for resurrection for lots of reasons. We would want our family and friends to be among the resurrected, perhaps our fellow countrymen and perhaps all good people around the world, but many we would vote out of heaven, for sure. The Bible has a lot to say about life after death and resurrection. It defines the qualifications for participation, for judgment, for eternal reward, for destruction. Many Christians find solace and comfort in resurrection hope and emphasize this above all other Christian dogma. Other Christians emphasize this life and the Christian's obligation here and talk little about the hereafter.

I have observed that the Christian hope of life after death brings a great deal of comfort to many on their death bed. Grandma Cauble talked about heaven much of the time as she approached the sunset of life. Others somehow don't feel too secure about their eternal destiny in as much as they have not stood before the judge of all spirits. I find that I am more oriented to this world and do not spend a lot of time thinking about the hereafter. If and when the sentence of death is placed on me and I have time to reflect, I suspect that I will adjust my priorities of contemplation.

Resurrection of the body, as Jesus demonstrated, strikes us as the greatest of all miraculous events and so it was. But somehow I find that there are "miraculous" events all around us every day that are surely worth our notice. There is the miracle of conception and new life as an expression of a relationship between man and woman that never ceases to be anything but "miraculous." There is the miracle of resurrection as a chemically dependent person finds release and becomes a productive and lovable person. There is the martyr who willingly lays down his life for a cause greater than himself strengthened in many cases by a firm belief in the resurrection and the hereafter. The intricacies of the human organism, the amazement of the physiology, chemistry, anatomy, immunology and functioning of the mind and its inter-relations with the body; all of this to me is as miraculous as perhaps the resurrection.

The bottom line of what I am saying is that I am convinced that the architect of the universe and the one who Jesus called father and the one who thought of relationships, love and family is planning a homecoming for humanity, someway. Can I prove that? No! But it makes sense and it seems right.

Founded in 33 A.D.

Recently, I was driving through a town in Georgia while on vacation and I noted on a church sign that the congregation was founded not in the 1800's or 1900's, but in 33 A.D. Now that struck me as highly unusual for a Protestant church to date itself even before the reformation. I know what the congregation meant by that, however, and I think I understand where they are coming from. They are simply saying to the community that the local church at that spot had its roots at the time of Christ. Now in a sense, that is true, for all Christian churches have their roots in Jesus of Nazareth. But I also realize that the congregation with the 33 A.D. sign meant that that church and all sister churches had their roots in Jesus, while all the rest of them, not of that particular variety, had their beginnings much later. Basically, they were saying, "we are the original, the oldest and consequently, the true Church, and all others failed to meet this standard of excellence and truth." If a person really believes this about his church, it can be invigorating. It can generate enthusiasm and the members can feel very good about their position in the Christian world under these circumstances. The problem is, and it is a big one, that that kind of an attitude fosters the idea that all churches not of their variety, are badly missing the mark, even to the point of total failure and rejection by God. This means that all church members other than those of the "true church" are objects of missionary activity. To me, this would be a depressing concept rather than an invigorating one. To believe that the members of only one Christian church are heaven bound and the rest are lost, is a dreadful thought. And not to mention all the adherents of non-Christian religion.

This position seems to be a common thread throughout much of life, not just limited to religion and churches. How many doctors are prejudiced into thinking that their method of treatment is the only acceptable one? How many teachers, lawyers, businessmen, parents, administrators, feel their way is the best, if not the only proper one? Our opinions and prejudices are a reflection of our experience in life in combination with our inborn tendencies produced by the genes. It is often true that we have violent differences of approach and opinion on a subject because we are simply coming from a different world than the next person. And so I believe that to really communicate and understand each other, we need to recognize this principle. We simply must try, as much as possible, to see the situation as our neighbor sees it, not that we necessarily agree with it. If we can really understand where the other person is coming from despite the fact that we do not necessarily agree, this will foster human relations and good will, I believe, in a remarkable way.

A Campbellite's Spiritual Journey

I have been a family physician for over forty years, and I have lived long enough to have some sense, to have some judgment, to know why and how some things fly and why some things crash. I have learned to like people, most of them. Some I have loved, some I have admired, some have been role models. Family is precious. So are friends. I have found it more blessed to give than to receive.

Not let's talk about my spiritual journey. When I talk this way I think about church, sermons, preachers, prayers, communion, baptism, commitments, beliefs, attitudes, hopes, fears, struggle, God, Jesus and the Bible. Life is a pilgrimage, a journey, a brief sojourn for all of us. Our bodies change from infancy to childhood, adolescence, adulthood and maturity. My body is not exactly as it was when I was in grade school, for sure. So, too, my concepts, my beliefs and understanding are quite different as contrasted with my certainities of college years. How and why this switch? I suppose I would be considered a liberal by some fundamentalists and if that is the case, I'll accept the tag. In some areas of my belief and attitudes, I am not so cock sure as I used to be. In other areas, I am more sure about things and this is my brief story.

My church journey began with the non-instrumental church of Christ as a boy. In college at Wheaton I was exposed to the interdenominational, evangelical point of view. After that, I rubbed shoulders, sang and prayed with American Baptists. Then for twenty years I was deacon and Sunday school teacher in Southern Baptist Churches. For fifteen years, I have once again been a Campbellite, but this time I returned to the Christian Church (Disciples of Christ). I am spiritually at home. I am with a non-judgmental, accepting and loving people. I delight in that.

In my earlier spiritual journey, I, like all evangelical fundamental people, believed that to be a true Christian, it demanded a belief and a loyalty to an inerrant Bible. That is, the belief that the scriptures are literally true in every detail, both historically, scientifically and theologically. Adam and Eve, in that concept, are regarded as real people. Jonah was literally swallowed by the whale. The children of Israel were indeed instructed by God to kill unmercifully their enemies and not leave one person or animal alive. According to this inerrant

Bible view, we must believe that the people of the Third World, who have never heard of Jesus, are destined to spend eternity in hell. I can't believe that. A God like that would be no friend of mine.

In no way do I wish to imply that those who believe in an inerrant Bible are unintelligent or hopelessly prejudiced. Believing in an inerrant Bible gives one a commitment to a lifestyle that can be beautiful. But, alas, I have noticed that the lifestyle of some inerrantists is very similar to the Pharisees of Jesus' day. If God intended for any religious holy book to be inerrant, then people would eventually accept its truth, despite lack of compliance. Truth does surface. We don't argue about the force of gravity or the fact that the world is round. I can't imagine God giving us an inerrant book such as the Bible that is the subject of such divergence of opinion and belief. Intensely committed people of various religious traditions vary widely about the interpretation of scripture. To me, it is a form of extreme religious arrogance to say that my understanding of scripture is truth and anyone who differs is wrong.

I believe the Bible is a precious document that contains virtually all we know about the Galilean carpenter whose followers turned the world upside down. It contains the witness of Jesus' disciples and their interpretation of Jesus. It contains the theological position and interpretation of Jesus by the great missionary, the Apostle Paul. It reveals the history of the ancient people of Israel and the evolution of their understanding and relationship to God. I believe in the uniqueness, the simplicity, and the majesty of Jesus of Nazareth. The Biblical writers have given us their interpretation of him and their witness has stood as a beacon to humanity for centuries. Because of their written testimony and its faithful preservation by his followers, the Bible is with us to this day. The disciples of Jesus knew him, experienced him, interacted with him. They talked with him, listened to him, were amazed, bewildered, and were filled with awe. They saw his compassion, his acceptance of all people, his identification with the losers, the sinners and the poor. They winced at his anger and disgust with the religious legalist of his day. They knew he was courting disaster as he attacked the religious power structure. He was an enigma. He was unorthodox. He was rejected by his hometown friends and acquaintances. His own brothers and sisters stood back with uncertainty. The cruelty of the death of one who lived so majestic a life is a terrible indictment on mankind, yet triumphantly the scriptures witness to the resurrection event, and the world, as a result, has never been the same. The resurrection hope accordingly is ours and we can face our own death as we would the sunset of our life knowing that morning will come.

I am tired of seeing fences erected around Christian and religious groups. I would rather be a destroyer of fences than a builder. I am tired of the eternal bickering among Christians, each group feeling that they have a special insight as to what true doctrine and spirituality is all about. I am tired of seeing so-called devoted Christians verbally clubbing each other with the cross of Christ and the Bible. I am tired of seeing churches divide and subdivide into splinter groups, each feeling that they and God have a special relationship above all others. Now I have lived long enough to know that we cannot always agree, nor can we always work together. We must go our separate ways at times, but we can live and let live. We can worship and let worship. We can respect our fellow Christians though they be "wild-eyed liberals" or "feuding, fighting fundamentalists." If we Christians can't show the world that we can love and accept one another, is there any hope for the world? If we can't or if we won't set the example for the world community, then who will?

■————————————————————————■

Preachers

I am not just talking about the clergy, the men "of the cloth," the evangelists, the men who remind us that "payday" is coming someday. I'm talking about all those who have a message for humanity and give out advice with conviction and enthusiasm, whether it be the printed word, the radio, the tube, or the speech from the courthouse lawn. The libraries are full of books on "how to do it," "how not to do it," "how to succeed," "how to hang on," "how to be made whole," or "how to bring heaven on earth in ten easy steps." Now I want to first off admit that there is a lot of good advice out there. Norman Vincent Peale's book of many years ago, *Power of Positive Thinking*, is a case in point. This book has helped many a weary traveler along life's rocky road. Doctors have written books of advice by the ton. Psychologists have ground out material of value. Certainly our childhood church school teachers have helped many a sapling grow a bit straighter. Our preachers have convinced many a hell-bound sinner to clean up before it is too late. Often our various preachers, advice givers, map makers of life's road, have had a personal experience that has propelled them from podunk to big city and they are ready to tell humanity that they can do the same thing.

Now that is exactly where I have to slam on the brakes. It just isn't so for everybody. The poor guy who hasn't got any gas in his tank, can't exactly be turned on by the preacher or the advice-giver who tells him how to go sixty miles an hour instead of thirty miles an hour. What I am trying to say I suspect you have already figured out. So often we feel that our experience can be everyone's experience. Wrong! So often we take twenty-five cents worth of truth and make it total truth for all at any age. So often we feel that everyone should want to climb the mountain we have climbed and if they don't, there must be some deficiency there. Wrong again. Some folks are made to stay in the ruts of life and they seem quite happy. Some persons simply don't want out of jail and if they are forced out, they come right back in. Why should they want to be in jail? Why not? It is secure, there are three meals a day and you don't have to make too many decisions. I guess the bottom line of what I am trying to say, you have already guessed. If you have achieved something, if you have climbed a mountain and have come out of a hole, and if you are bound to tell the world about it — fine! But somewhere in the essay on success we should make it clear that some readers may not want to do what you have done, may not need to do what you have done, and may, for one reason or another, be unable to do what you have done. If you make it seem possible for most everyone to achieve what you have done, then you have done some folk out there a disservice for sure. Giving advice, handing out life's road maps, preaching sermons, evangelization, whatever — I like this metaphor the best. To give out the good word is best described to me as one hungry person telling another starving person where he found food.

—3—
Malpractice Woes

To my lawyer friends and acquaintances: It is obvious that I have written this section with my emotions on edge and I will doubtless generate some heat from the legal profession. Although I make no apology for what I will say, I do recognize that there are ethical and unethical attorneys the same as can be said of doctors, clergymen and whoever.

The Malpractice Mess

There is a disease which is presently out of control and I am not speaking of AIDS this time. The disease is attacking doctor-patient relationships. The disease is characterized by fear and anger. The disease is called malpractice litigation. In Indiana, it is still under control, but in some states it is rampant. Doctor-patient-attorney relationships are under attack and are getting sick and in some areas sick to the point of requiring transfer to the critical care unit where emergency measures can be carried out. Medical practice is changing rapidly because of the malpractice mess. The following events are now happening:

1. Doctors are leaving some states where the malpractice premiums are the highest.

2. Many older doctors, still able to give a lot, are simply taking early retirement and will not subject themselves any longer to the chaos.

3. Family doctors are quitting obstetrical practice because of this situation.

4. A number of obstetricians who also do gynecological surgery are completely quitting obstetrics in order to do surgery alone.

5. Family doctors are referring many patients to specialists simply out of fear which, of course, increases the cost of medical care dramatically.

6. Doctors are ordering numerous tests and x-rays simply out of fear, which further drives the cost spiralling upward.

7. When doctors become obsessed concerning their own safety as well as their patient's safety, bad things can and do happen.

8. As the malpractice premiums skyrocket, fees go up and when fees go up, patients and third party payers get more and more upset and angry. This sets the tone for retribution in the form of more and more litigation. The obvious rationale is that if the surgery or the treatment costs that much, then it had better be perfect or else!

Why are we facing this dilemma? Why is the situation out of control? Why are we apparently helpless to bring about a solution? I believe that all parties involved have to share in the blame as in most disputes. The medical profession has made its contribution. In the first place, we doctors are not recognized to be the most humble profession in the U.S.A. To the contrary, we are too often arrogant and proud and conceited. We are intelligent, highly trained, and many of us, rich. We probably make more money than we deserve, as do a number of other professions for that matter, not the least of which is the legal profession. Secondly, medical costs have skyrocketed and that does not go over very well, but we Americans demand the best in everything and we object paying for it. Some doctors' fees are without question, exorbitant, and that gives the entire profession a bad name. Just like in national affairs, we demand services but we don't want to pay the taxes. It is a ridiculous position, but I am afraid we are guilty. We want the best hospitals, the greatest doctors, the latest equipment and we want the latest surgery, whether it is open heart, cataract removal, or face lifts. And we expect it all to come out perfect every time. Why? Because it costs so much and because we somehow do not expect the doctor to be perfect when he is working on John Doe, but we do expect him to be perfect when he is working on us.

It seems to me that a form of national health insurance will come into being and some form of socialized medicine will follow. The mess will then be government-regulated and hopefully brought under control. Medical care will then be available to all Americans and this will be good. The quality of care will likely deteriorate somewhat and bureaucracy will enter the scene as never before. In other words, the price to be paid for making care available to all will be a reduction of some services and further erosion of doctor-patient relationships as the government agencies gain more and more control. One can argue endlessly about whether this will be a step forward or a step backward. My own position is simply this. I am willing to further sacrifice my professional freedom and accept an income reduction in order to make my services available to all, providing that in so doing, the present malpractice chaos comes under control and I can again relax a bit and practice without constant fear of the threat of a lawsuit.

What Has Happened to the Country Doctor?

Fifty-six years ago I got "double pneumonia" and had a near death experience. I was out of school for several weeks and very ill for two weeks with a high fever and delirium. It was touch and go during this time. Our family doctor was a D.O. (Doctor of Osteopathy) and he did his best. There were no osteopathic hospitals in Louisville, and consequently, he made home visits on his seriously ill and bedridden patients. He saw me several times and did what he could. There were no antibiotics. I basically had supportive care such as it was and was surrounded by family and soaked in prayers. I made it obviously but I went back to school weak and a ghost of my former self.

The doctors a half century ago made many home calls. Hospitals were for the critically ill, the injured, those for major surgery, and for those who wanted to die in a hospital setting. Sophisticated diagnostic procedures and sophisticated surgeries and medications were unknown. Disease processes were only vaguely understood. Monitors, computers and fancy equipment were unheard of. In that day doctors were more apt to rely on clinical judgment in diagnosing and treating. As the old saying goes, "Doctors flew by the seat of their pants," not by instruments. There was a closeness between doctors and patients that perhaps no longer exists in many areas now. As medical science has advanced and as we have been able to do the impossible often, and as brain surgery, heart surgery and transplant surgery have mushroomed, the gulf between doctor and patient has widened. The art of medicine is being replaced by the science of medicine. Doctors have tended to become prima donnas and have alienated their constituency often. Some doctors have gone after the buck and have become rich. Some doctors have become unethical and appear to be more interested in fortune than fame. Alas, some surgeons have become aggressive and operate when medical treatment would be preferable.

Along with these factors, other changes have come about which have added to the problems of medical care delivery in the United States. Medicare, Medicaid and private insurance carriers have begun to monitor and set the policy for the way medicine is practiced in the nation. This has led to Peer Review Organizations, DRG's and all sorts of rules, regulations and red tape that "drive the doctor up the wall." On the one hand there is growing pressure to keep the patient out of the hospital and on the other hand, if something thereby goes wrong, tragic results may occur for the patient and the doctor.

Because of all these factors, applications to medical school are now down, perhaps for the first time. Doctors are retiring earlier, and physicians practice in fear as never before. How would you feel if the pilot of your aircraft was under constant stress and fear? Would you feel happy and relaxed in the plane? My friend, that is the way it is getting to be with your doctor and that is not in anyone's best interest for obvious reasons.

So today as always, rapid changes in the health care delivery system are upon us and have to be dealt with. Despite all the marvelous advances in medical science and surgery technique, despite all the new diagnostic equipment available to figure out our diagnoses, despite the marvels of new hospitals and well-trained doctors, nurses, technicians, aids, therapists, counselors, rehabilitation people and all the rest, there is nothing that can take the place of the spirit of tender care that can and should exist in a hospital setting. Machinery comes and goes, techniques change, therapies are ever improving. And finally abideth brilliant diagnoses and lifesaving therapy and compassion, but the greatest of these is compassion.

■———————————————————■

—4—
A Doctor's Life in the Trenches

Conclusions From People Watching

1. **In the matter of religion.** The religious faith that most people follow has not been determined by a method of selection such as we use when we go through a cafeteria line. Our options are strictly limited in this regard. First of all, many of us have found ourselves involved in a particular religious faith simply because of geography. If we are Americans, we are apt to be Christians. If we are Israelis, we are apt to be Jewish. If we are Indian, we are apt to be Hindus and if we are Iranians no doubt we will be Moslem. As Americans, the type of Christianity we are involved in also is affected to some degree by geography. If we are southerners, we are apt to be Southern Baptist. If we live in Salt Lake City, Utah, we are apt to be Mormons. Another force that directs our selection of religious preference has to do with our own individual needs

as people. If we need a faith which is rigid, absolute and makes claims to have all the truth, then, no doubt we will be fed and nourished by Orthodox Christianity and fundamentalism. If we by nature are of a more liberal spirit, and our needs are more fulfilled when we see cooperation among diverse groups, then we are apt to be involved in liberal Christianity. And finally, our lifestyle and behavior often is a determining factor in what religion appeals to us. If divorce and remarriage has been part of our life, then we are surely not going to identify with a religious group that condemns divorce. If we believe in open marriage, then we are apt to select a religious group that likewise accepts that behavior or opt for no religious conviction whatsoever.

2. **The kinds of doctors we select.** First of all, we select a doctor who is available to us. If we live in Salem, we are apt to have a doctor in Salem rather than depend on somebody in Louisville for all of our needs. We often go to the physician who has been recommended to us by a friend. We tend to stay with the physician who reasonably meets our needs. If we need a physician who allows us to participate somewhat in our own medical care, then we will find a physician who is comfortable with that. If we need a physician who directs every phase of our medical life and who calls all the shots, then we will seek out and be most comfortable with a dictator doctor. If we have a serious emotional problem we will certainly select a doctor who is empathetic in regards to emotional illness. There are some physicians who are uncomfortable with people with emotional problems and simply let them know in one way or another that they are not welcome. We get the message real fast. We tend to select the physician with whom we feel comfortable and confident.

3. **Obesity.** Although in America we have our homeless and we have our hungry, by far our greatest nutritional problem is obesity rather than starvation. An hour on a Florida beach or an hour in a crowd of Americans coast to coast will soon reveal the fact that the stores that specialize in clothes for big people are doing a land office business. The diet and

weight reduction programs and establishments around the country are prolific and doing a hefty business, especially after the holiday season. There are hundreds of super specialized diets to produce magnificent results in a short time available. Most of them don't work. Most of them don't work because patients don't let them work. Like any affluent society, most Americans want somebody else to do the work for them in getting their weight off. Every doctor has many patients who need to lose weight and who want the doctor to participate in and do much of the work in achieving that result. They want to swallow a pill and lose their appetite and therefore, escape the necessary ingredient called discipline. The principle reason for obesity, in most people at least, that I have observed, is the fact that the patient selected the wrong parents. It is, like so many conditions, a family-oriented condition and if fatness runs in the family, look out, you've got trouble. You are born with a built-in handicap which can be managed with sufficient discipline, but I have found that few have that kind of determination because it will be a life-long struggle. There are a few who, like Olympic champions, make the grade and do a beautiful job, but it requires constant discipline and constant attention. There are those people who can sit down anywhere, anytime and eat anything and never gain a pound. There are other people who simply smell good food and gain weight. That is the way it is and we simply have to accept the fact.

4. **Disease runs in families.** In medical school, we were taught always to take a family history when talking to patients. That is, we were instructed to ask what disease close members of the family had suffered or died with. I wondered at the time how necessary that was. Now I know after forty years of practice, that it is absolutely essential to know these facts. Basically, if you want to know what is going to happen to you, look around and see what has happened to your relatives. This is not iron clad and absolutely certain, but one certainly can get a fairly good idea of what one is likely to encounter along life's road as far as diseases are concerned. Cancer runs in

211

family, heart disease, high blood pressure, as well as obesity, emotional illness, diabetes, tallness or shortness, personality, beauty or the lack of it, and the list goes on and on and on. If your parents are brilliant then the chances are you are going to have a high intellect. If your parents are dull and limited, you don't have a chance usually to excel in intellectual pursuits.

5. **Women in prison.** A visit to your local detention center or a visit to any correctional institution or penitentiary will reveal females in abundance just like males. But I have noticed in my practice, that there are many women who are locked in prison but not in the detention centers, as such. There are a number of women who are incarcerated in a prison of their home, chained as it were, in a disastrous marriage relationship with no hope of escape. For one reason or another, the marriage relationship exists only because, for the woman at least, there is no alternative. She has children to be responsible for and would have to earn a living independently and would have to survive emotionally were the marriage to dissolve. Many women simply lack the ability or the skills or the determination to get out of their prison and so they cope with their situation in various ways. Often the coping mechanism is satisfactory and they endure. Sometimes the coping mechanism brings about intense suffering and is a disaster itself. It may lead to chronic emotional illness, it may lead to abusive behavior directed toward the children, and of course, it may lead to alcoholism, drug dependency or codependency. Women in prison have three ways to go. First of all, they can remain in prison and accept the consequences, whatever they may be. Secondly, they may seek counseling and perhaps achieve, along with their spouse, some degree of improvement in their relationship and the relief of suffering for all concerned. Third, one may gather the strength to leave the relationship and go it alone and try to find a better life. I have no special secrets to leave with you, my reader, but I do have a message. Let us try to be nonjudgmental and let us try to be supportive of women in prison and let us remember that if we are enjoying a good relationship with our spouse, it is a marvelous blessing that not everyone is able to enjoy.

6. **Amish children.** I have jokingly said that there are two ways to get to see your doctor real quick when you are caught in a traffic jam in a busy office and everything is running from one to two hours behind schedule. If your body odor is overwhelmingly impossible, in my office at least, you are ushered in very quickly. Also, if your children are literally tearing up the office, you likewise can get on the express train and have a quick visit with the physician. Rowdy children are not unusual in the American family. A hundred years ago evidently things were quite different. The pendulum evidently has swung from rigidity and austerity to the opposite extreme and often the kids are in total command of the situation. Not so with the Amish. I go into a room where an Amish family is waiting and there will be mother and dad sitting perfectly quiet, usually not talking, and anywhere from one to three kids, likewise sitting there not saying a word, perfectly behaved. We regard the Amish as different, if not peculiar. That may be true, but I sure do like them and find them delightful people and certainly when it comes to illness, you can be perfectly sure that when you see them, they are sick and usually sick with good reason. The children cooperate for the most part and are quiet and disciplined and behaved. They tend to follow instruction and generally speaking are regarded as excellent patients and they pay you. I like the Amish. I think Americans desperately need to return to some of their disciplines and life would be much simpler for all of us.

7. **Follow the leader.** There are a few Americans who delight in being different and delight in shocking people and are apparently nourished by a life of "screwball" activity. However, the vast majority of us follow the leader. We do what others are doing — we fit into the crowd, we don't want to be different, we want the acceptance that sameness seems to bring and if we do have an independent thought, so often we don't have the courage that is required to carry out a different sort of behavior. Take blue jeans, for instance. Most women patients that I see under fifty at least, are wearing skin tight blue jeans. If I need to examine part of their anatomy

underneath the blue jeans, requiring removal, I request that they remove them and I will be back in the room in at least half an hour. The jeans are skin tight and it is no small undertaking to remove them. If it were fashionable for men or women to wear rings in their noses, I am sure that the style would sweep the country. I am not objecting to this human trait. I am just making an observation. There are times, however, when it is obvious that a willingness to be different can save our lives or make our lives much better. Many of us simply do not possess the strength of personality or character to be different and thus enrich our lives or even save our lives.

8. **Old folks don't use canes.** The bone setting doctors have made a living on broken hips and broken extremities because many old folks are too proud to use a cane. So often our senior citizens pick up a cane or a crutch only after a disaster has occurred. This is a very human quality and many of us possess that characteristic. We don't want to admit we have a problem and we don't want to admit a lot of things that we should. In trying to cover up our deficiencies, sometimes disaster awaits us. If we have an emotional illness and are ashamed to seek help, delay can be a very serious mistake. If we are fearful to present ourselves to the physician when we suffer pain and disability and put it off, a delay can bring disaster. Some of us are so stubborn that we don't want help with anything and as a result, we suffer the consequences.

And finally, let me make this observation. It is easy for us to notice the characteristics of others particularly when they are offensive and bother us. Very often we do not recognize or are aware of our own peculiarities which tend to drive others up the wall. It is as if our sensitivities directed to others are working one hundred percent but our awareness of our own selves is seriously impaired. Maybe this is a blessing. If some of us knew the truth about ourselves, it would be more than we could take.

The Sick and the Pseudosick

A doctor never knows what is going to come in the front door. Maybe it is a good thing he doesn't. Most of the people are sick. Some are nervous, depressed or disturbed in some way. Some are injured. Then there are a few who fall into the category of pseudosick. Pseudo means false and so these folk are sometimes malingerers and sometimes they are those who are what you might call professional patients. They are always sick or going to get sick or recovering from something or other. They simply are sick for some strange and unknown reason. There is what we call secondary gain to be derived from an alleged illness. Then there is the "far out" patient. By this I do not mean the genuinely psychotic patients, I mean the far our patient with a bizarre story. Among these are the professional collectors of narcotics who pass as sick persons and make an attempt, often successful, to get drugs from the doctor.

Almost every doctor has had the experience of being confronted with one of these experienced narcotic collectors who presents himself with the need of pain relieving medications. I suspect that doctors get "took" more often than they would like to admit. These characters present themselves in a very convincing manner and the first thing you know you are believing their story and wanting to be of help. The compassionate doctor especially is vulnerable. I have been hit twice in recent years by such characters, once I was "took" and once I smelled a rat and sent the patient out on his way empty-handed. Family doctors have their share of patients who seem to require, for one reason or another, a lot of drugs, especially pain relievers, tranquilizers and sleep producers. Sometimes these people have organic or physical ills. Sometimes their ills are primarily emotional and sometimes they have personality disorders. At times such a person may have all three problems. In that case, pity the patient and pity the doctor.

Not long ago my receptionist got a call from a patient in a nearby town. She needed to see me that day. She had recently moved from California and needed a family doctor.

She had heard about me and started bragging and blah, blah, blah. She had far-advanced cancer and was on various medications and needed refills. She was given an appointment and she came. When I went into the room she introduced herself, was polite and knowledgeable about her lung cancer and was very personable. She gave me a discharge summary from a hospital in California and it did confirm her oat cell carcinoma of the lung, her state of having received maximum therapy both by irradiation and chemotherapy. All that was left for her was to control her pain and keep her comfortable and so, obviously, she was wanting her pain-relieving medication along with other things. I suggested that she be examined and so she got up on the exam table and as she did she described not only pain in her lung but also abdominal complaints. Her lungs sounded remarkably clear. I removed her turban that covered her alleged bald head that she had suffered because of chemotherapy, but there was still a fair amount of hair there. I wondered about that. I next examined her abdomen and she was big, distended and her abdomen was firm. I felt something move. I listened. I heard a fetal heartbeat. She was obviously pregnant and near term. I so informed her. She reeled in stark disbelief. She said that was impossible, etc., etc., etc. At this point I advised her to go at once to the hospital for a chest x-ray to see how bad her lungs were, knowing all the time that she was almost surely a fraud. It turned out, surely enough, that she did not go to the hospital. I was right. I then called my colleagues and told the other doctors in town about her and that she might be visiting them in the very near future. As I called one of my doctor friends, she happened to be there at that very moment with the black turban on her head sitting neatly waiting to be seen by the physician and so obviously he did his stuff and ran her off.

Why do people do such things? The reasons can be many. First of all, a good actor or actress can fool many doctors and get prescriptions for lots of drugs that bring good money on the street. Then there are those addicts who need the medication themselves and need extra money from the sale of collected drugs to sustain their habit. Then there are those who simply enjoy being deceptive and have a virtual compulsion to try to outwit the doctor.

And so the doctor has to be a detective, a diagnostician, a compassionate listener, a man of patience, a man of smarts to be a good physician. Many booby traps await him and God help him not to set his foot on one too often.

■———————————————————————■

AIDS is Real

Homosexuality has been with the human race for as long as recorded time. It involves a small percentage of the species. The cause of this minority behavioral orientation is unknown. It rarely can be treated successfully. Once sexual orientation is directed toward a member of the same sex, it is powerful and ongoing. It leads to problems. Socially it has significant problems and now with AIDS on the scene, the medical problems are critical.

Many religions condemn this kind of sexual behavior and certainly the Christian religion does. The Apostle Paul in the Bible speaks out clearly on the subject. Psychiatry attempts to take a non-judmental point of view of homosexuality. Society still, by and large, condemns it, except for the ghettos of homosexual subculture. Persons pay a terrible price for this kind of behavior. Minorities of any kind often have been persecuted, ridiculed and subjected to mistreatment and malice.

I personally try to take a nonjudgmental stance though I am a Christian and I hold the scriptures as my guide and inspiration. I am aware that the Apostle Paul's comments on homosexuality were conditioned by the understanding of the First Century rather than the Twentieth. Although at one time I would have firmly believed that what Paul said in the First Century would be true for all time and eternity, I can no longer hold these views in the light of my experience and in the light of reality as I have observed it. Whether homosexuality is implanted by the genes, whether it comes because of our environment or whether it is a result of multiple factors, I am convinced that the individual has little, if any, real control over his sexual orientation. Though my thinking is somewhat liberal and represents a more understanding attitude than many people have, I still have my hang-ups. I find myself easily being friendly and accepting of my homosexual patients however, and have no problem in the doctor-patient relationship.

In an area that is clouded with mystery, in a situation where all the facts are not in, in an area of human behavior where the best of minds clash, I think it prudent that we all walk the nonjudgmental path. I think Jesus would be friendly to a homosexual and would eat and visit at his or her house and would love them as he loved the heterosexual.

It goes without saying that promiscuity, either by the heterosexual or the homosexual, is fraught with hazards both to one's social structures, not to mention one's health. To be promiscuous is to flirt with death, both socially and medically.

It is Impossible With a Few Exceptions

Yes, that is exactly what I believe about stopping smoking and quitting eating. Nicotine addiction and obesity are plagues that afflict a lot of Americans, as we all know, and after 42 years of suggesting to countless people that these conditions should be eliminated, I have decided to quit preaching. It is impossible for a fat person to get skinny and stay there or a heavy smoker to quit and stay quit — with a few exceptions. It is estimated, currently, that of one hundred people who make an honest and determined effort to quit smoking, that by the end of the year, eighty are smoking. Nicotine is an amazing drug for the present age, apparently. It produces a state the people enjoy and once addicted, the withdrawal signs that develop with an effort to stop smoking, seem impossible to deal with. I have seen people dying of emphysema and breathing oxygen twenty-four hours a day and literally beg to come out of oxygen in order to smoke. It is like a rattlesnake-bitten person dying of venom and lying in bed with rattlesnakes at the same time. After a full-blown heart attack, fifty percent of the victims continue to smoke, despite the fact that their addiction is contributing to an early death. Cancer victims continue to smoke. I have heard people tell me, in all honesty, "Doc, if you take away my cigarettes, you have taken away my best friend." The addiction to nicotine is one of the hardest to break, without question. It can be tolerated for long periods by the victim and by society, whereas other addictions may well do you in much sooner. Cigarettes are available, socially acceptable and portrayed as smart and sexy. I have about given up trying to get people to quit. The person has to want to quit in the worst way if he has a ghost of a chance to stop.

Millions of Americans are fat. Few are able to lose weight and keep it off. In the first place, it is a family-oriented disease and the habit pattern of overeating is virtually impossible to break. Eating is so much fun. We have more food in America than we can eat. Etiquette demands that we eat almost constantly some days, and often we have a distorted body image and don't realize what a condition we are in. People can get weight off by heroic measures but usually they back slide in time. And so a second fact. It is impossible to lose weight over the long haul with a few exceptions.

Now there are a number of other habits or dependencies that we have which are dangerous in addition to smoking and overeating. Drinking booze to an excess is a problem to deal with, but I do believe it is more amenable to breaking the habit than to overeating or smoking. For one thing, people come down on you so hard if you are an alcoholic that they may make life miserable for you if you continue to drink. And then the alcoholic stands a chance of being maimed or killed. And so we have constraints about drinking which I believe make it easier to quit than other habits. Some go through withdrawal (DT's) and this is a bit of hell on earth for sure. But despite all this, significant numbers of people quit. With the help that AA's are giving, and the mutual support and caring, people can quit drinking, and do.

Many of us who smuggly pride ourselves because we are not victims of serious addictions, do have other addictive problems which maybe are worse. The gossip addiction is rampant and lethal to the reputations of many, and even the best of citizens and religious people engage in this addiction without qualm of conscience. The addiction to money is another one that many have. The addiction to be promiscuous sexually and to engage in abusive behavior is with us and hard to understand. The tendency, or I should say addiction, to talk and rarely to listen is widespread and long-lasting. The addiction to make money at all costs is prevalent. The gambling addiction is to be reckoned with. And so there are reasons why our behavior is often addictive and destructive. The reason may lie well beneath the level of the consciousness, but it is there. Yes, we have to hold people responsible; but when one is firmly addicted, let us who are without some addiction or compulsion or destructive tendency, cast the first stone.

Millions Down the Drain

As medical director for a 130-bed nursing home, as a physician for forty-two years, I speak with some degree of knowledge on a subject of considerable importance and variance of opinion. It is a sensitive issue and if I wanted to avoid arousing passions, then I'd better shut up. But I won't. I'm old enough now and secure enough to say what I strongly think and feel, and let the chips fall. Matter of fact, I don't have to lick anybody's boots, either. And you know, it is still a country where you can pretty much say what you wish. You can say words of wisdom or you can make a great big fool of yourself if you so choose. So here goes.

Hundreds of thousands of "dead" people are being kept alive for various reasons in the nursing homes across the United States at this very moment. I maintain it is a waste of money of monstrous proportions, is inhumane and is inflicting unnecessary suffering on our demented and helpless aged who are at the mercy of care givers. The quality of life of these poor souls is zero. Yet they are kept alive by various means for months and years.

Here is John Doe Senior Citizen. He was president of the bank, elder in his church, raised a family to his credit and is a model citizen. He is ninety years old. For five years his dementia has put him in the nursing home. He is disoriented. He doesn't know who he is, where he is or who you are or what year it is. He is too weak to eat. He is bedfast. He lies there. Because he can't eat, a feeding tube goes into his stomach through his nose and he gets a continuous drip of liquid food. He is turned to prevent bedsores. His pacemaker is going. He gets pneumonia and is moved to the local hospital and spends a week there. He returns to the nursing home. This scenario goes on and on and on. Who benefits from this? Does John? No! The nursing home does. They make good money. Medicare gives the doctor a tip, but that is about all. Small wonder that doctors fail to become very enthusiastic about nursing home practice in this setting. Does the family benefit? Hardly. It costs thousands of dollars to finance this. Eighty percent of our nursing home residents run out of money before they die and the taxpayer takes over, paying astronomical sums of money.

So why on earth do we do this? Well, for one thing, nursing home administrators are scared to death not to. To do otherwise might mean a complaint and then in comes the lawyer and the lawsuit. So legally we are intimidated. Then too, families sometime get all bent out of shape and can't let old John go on to his reward.

What can be done about this? In the case of John Doe Senior Citizen just described, I would remove the feeding tube and let nature take its course. I would do this providing the family was in agreement. Our nursing home at present won't let me do this even with the family's demand for such removal. After three days of inadequate fluid and nutrition in our nursing home, I have to write an order to support life and nutrition. It is out of my hands. Reason? 1. Legal worries. 2. Let's face it. The nursing homes make their living that way.

I hope the day will come when we will allow sanity to prevail and not continue to prolong the act of dying of our demented senior citizens. If a man on the battle field was mortally wounded and there was no hope of his survival and he was suffering, would the medic keep supporting his life with whatever it took only to see him moan in pain and continue to suffer? Of course not, he would give him a dose of morphine and repeat it until he peacefully died relatively free of pain. The medic could leave the scene then with a clear conscience knowing that he had made his inevitable death easier. At the present time we are letting our patients suffer in nursing homes more than we realize. Oh, we say they are not suffering. I say they are suffering and I for one will rejoice when we discontinue this barbarous practice of keeping away the death angel. Let the death angel of mercy do his work. Death is our friend at a time like this, not our enemy. I suspect the majority of Americans believe in life after death, but we certainly don't act like it.

Cancer War

When I graduated from medical school, we had declared war on cancer, but the battles were not going too well. So often, the enemy was victorious. We had surgery and we had irradiation of sorts. But chemotherapy was only a newborn babe, so to speak. The only chemical weapon we had was a drug called nitrogen mustard and the side effects were bad. Cancer of the lung was not very common forty-five years ago, cancer of the stomach much more common than today. Of course, as today, we had skin cancer, bone cancer, brain, bowel, liver and kidney cancer. Most any organ could at times be the site of that dreaded monster. The cause of cancer was then unknown. Today we understand that cigarettes and alcohol play a significant role in cancer but beyond that we know very little. For sure, heredity plays a big role as it does in almost all diseases. Today we estimate that fifty percent of cancers can be cured but that figure is deceptive because it includes skin cancer. This makes the statistics much better. Excluding skin cancer, the cure rate, I'm confident, would be much less.

What on earth is cancer anyhow? Cancer, to put it simply, is a mass of cells in some body organ that has broken all the rules and has gone crazy. The growth invades structures and interferes with normal body function. To make matters worse, it spreads in the body by way of the blood stream or the lymphatic system and it seeds other areas. It's like a weed growing in a lawn. Not bad to start, but the weed seeds eventually spread to the rest of the lawn and finally chokes out the grass and you have nothing but a weed patch and a dead lawn. That is what cancer is. We can cut out the weeds, and sometimes we get them all. That's surgery. We can spray chemicals and occasionally kill all the weeds and win, and that is chemotherapy at its best. But so often in the weed killing process, we kill some of the lawn. If we keep on with the weed killer, we may kill the entire lawn. We do this with chemotherapy sometimes. Trying to kill the cancer, we kill the patient unavoidably. Chemotherapy is sort of like standing a hundred yards from a guy with a rattlesnake coiled around his neck and ready to strike. We have an automatic rifle and we take careful aim and start shooting. We may kill the snake and win. But alas, one of the bullets may strike the victim and we lose him, too. So chemotherapy is in the infancy stage and adulthood is yet in the distance.

Our batting average with some cancers is now pretty good. With Hodgkin's Disease and leukemia we are doing better, much better. Some leukemia patients are cured even. Patients have to go to hell and back though to get the job done. A leukemia victim will have to undergo chemotherapy that wipes out the entire bone marrow. Then a bone marrow transplant is given intravenously later and if it takes, the patient may be cured. Fantastic, amazing! It is like taking a weedy lawn and killing everything, and then we resod the lawn and we have restored life and beauty. It is almost like rising up out of the grave.

Charlie, a doctor friend of mine, this year has withstood the ravages of cancer of the pancreas and is back at work almost as if by miracle. He had to undergo several hours of surgery and he had lots of things removed and was hooked up again. After a stormy post-operative course, he crawled back to some degree of stability. Then followed a series of complications and devastating problems that were life-threatening, each one. He rode out the storms. On one occasion I visited him in the hospital room and it was obvious that my visit must be a short one. Oxygen was going, he had fluid around his lung, his heart was laboring, his abdomen was a nightmare, he couldn't eat, he was being given TPN (total nutrition by vein), and he was getting blood, several units. I had a brief word, took him by the hand, and we prayed together. I left not knowing if I would see him again in this world. I went again a week later and he was out of bed and trying to walk. Unbelievable, and his recovery continued. Now he is back again seeing sick folks. His future is uncertain, but so is mine and yours.

And now about my doctor friend, David, about whom I have recently written. Cancer in the bone, unrelenting pain, IV morphine to control it. Irradiation to kill the cancer cells. And the latest word from David is that he is out of the hospital, up and about, and ready to drive his car to town.

Life is struggle. Something is eating on everything. When cancer starts, it is a battle between our immune system and the cancer cells. Sometimes the immune system wins and kills the cancer. But sometimes the cancer wins and we go down. Of all the weapons against cancer, our immune system still contains the best soldiers in our arsenal. It is said that cancer cells are formed every day by everybody, only to be zapped by our immune system if it is working well. Surgery can help or sometimes cure, chemotherapy can help and sometimes cure, irradiation can help and sometimes cure. But our immune system is still our best weapon against cancer overall. Research directed toward enhancing our immune system, to beef it up when it is failing, may be another weapon in this life and death struggle for survival.

P.S. Charlie lost the battle and died after a few months of improvement.

David recently died, too, the day after Thanksgiving. Both docs fought like tigers until the whistle blew for them.

■———————————————■

—5—
A Country Doctor's Ideas and Philosophy

Discipline — Yuck!

Discipline is like castor oil, it is awfully hard to take but it can be very good for you if you need it. We are introduced to discipline in infancy and childhood and universally we find it difficult to accept, at least in the beginning. The young child wants to run free and unhindered and the young colt resists being saddled and ridden. Staying home and studying for a test while your friends are out enjoying a wonderful party never was very popular. Coming in at midnight from a high school date when the rest of your friends are staying out all night is truly disgraceful!

Rational people, nevertheless, recognize the tremendous value of discipline in life and truly have to admit that for life to be successful and rewarding, discipline is a necessary ingredient. Certainly, to obtain an education, the discipline of study is obvious. To maintain a healthy body, the discipline of good health habits is essential. We must eat in moderation, exercise in adequacy, and get the necessary rest. For good mental health, we must be able to shift gears, rest our brains with proper recreation, and learn to think positively.

Just as driving fast with acceleration and little braking can be thrilling, so can living it up with the undisciplined life. For the moment it can bring a lot of excitement, exhilaration, fun and ecstasy to life. A life of rigid and total discipline can be very drab indeed. A life devoid of discipline and lived in total abandonment to our pleasures for the moment can and will bring disaster. We all recognize the need for balance in life. We all affirm that a life of the proper mixture of discipline and restraint along with a life of enjoyment, freedom and pleasure is indeed the essence of the good life. How to achieve this balance is where the problem lies. Some people come equipped far better than others to achieve the good life and bring together the proper balance. Some indeed come into this world with intellectual restrictions to the point that the good life is impossible. Some are handicapped with a genetic personality disorder that makes the good life virtually impossible. Some have had turbulent childhoods and environmental factors which so altered their developmental processes that the good life is beyond them. If one is indeed blessed by good genes, by a good childhood environment, by adequate intelligence, surely one is in a much better position than many others to achieve the good life and bring it about by a proper mixture of discipline along with fun and pleasure.

The doctor's life with insufficient discipline is like walking through a mine field stepping on booby traps. After eight years of medical school with intensive study and three to four years of residency training for one specialty, the doctor is tempted to quit his studying and do some coasting. However, it is recognized that continuing medical education all one's professional life is absolutely essential if one is to be a good doctor and to be successful. The rapid changes in medicine make this mandatory. Study must be continued by attending medical meetings, by reading journals, by doing correspondence study courses, or by listening to teaching tapes. All of this can be a form of drudgery or it can be a happy existence depending on our attitude and our motivation. In any event, it is absolutely essential.

In order to survive the anxieties and frustrations of doctoring, one has to develop a sense of positive thinking, equanimity, and the ability to proceed despite fears and anxieties in an emergency situation. This requires the discipline of doing when we think we can't do. It requires the discipline of action when we feel we can't. It requires the discipline of moving on in a situation even when we are not absolutely sure.

The good doctor needs the discipline of being quiet and listening to his patient and to hear him out, even when the story is dull and repetitious and lengthy. The good physician will strive to maintain the discipline of restraint even when the patient may be unpleasant, boring, or provocative in his actions or statements. None of these disciplines are easy. They are all tough. Few of us attain them to the degree that we might like.

———————————————————

Freedom and Permissiveness

We Americans make much of our freedoms and shout it to all the world and that's okay. I like it. It's great. I wouldn't live anywhere else than the good ole U.S.A. It is our privilege to say what we like, live where we wish and get the best job that is available and for which we are qualified. It is good to be able to leave this country if we wish and return when we are ready. It is comforting to go to the church of our choice or not to go if we don't want to. It is especially reassuring to know that the F.B.I. is not on our trail for the slightest reason. Our forefathers planned for this and we have maintained it. For all of this we can be justly proud and thankful.

Are there some negative aspects to our freedom? I think so. When a pendulum swings, it often swings too far. I believe our freedom pendulum has done just that. We are indeed a free people, free to buy all kinds of guns and shoot each other. Our murder statistics are skyrocketing. Our freedoms have led to permissiveness in many areas of life. We make fun of totalitarian states, but they do not suffer the effects of permissiveness perhaps as much as we do. When China was plagued with opium addiction, it didn't take the government long to clean out the mess. They simply lined up the offenders and shot them. Now I am not for one minute advocating anything like that for this country, but we must get serious about punishment, very serious.

Our freedoms have given us permission to do our own thing and that is okay, but we must remember that we are also free to abandon restraints, abandon discipline, make light of code of ethical behavior, and do what comes naturally. We have done this for the last two generations and has it brought us to heaven? Quite the opposite. Alcoholism is at an all time high; drug dependency is out of control. Our homes have reached a new level of instability and problems of multiple marriages and divorces with children sandwiched in between abound. The price that is paid for this type of behavior is very high indeed for individuals and society in general.

Although some of our problems in America are related to poverty, inadequate education and discrimination, many relate to our materialism, our lifestyle, the disintegration of authority figures, and the rapid changes in all aspects of life and living.

The conditions of America today in some ways remind me of the patient who goes to the doctor with a number of complaints. He is too fat, is diabetic, has high blood pressure, drinks too much, eats too much and smokes too much. The doctor puts the patient through a battery of examinations and x-rays and comes up with a diagnosis and recommendations. The patient is to stop smoking, go on a diet, eliminate fats and cholesterol foods, cut down on salt, get exercise and stop drinking. In addition, various medications are prescribed. The patient is pleased to take the medicines as prescribed, but the tough part, the dieting, the drinking and smoking cessation and the exercise does not appeal to the patient whatsoever. As a matter of fact, the patient refuses to do his part. He does not lose weight, does not go on the diet and does insufficient exercising. It seems to me that this is the way we Americans are behaving regarding our problems. We simply do not possess the will as a nation at the present time, to deal with the problems at hand.

Perhaps it will take a national catastrophe to bring us to the point to return to a lifestyle which will include respect for authority, a return to disciplined behavior and contentment with values in life rather than things.

It is most interesting to me to see what strict adherence to the disciplined life will bring about. Take the Amish culture, for instance. Discipline is the rule. Simplicity and respect for authority, godliness, honor and honesty prevail. I am not suggesting that all of America become Amish, but I am saying that the things stressed by the Amish make for stability and peace. If some of their attributes were injected into American culture, it would do a lot, in my judgment, to healing our ills.

■————————————————————————■

Right to Life and Right to Death

I am going to venture out into two controversial areas and state my views for whatever they are worth. I speak as an American Family Physician, having practiced forty-two years. I have served in an area of great medical need among a disadvantaged people. I have also served in a small county seat southern Indiana town. I am a Christian, a member of the Christian Church (Disciples of Christ). I suspect I would be called a liberal by the religious right.

First of all, what about abortion on request. I have reached certain conclusions. Surely abortion on request, along with the "pill," and the culture's acceptance of a more liberal lifestyle have brought about a drastic change in American behavior. The disciplines that once were operative to prevent pregnancy have now been removed. It is like a car going downhill and the brakes are gone. It goes very fast. A new era of sexual freedom brings along with it, perhaps, a new source of joy and fulfillment to many people. On the other hand, at the same time, there is an increase in alcohol and drug addiction to an all time high. The stability of the home is weakening and the specter of AIDS is haunting us. Is the joy and fulfillment that sexual freedom has brought worth the price that we are paying?

America is at war over the abortion issue. We are at each other's throats. To destroy a life is a dreadful thing. On the other hand, children born who are not wanted can lead to dreadful things. Criminal abortions can lead to horror. I cannot see a good answer to this dilemma. If the women of America were voting on the issue, I suspect the vote would go for abortion on request. I am presently of the opinion that outlawing abortion would bring on more problems than it would solve. I firmly believe that a viable fetus should not be destroyed, unless the mother's life is endangered. As time goes on and more is learned, my present conclusions may be changed. I try to keep an open mind on this very sensitive and controversial issue.

Now what about the "right to die?" My inpatients now are primarily nursing home patients and I have over a hundred such patients at any one time in our local nursing homes. Many people have virtually zero quality of life. The intellectual function is gone. They are incontinent of urine and feces and they are helpless. Some have feeding tubes in their stomachs to maintain nutrition. I believe this is inhumane. The only one profiting from such a situation is the nursing home. Several factors promote this activity. 1. First of all, many nursing homes have rules that say that nutrition must be maintained even though the patient is in a vegetative state and quality of life is zero and so, when the patient no longer is able to eat, down goes the feeding tube for weeks, months or may be years. 2. The family feels guility about not maintaining life under the artificial atmosphere of maintaining nutrition as described. 3. The doctor is afraid not to maintain life under all circumstances because of many reasons. As a result of all this, many are keeping people alive who have no life. Much of this is tax money and we desperately need to divert this money into other channels. We must come to ourselves, wake up and do what needs to be done.

Heroes

Heroes we love — we remember them, we write about them, we display their pictures, erect monuments to them and hallow their memory in many ways. We sometimes let our praise run wild and make them something they are not. We even worship them at times and in various ways. Among others, there are three common threads that often go into the fabric of hero making. As I see it, these three are courage, control and compassion.

Courage. Ephraim McDowell, M.D. was a frontier surgeon in Danville, Kentucky, in the year of 1809, and possessed courage to a remarkable degree. A patient by the name of Jane Todd came to him one day with a huge tumor in the abdomen. He knew that this would cause her death soon and her only hope would be surgical removal. The problem was there were no hospitals and no anesthesia and a tumor such as this had never before been removed in the annals of medicine or surgery. He decided to offer to Jane the opportunity to undergo a possible life-saving, but very scary and uncertain, surgical procedure. She had the courage to say "yes" despite all the advice she had to the contrary. Ephraim McDowell had the courage to go ahead despite the ridicule from everyone and despite an angry mob outside his office ready, perhaps, to lynch him if the operation failed. She did submit and he did proceed. She made it through and it was a glorious success. How we admire that kind of courage both on the part of Jane and her physician.

The above story is an indication of courage in a large package and very unique and fascinating, but I have in my forty-plus years of treating patients, seen everyday bits and pieces of courage that are heartwarming and inspiring. I have seen the courage of my beloved mountain patients as mom looked after a brood of twelve children and dad got up early on a snowy morning and went to the coal mines and worked out a shift amid coal dust and danger. I see the courage of Washington County farmers, who day in and day out, struggle on to make a go of things, battling high costs of operation and low prices as he sells his produce. I have seen the courage of local folk as both husband and wife would work an eight hour shift, forty hours a week at the Cabinet Factory and then have to manage a household, raising the kids and trying to keep their noses out of the water. I am fascinated by the perseverance and courage of the alcoholic and drug dependent person who manages to make a living and keep things going despite a terrible problem. I am amazed at the grit and courage of the spouse who lives with an alcoholic and is determined to keep the family intact, despite it all.

I stand in respect, honor and on occasion, awe, at the courage of countless cancer patients I have known and treated in the past years. These patients have been given their diagnosis, and have accepted their treatment and their pain and weakness with equanimity and courage. I shall never forget a select few who have literally pushed me up, so to speak, as they went down. And then there are the stroke victims, many of these have fought back like tigers to maintain as much independence as possible, and faced life with serious limitations without crying and begging for sympathy. Our hospitals are filled with patients who have mustered the courage to face extensive and dangerous surgery. I think of the patients who are waiting for a telephone call to say that a donor heart is ready for them to undergo a transplant.

Our psychiatric hospitals contain thousands of patients across America who have faced life with great handicaps and have gone on. When released and improved in their condition, they will return to face a world of problems again with courage and determination. I think of the thousands of courageous men and women who attend AA meetings and Narcotics Anonymous Meetings week after week with the courage that all these people represent.

Courage comes easier for some people than others, of course. What makes up the fertile soil in which courage grows? Positive thinking, support of intimate friends, religious faith and conviction, a willingness to accept a possible failure and still go on. Perseverance and a refusal to quit.

The courage of the martyrs is that of a special quality. It is that ability of the martyr to say that there is a cause greater than himself for which he is willing to give his life. We are aware of this on the battlefield, we know it existed in the hearts of countless persons through the centuries as they went to their graves with full knowledge of what lay ahead and determined to pay the supreme price for their beliefs.

Perhaps in the life of Jesus of Nazareth, we see coming together in focus, courage, control and compassion in an unparalleled way. Yes, the hero of the Christian faith is this Jesus. He has not been remembered for his wealth, his academic degrees, his books, his oratory or his political power. He is remembered and revered and worshiped as the unique Son of God because of his identification with the outcasts, the worthless, the poor and the losers. The world will never forget the man of Galilee who let us know what God is like, who lets us know what love can do, who loved and showed us a lifestyle that could bring a measure of peace, of hope, of purpose in this world, such as nothing else could do.

Control. If courage is the acceleration, then control is the brakes. A beautiful Jaguar without brakes does present a problem, and so courage, to be effective and purposeful and successful, must be tempered by control. When we see the beautiful and sleek and powerful auto moving majestically down the interstate with perfect control, it is impressive for sure. Unbridled courage can, and does, lead to disaster. Can you imagine the tightrope walker leaving his balance pole behind and going it alone over the wire — no way! Can you imagine the detective going on a narcotics bust, forgetting his bulletproof vest? If the executive on his way to the corporation summit starts to knife those around him, he may, in fact, be fatally knifed himself enroute. If Jesus had called a legion of angels to wipe out the Roman authorities and take him off the cross and press on to political power and glory as the people wanted, then his magnificent mission of supreme love would have been reduced to ashes.

We must bridle our courage with control if we are to achieve our purpose and arrive at our goal. It is hard to do this. We fail many times. We keep trying. The ones who make it to the top, who win our love and admiration, combine courage with control and discipline in an effective way.

Compassion. Now I'll admit that not all our popular heroes are remembered first and foremost as compassionate men and women. Our military heroes certainly are not remembered essentially for that, namely, we remember them for their courage and their genius. Our medical heroes, such as Jonas Salk of polio vaccination fame, and Joseph Lister who made modern surgery safe, we honor primarily for their marvelous contributions to the welfare of mankind.

Our athletic heroes we honor because of their fantastic ability to coordinate their minds and bodies and bring glory to our teams. Our heroes of the arts, the stage and television we honor because of their ability to entertain us and capture our attention.

But for some reason, the heroes that somehow occupy the front rows, the ones who demand our utmost respect, even our worship, are those who use their ability and talents for the good of mankind and were known as men and women of compassion. For the Christian, in a class all to himself, it is Jesus of Nazareth. For the Jews, it is Moses. For the American, it would be Abraham Lincoln. For the Catholic, it might be Mother Theresa. For all of us, it would be the certain person in our lives who loves us as we are and tells us so by words and deeds and who is always there when we need them most.

———————————————————

Excuses I Have Heard

I reckon I have heard about all the excuses thought of by mankind in the past forty years of medical practice. Patients want to lose weight and they don't and there are excuses. Patients want to quit smoking and they don't. People want to quit drinking and they don't. Patients want to quit cholesterol and fats and they don't. And usually I hear a lot of reasons why these goals are not achieved. Excuses are sometimes valid and most are not. The truth of the matter, as I see it, is that we fail to achieve our goal because the temptation to fail is too great and we simply are unwilling or, perhaps, unable in some cases to pay the price for victory.

As far as the weight reduction business, I hear so often, "But doctor, don't you think a lot of this weight is water!" "But doctor, honestly, I don't eat all that much." And then there is the guy who eats another piece of pecan pie and walks around the block assuming that will balance it out. The truth is we would have to run several miles to work those calories off.

And then there is the guy who comes into the office and is placed in the exam room. The nurse does the preliminary exam and takes the history. He tells her he has a private matter to discuss with the doctor. Usually that means he has symptoms of venereal disease. I discuss the matter with the patient and surely enough, it is evident that he has caught a sexually transmitted disease. Whereupon he says, the girl absolutely was clean and pure, she couldn't possibly have given him anything. He assumes, of course, that she has been with him alone and no one else. It sort of comes as a shock that this has happened. His girlfriend, on the other hand, assumes that he likely has caught the disease not from her, but from someone else. It sort of gets complicated after a while.

I do believe that breaking the smoking habit is almost impossible for most people. Excuses really do not need to be given and actually I don't hear them too often. It is simply a matter that after two to three days of smoking cessation, the average smoker falls apart and goes bananas and resumes the smoking before he "loses it," and the motivation to quit smoking is not as strong as the motivation to quit drinking. Significant people in the lives of heavy drinkers finally gang up on the drinker and lower the boom and give him virtually no choice in the matter. Not so with smokers, and so they continue their habit.

Then there is the matter of remembering. I tend to remember for sure the things I want to do and forget those things that don't especially turn me on. I think that is a common human trait for many of us. Committee meetings I may forget for sure, but meeting a friend at a certain time and place I am sure to remember. I remember meal time without much trouble, too.

There is all the difference in the world in the presentation a patient makes to the doctor when he comes in for a physical for disability and when he comes in for insurance qualifications. The disability patient usually has a bit of a depressed look on his face, is a bit stoop-shouldered and recites a litany of complaints to fill a medical text. About everything has gone bad in his body. On the other hand, the candidate for insurance qualifications comes in smiling, his shoulders squared and stating he never felt better in his life. This is all so human. All of us are likely to simulate this stance to some degree.

The self employed man gets sick or injured and he is back on the job dragging himself from pillar to post. The salaried man with lots of paid sick time, grunts and groans forever it seems, and this is also human.

The doctor in the military doesn't have to "kow tow" to the patient. He can kick the balky sailor in the seat of his pants, so to speak, and not listen to his bull. In private practice, on the other hand, the doctor is usually the friend and advocate for his patient and is more inclined to see things the way his patient wants him to. Doctors want to keep their patients happy for obvious reasons and don't especially want to incur the wrath of his patient who might be inclined to bring a lawsuit if the doctor has made a mistake.

Basically, we are all more or less self-centered and looking out for our own interests. We are prejudiced and egocentric, all of us, to some degree. The doctor has a responsibility to his patient, but also to the insurance company, to the factory and to all concerned in medical matters. Consequently, the doctor can't always keep everyone happy in all situations, far from it. We simply have to make our judgment calls as best we can, give our reasons and let the chips fall. In so doing, there sometimes is satisfaction with all concerned, sometimes dissatisfaction with all concerned and sometimes the decision is split, that is, the patient is happy but the factory personnel officer or the insurance company is upset. We all have an axe to grind and that is the way life is.

Having One's Own Way

Someone said to me recently, "You are used to having your own way and I am not. Your reactions, therefore, are different from mine in this situation." That, of course, got my attention and really started me to thinking. Do men generally get their own way? Do fathers get their own way? Do doctors get their own way? Certainly, authority figures of the past generally got their way, the fathers, the breadwinners, the teacher, the principal, the policeman, the boss, the lawyer, the doctor, generally got their way. Times have changed drastically in recent years and we are all aware that a new day is upon us and old relationships have been restructured.

I am a solo doctor. I am the boss of my office. I am fully responsible for all that happens and thus I am given full authority in the decision-making process there. If I take the full burden of responsibility, then I must have reasonable freedom to call my shot and exercise my judgment. At home it is quite a different matter. I am not fully responsible and, as a result, I am not the overall boss. My wife and I bear the responsibility together and have to work as a team.

In the practice of medicine, obviously the vast changes in the delivery system will mean changes for the doctor, and he will not "always get his way." Peer Review is telling the doctor he must do certain things. Medicare is telling the doctor he must do certain things. Medicaid is telling the doctor he must do certain things and third party insurance payers are telling the doctor he must do certain things. Patients are telling the doctors what to do for they are more knowledgeable and sophisticated. To be stripped of one's authority is always a painful thing and many physicians are experiencing pain and frustration as never before as the system rapidly changes. As patients are becoming more knowledgeable and sophisticated, doctors are having to make themselves better understood and adopt the changes that make that possible. As I am confronted with one frustration after another, I realize that to reduce my own pain, I need to align myself with reality, accept the situation as it is and as I must, and shut up my complaining and be grateful that things aren't worse. In short, I need to rejoice that I have as much as I have. Maybe I can. I hope so. I'll give it my best shot.

It is a Good Morning!

It is 5:30 in the morning and I am up and stirring about, pajamas, robe and slippers on, waiting for the gas furnace to do its thing and dutifully to make this 117-year-old house comfortable. When grandfather-in-law, Jonas Berkey, built this ten-room house here in Salem, Indiana, it was not heated with a gas furnace, for sure. It had a stove in most rooms and wood and coal were burned and that took a lot of work to keep all those stoves going. And so instead of firing up all those stoves, I sit here and wait for the place to get warm, having kicked up the thermostat. Just another reason why we Americans fail to burn off our calories and have a fat problem.

Yes, it is a good morning. I am waking up in America. Millions are waking up in the third world and they are hungry, always hungry. Not too good a morning there. The morning for me is the beginning of a day in which I will make rounds at the nursing home, see a bunch of patients at the office, attend a committee meeting tonight and generally perform as a useful and productive citizen of Washington County, Indiana.

There are those waking up in prisons of one kind or another this morning, not such a good one for them, for sure. There are those waking up in psychiatric hospitals and facing another battle with mind and emotions. There are those waking up in general hospitals, facing another day of pain, discomfort, uncertainty and fear. Some await their trip to surgery, be it brain, bowel, breast, heart, lung or uterus. Some wake up with their cancer and another day of struggle for survival is upon them. Not so good a morning for them.

There are those waking up in missions for the homeless. They are there for many reasons, whatever, not such a good morning. There are black men of South Africa who wake up in a gold mine dormitory away from their family and let us smug Americans not forget the America Indian is waking up, too, in situations that he didn't ask for, but were forced upon him.

241

The bottom line to all of this is simply that I am a million-aire, not according to my banker, but according to me. I have my right mind. I have my place in the sun. I am a respected citizen of this town. I have family, friends and all that one could possibly want or need for the good life. I need love and I am loved. What more could I want? "Good morning, have a good one!"

■———————————————————————■

Marriage — Good and Bad

Although marriage counseling is not my stock and trade, I have been a marriage observer as a family physician for over forty years and I am a married man of over forty years. I am qualified to speak on the subject, I suppose. So for whatever it is worth, here goes.

Marriages and home can be heaven or they can be hell. They can be stable or unstable. They can be heaven for children or a nightmare. They can be successful and long-lasting or end in failure and frustration. It is usually, for many couples, somewhere between the two extremes like most things in life. There can be good times and bad times, peace and war, times of success and times of failure. For sure, marriage in a stable home where love is found provides the best nest for our young. Despite the fact that marriage so often in these days ends prematurely, and despite the fact that the home environment is often turbulent, and despite the fact that love does not bind the marriage together so often, children often do weather the storm and make the grade.

Some marriages that I would call good ones are composed of husband and wife, both of whom have serious problems. They come to depend on each other, need each other, and somehow help each other through the agonies of life. I think of the wife who has serious health problems and is often, in addition, a nervous wreck. The husband sometimes helps in an amazing way and obviously feels good about his role with the situation. And then, too, I think of the wife who has an alcoholic husband and who wisely and patiently steers the ship through the shoals and around the rocks of life's journey. Marriages where serious problems exist and yet go on, indicate that a team can go on to victory despite serious handicaps. I think of the wife with recurrent manic depressive illness and the resultant chaos that erupts. The husband sometimes will keep the household going by almost heroic measures, long hours and hard work. I think of the marriages which have significant problem areas, where love is sporadic and partial, where cooperation is minimal and where harmony is scanty. And yet in these circumstances, the marriage goes on because the couple has opted to make the best of a bad situation. I think of the marriages where there is infidelity and the problems that arise, and yet survive.

I would like to mention two characteristics of a good marriage among many others that I have observed. First of all, I think it is essential that each spouse give freedom to the other to do their thing. That is, that one does not demand that the other conform, but can enjoy reasonable freedom to fulfill one's self. And secondly, I think communication is vital in a marriage relationship. Praise helps for sure. Constructive criticism in the right spirit does, too.

A pitiful situation that all of us are aware of is that in which a wife is abused in many ways and is unable to get out of the marriage. She has no skills for self-support, she is plagued with low self-esteem and there is depression and misery added on. In jail she is, for sure. I can understand how murder does happen after years of this. I think of the man who has a disabled wife, both mentally and physically, and has to assume all or most of the load. I can understand why he is tempted to fly away and sometimes does.

The ideal marriage, most of us would agree, would be the one which lasted throughout life, which survived all the vicissitudes and turmoil, and which rejoiced in all the joys and successes. Children would, in this marriage, be reared in an atmosphere of love and acceptance and encouragement. However, I know and you know and we all know that the ideal is not always achieved. Over one-half of the current marriages end in divorce. Many couples live together for varying periods of time without the formality of marriage. Other marriages begin with reasonably good prospects of success, but end after a few years. Often this comes about because as persons grow and develop and mature they grow in an entirely different direction. Reconciliation may not work and inevitable divorce results. Breaking the marriage vows by seeking and finding intimacy outside the marriage for various reasons can and does cause many divorces.

Surely we all can agree that if society was blessed with ideal marriages primarily, then it would indeed be a different and better world. This is not likely to happen. That being the case, we simply must accept the situation as it is. We can aim and strive for the ideal. If divorce does come, much grief can be spared if it is carried out without turmoil and bitterness. Too often, children are caught in the cross fire of an ongoing battle between husband and wife. This does not need to happen and the entire divorce problem could be improved greatly if this alone could be eliminated, and it could be in my judgment! Those who have had the blessings of a stable marriage could improve the entire scene by taking a nonjudgmental stand regarding those couples who are less fortunate.

■————————————————■

Hungry Children

One of my most vivid memories in my early childhood included scenes from the Great Depression beginning in 1929. The financial crash came when I was a first grader. I lived in Audubon Park, a subdivision of Louisville, Kentucky, and most of the residents there were professional or business people who owned their own homes and were upper middle class.

Across the Southern Railway tracks was Camp Taylor. This was an Army camp in World War I and afterwards it was inhabited by residents of the blue collar class of workers. The depression was rough and every class suffered, but especially the blue collar workers. Children came from Camp Taylor regularly to Audubon Park to beg for food. They came to our door, sometimes almost daily. There was no welfare, no food stamps, no social security. It was "root hog or die" in those days. The children came to us regularly because mother was generous and she quickly became known for that. The kids always asked for milk. At times the kids would become more aggressive and ask for certain foods. Dad didn't think too much of that but said nothing. One day one of the children said to mother, "Mrs. Martin, daddy wonders if you wouldn't have your milk man simply deliver the milk to our door and save us the trouble of coming over here and asking for it." That really got dad and he let it be known that he was much perturbed. People came to our door and wanted to work. Plenty of hitchhikers were on the highways. A lot of men rode the rails and became hobos. Homeless people were in abundance and soup kitchens became common. Banks failed everywhere and people lost fortunes. Suicides were common as people gave up all hope. Businesses failed across America. Plants shut down and those that survived were rolled back to a fraction of their former business. Slowly the depression began to lift in the late 1930's but in no way did the standard of living then compare to now. In high school, in the late 1930's, no one had a car to sport as they do now. We had bicycles and were glad to have them. I had hand me down clothes. My suits were made from dad's suits cut down to size. We had one car and kept that one twelve years. Two car garages were a sign of wealth in those days. Vacations were short, if any, and did not involve anything fancy. Motels were just beginning. Mostly there were tourist homes and cabins for night lodging and it wouldn't be over $5 a night for a family.

Children had few toys and they often made their own and perhaps enjoyed them more. Those who lived through those

245

days have a different perspective on money and wealth than those who missed it, for sure. The reasons are obvious. Today we are rich but still not happy. More drugs and alcohol than ever. Wealth can be glorious, but often it is not.

■———————————————————■

Shut Up!

Most of us are experts at judgment. We become aware of neighbors' entanglements and we pronounce judgment. We read about an impending divorce of a well known couple and we know exactly the problem and why things went wrong. We become aware of a boy's difficulty with "pot" and police and make careless remarks. We speak with disgust at the alcoholic's behavior and have the answer to his problems and we tell him to just leave it alone. As I see it, until and unless we have had a similar experience to that of our fallen neighbor or youth or whoever for whatever, then we should be cautious about our judgments. Otherwise, we simply reveal our prejudice and ignorance.

I had one view of the malpractice situation until I got sued myself. It looks a lot different now. As physicians, we view illness and injury in a certain light, but as patients we have some other thoughts and ideas. If I have had a solid marriage, I see divorce one way, but if I have been through a divorce myself, no doubt, I have a better understanding of the situation. For the first fifteen years of my professional life, I worked more for love than I did for money. I worked in an impoverished area where people simply could not pay me. And so I look at a doctor's income from a different perspective than those who have spent their entire career where income has been tops. As a father of four children, I can look at youth with their challenges and problems a bit differently than I would if I had never fathered a baby. A minister with a family can understand family problems better than a priest who is celibate. A female who celebrates twenty-five years of marriage "made in heaven" has, for sure, a different perspective than the unfortunate housewife who has lived for twenty-five years in hell. If one has gone through bankruptcy, he views money matters and finance differently from a person who has been on financial easy street. A recovered alcoholic has a different concept of alcoholism than I would have, without doubt. And the comparisons could go on and on.

Suffice it to say — let us be cautious about our judgments and let us be especially careful in acting like an expert when we haven't the faintest idea of what we are talking about.

Does a Dead Dove Matter?

This morning as I drove to the hospital, I saw two doves together in the middle of the road, obviously mates, enjoying the spring weather and each other. I got dangerously close before they decided to make way for me, but the delay was too long and one of the pair didn't make it. Feathers flew and the dull thud as my car struck one of the doves told the story. I hated that, I feel bad whenever I think about it today. They apparently were absorbed in each other to the point that approaching danger was disregarded until it was too late.

This scenario is all too often seen in the human family, as no doubt you would agree. The student becomes absorbed with his girlfriend, and alas, the study for the exam time is short circuited and the test is failed. This delay to do the right thing is seen all too often in the doctor's office. Symptoms are noted by the patient, but he does not respond and go for a check-up because of so much involvement with everyday passing commitments. When finally the symptoms become intolerable, action is taken, but by then the cancer is out of control and it is too late, too late.

Human nature is such that we tend to put things off and we delay and let things ride because to do otherwise involves work and effort. By nature we tend to do what comes naturally and inertia is hard to overcome. A relationship develops between two people of one kind or another. There is brother and sister relationship, husband and wife, doctor and patient, counselor and counselee, attorney and client, boss and worker. In all of the relationships, guidelines, disciplines and rules are a necessary part without which the relationships could get all messed up. Husband and wife must, and do, develop relationships constantly in the work a day world. Some of the relationships have the potential for intimacy to develop insidiously and in a direction that could bring conflict and chaos. Discipline is the ingredient needed to keep the ship on course, but such disciplines are sometimes difficult to employ and it would appear that the course of least resistance is often the road taken. Easy to understand, for sure. How much like the two doves we are. Approaching danger sets off our alarm but we delay because we are so human and, alas, it may be too late by the time we take action.

The Ultimate Gift

I have been the recipient of a lot of very wonderful gifts in the past forty years of practice. Patients have brought me garden produce in season for years and how we love it and appreciate it. Hunters have brought me venison, mushroom pickers have brought me the fruit of their labor. Jellies and jams have come in at various times. At Christmas, candy, cake, cookies, come in in abundance. I have received scarves, caps, gloves, ties, many of them homemade, through the Christmas season. Beautiful tablecloths grace our table made by the hands of an appreciative patient. Flowers have come when I was ill with a deep vein thrombosis at Norton Hospital three years ago. I received over 300 get well cards during that time. I have received letters of appreciation through the years from my patients and some from nurses who have worked for me. Two in particular I can remember and never forget. They simply opened their heart and let me know how they felt about the time and experience they had during their working days at the office. They expressed their difficulty in saying good-bye and the fact that they perhaps would not again experience the same fulfillment as they had while working in this office. This, to me, is about the ultimate gift from an employee. I love it. It makes the effort worthwhile. The greatest gifts we can bestow on one another are the gifts of some portion of ourselves. We give of ourselves when we take time to understand. We give of ourselves when we can be a bridge over troubled waters for someone we love. We give of ourselves when we listen to another's grief or heartache. We give of ourselves when we love someone despite the circumstances or despite what they have done or have not done. We give of ourselves when we give and expect nothing in return. That person may express their appreciation and say with regret, "You do so much for me, I can give you so little in return." The truth is, the appreciation expressed, the love that is so obviously there, is all that is wanted or needed in return. That makes it all worthwhile and that is the ultimate gift.

For Love Or For Money

Perhaps the thing in my life that has provided the greatest fulfillment is earning a living at something that I immensely enjoy. I think many doctors can say that. I don't hold this up as a virtue necessarily, it is just a fact. The need to be needed is present in most of us to some degree and in some of us to a great degree. One's feeling of self-worth is bound so tightly to one's occupation in life. Witness the depression that occurs when one is out with a prolonged illness or enters a retirement that is not fulfilling. When we are busy at something we enjoy, we can bear pain, disappointment, frustration, depression and about any obstacle much better, and so if we earn our living at something we love and enjoy, we are blessed beyond measure. To have to work day after day doing the same thing a robot could do would, I think, be degrading if you think about it long enough. To earn a living in a business that hurts people or kills them would be a major problem to many of us, for sure. I am glad I don't have to sell tobacco, whiskey or peddle narcotics to make a living. Having said all this, how would it be to earn a living as a criminal, living a life of deception, lying, cheating, stealing and breaking all rules of civilized society?

Yes, I love what I am doing — I am fulfilled, I am needed, useful and respected. Despite the fact that my freedoms are increasingly restricted, despite the increasing expectations of the public and the deterioration in doctor-patient relationship, I would go to medical school again if I had to start over.

The first twenty years of my practice I was in an impoverished area medically and economically speaking. It was rich in culture, tradition, and human relations and that was rewarding. I was employed by a foundation in the mountains of eastern Kentucky and I went to work for essentially a school teacher's salary. My friends thought I was crazy, had rocks in my head. But I had always thought that this sort of life would bring fulfillment of my drive and purpose in life and so I went for it. I flourished. I found my place in the sun. My self-esteem rose (it needed it). We didn't spend much money because we didn't make much. Simple as that. But we had enough of what we needed. One car, no fancy clothes, simple vacations, simple lifestyle, no extras, only basics. But we were happy if not joyous. We were filling a need where few would venture. We did a job that others did not want to do. If you have not had that experience, you have missed one of the best things life has to offer. For the last fifteen years I have also worked in an area of need but also in an area where people could adequately pay their bills. Consequently, my income has risen to the expected level of most family doctors which is more than adequate. I have two homes, two cars, have a rental duplex complex for community use, give considerable money to family and church and charitable organizations. I have literally worked night and day in the process. I have had little time for anything but work, work, work. Have I enjoyed it? Yes. Would I do it again? Yes. I have been exhausted many times and experienced one stretch of disabling depression requiring eight weeks away from practice. But the truth is, every responsible position in this world requires blood, sweat and tears. It requires discipline and hard work. It requires us to take the bad with the good. I know of no job or position that is all honey and roses.

I'd admit that having more than enough income provides things we all like. We like the deluxe features of life, nice vacation trips, stylish cars and a get-away home on the lake. We like money to give our children the things they need and an education if they want it and will take it. Money is good because we can help support worthy causes and institutions and assist in our own way with the poverty out there in the world.

And so I have been fulfilled in my earlier professional life where I worked more for love than for money. Also, I feel good about the last fifteen years where I have worked for love and for money. If I couldn't have had both experiences, if I had to choose one, I would work for love and not for money.

■———————————————————————————■

A Lot of Fun

Every Sunday afternoon for fifteen years I have reserved an hour or two to do my dictation of letters, insurance reports, reports to the welfare and social security, reports to attorneys, chart work in the office and you name it work. This is not exactly the happiest time of the week. As a matter of fact, I dread it. But it has to be done faithfully. I dutifully go through the routine. At the conclusion of my work I have, through the years, engaged in a project that has brought to some people and to me, some genuine pleasure. Since I have an excellent secretary, my daughter, who does my transcribing and letter writing, I am able to get a lot done by way of dictation. I scan the local newspapers each week and write notes of congratulations to those patients of mine who have done something noteworthy. This includes athletic awards, scholastic honors, beauty queens and so on. I have made it a point of writing letters to the families of my deceased patients. Furthermore, I have written letters on behalf of our church in appropriate situations. People tell me from time to time how much this means to them and the encouragement it has brought. Especially my letter carries a punch because of my demanding schedule. I have found, and I am sure you have, that recognition is a great thing and is the grease that keeps the wheels turning often.

I have written to prisoners and gotten appreciative letters in return. I have written to several men and women overseas in the military. All in all, the response from this has been gratifying and has added a real plus in my life.

When a patient writes a note of thanks to me, it is an unexpected and much appreciated gesture. Expected notes are okay, but unexpected letters carry a wallop and get one's attention. Try it — you may like it.

Cold Breakfast

One morning I was making rounds at the hospital and a patient was complaining that his breakfast didn't have his favorite cereal, he got grapefruit juice instead of orange juice, and besides, his eggs weren't all that good. I noted that he was obese, had gotten more than his share of food in his day, and all this, while starvation is rampant in many areas of the world. I can hardly take the complaining about food in the hospital. I wish I had the courage to tell the next obese bird who complains about the flavor of ice cream, that what he really needs is to have bread and water for two weeks and maybe after that he will stop his bitching. We Americans are blessed beyond measure, most of us. Unfortunately, we have too much food and too many automobiles, too much booze and too much tobacco, and we have pot, coke and heroin. As Billy Graham once said, "If God doesn't soon send judgment upon America, he will have to apologize to Sodom and Gomorrah."

We Americans have the world by the tail on a downhill drag so to speak. We have it made, most of us. However, we do live with uncertainty. We live with the possibility of nuclear holocaust. We live with a national debt that may, if it continues unchecked, put us into economic chaos one of these days. We do live with the knowledge of an army of homeless people that is a blight and embarrassment to this nation. We live with murder on the streets, narcotics in the vein, AIDS in the blood and with several million alcoholics trying to struggle and live. By and large, most of us have it soft. We live a life of luxury and ease, and we don't know what suffering, deprivation and hardship really is.

I suspect that the only hope for this nation to come to its senses is to have a national disaster that brings us to our knees with great suffering and takes away the things that we believe essential to happiness. Of course, I don't relish the idea any more than you do, but having lived through the depression during the twenties and thirties, I suspect I will be a bit more prepared for the bad times which may come than is the younger generation.

Come Along, Walk With Me

Someone once said to me recently when I finished telling one of my hair-raising doctor tales, "Oh, that I could have walked where you have walked!" That person has heard a lot of my tales and as a result expressed that sentiment and I could respond to that person and say, "I wish I could have walked where you have walked, too." Now it is true, we all can agree here, that some lives are more interesting, more challenging, more exciting than others for sure, but no two of us have exactly the same experience and walk in life. Surely the Russians walk in a different world from Americans. The black South African has a different walk from the black American. The Eskimo has a different walk from the Brazilian. The soldier in Germany and Korea guarding the line between freedom and communism has a different walk than the one who is parading a peace banner in front of the White House. The doctor has a different walk from the patient. The attorney has a different walk than the client. And on and on and on we could go with our contrast. We see things, and come to our positions based on our experience and our mentality and our prejudice. Especially the latter.

It would be, no doubt, good if every doctor could spend a week out of each year in the hospital and have to pay just as every other patient pays.

What I am saying is, well, you already know. You just can't know really a thing unless you have been there. Come along, walk where I have walked, come along and walk where I am walking. Come along and walk where I will be going next and I will do the same with you. Maybe, just maybe, we would have a bit better world that way. Correction. I know we would!

Penniless Millionaires

I have just come from a week's stay with the students at Southwestern Georgia University at Americus, Georgia. A lovely campus, 2,000 students and most of them not very well off financially. The countryside around Americus is not rich. As a matter of fact, much of it would be considered poor by American standards. There were white kids and there were black kids. They wore jeans, simple dress. There were not too many automobiles. Obviously not many kids were from wealthy homes. But these kids were happy, well behaved and studious and they were millionaires, though some of them, in reality, were nearly penniless, I suspect. They were happy and they were learning. They were looking forward to life and success, living in America with its marvelous opportunities. It was good to see them, talk to them and to listen as they responded to our question; see them smile and say "Yes, sir," and "thank you." It gives me hope. Ah yes! To have a sound mind and body makes one a millionaire. To be able to see is worth a million dollars alone. I saw one student groping his way along, shoulders squared, with a stick swinging out in front, guiding him along the campus. But most of the students were happy. They were not in a mental hospital or a home for the retarded. They were walking and running and playing tennis. They were not in wheelchairs; they were robust. They were not fighting cancer. They had hope of a good life and they did not live in a communist society. They had opportunity. They had friends. The black and the white students in the deep south of Georgia ate together, played together and studied together and faced life together. Yes, these penniless students were rich. Fifty percent of them work for minimum wage and are glad to get it. Some were on scholarship and others had student loans. Yes, they were penniless millionaires without doubt.

Soon I shall return to Salem, Indiana, where I will make rounds at the nursing home and deal with the host of problems there — wheelchairs, dementia, incontinence of urine and feces, pills, pills, pills and much suffering and misery.

255

Let us take care of these wonderful bodies, the most marvelous machine ever invented. It can repair itself and it can withstand punishment beyond belief. It can go on and on. It has personality and it has, I believe by faith, immortality. Let's take care of our bodies and be thankful and let us rejoice.

Old Can Be Beautiful

I still can't believe what I saw last night as I drove through Audubon Park in Louisville, Kentucky. Fairy land. *Better Homes and Gardens,* only real. Dogwood Festival time in one of the oldest suburban areas of the city. The place of my boyhood where I grew up, to boot. It didn't look that good fifty years ago. Age had given that place remarkable beauty. The trees were huge and the over-hanging branches formed a great archway for the street traffic. Dogwood, pink and white, seemed to be everywhere: Azalea and all shades of it, too. The yards were neatly groomed, the houses appeared to be freshly painted and the floodlights lit up the entire sub-division to a blaze of unbelievable glory. The homes were all well built and were fifty to 100 years old. No doubt in my mind, my boyhood home never looked so good as it did last night. It would appear that each home tried to outdo the others and get the grand prize. Cars were bumper to bumper, slowly moving and all taking in the magnificence of spring.

Surely in Audubon Park, "old" was not synonymous with decay. Quite the opposite. Old here meant beauty, enchantment and continual rebirth. This gave me a remarkable feeling of joy, of optimism, of hope, of expectancy, of satisfaction. So often in modern America old means wrinkled, gray hair, limitation, malfunctioning, dementia, ugly, useless and forgotten. Not so last night in that place of my youth. And that got me to thinking. Old often means something other than the undesirable and the ugly. What else is good about old?

As I walked into the huge pyramid at Giza, Egypt, "old" had a brand new meaning for me. Old meant permanent, survival, mystery and elegance. As I looked at the scroll of the Book of Isaiah, 3,000 years old preserved in Israel, old meant reverence, value, light. As we read our English Bible, we realize that old means eternal truth which cannot be destroyed.

As I compare myself today at sixty-five with the boy in Audubon Park fifty years ago, I can truthfully say that old can be beautiful. As a lad of fifteen, I was insecure, striving for a sense of direction, subject to lots of influences coming from all directions. Now at sixty-five my hair is gray, my skin is losing its elasticity and I am obviously giving evidence of mileage in more ways than one. However, I am finally taking care of this body of mine. I am keeping my weight down. I exercise daily. I go to the Y to workout. My cholesterol is normal. My shoulders are squared and my abdomen is firm. I still have my hair, my sight and hearing are acceptable and some say I don't look my age. I certainly don't intend to act my age! I keep up with my CME and I still see a bunch of people every day in the office. Yes, old can be beautiful. I have made it. I have arrived at a relatively secure place. I have an experience to share. I can help and I can be helped. Yes, old can be as great a part of life as youth, or perhaps greater. I intend for my journey to homeplate to be the best part of the trip. I have time now to smell the roses. I have time to give away some roses. I have time to appreciate and be appreciated. I can warn. I can suggest. I can recommend. I can counsel and I can teach. But if you know, I am still learning and I am ready to change my mind if I am mistaken. If you give me a warning, I hope I will listen.

American Style Civil War, 1989

In a recent message to whomever out there, I wrote about the modern American Civil War fought in the courtroom. I got that off my chest, not that my emotion will make a dent in the situation, but maybe collectively and eventually something will happen after we all get fed up to the eyebrows. Since then it has occurred to me that another war of Americans is being waged with considerable intensity and enthusiasm on the part of many. The communists have traditionally shot down the masses and kept them in line, until just recently, of course. But now the freedom-loving masses of Americans are shooting down our public officials, just the reverse of the communists, in an alarming and amazing way. The pendulum swings and when it swings, look out! Let one of our public officials look cross-eyed at a pretty girl and pretty soon it is all over town that he is sleeping with her. Let a public official drink a bit too much on derby weekend and pretty soon it is all over town that he is a confirmed alcoholic. Let some public official use his wisdom, ingenuity, work long and hard on a business deal and take a big risk, make a chunk of money and before you know it, he has cheated somebody somewhere or has used his influence and compromised his reputation. For crying out loud, folks. If we keep this up, nobody worth a cent is going to run for public office!

Don't misunderstand me, I am for law and order. I am for high standards of behavior. I am for the constitution, the flag, motherhood and all the rest, but let's quit eating our public officials alive. We have overdone it. We have gone berserk. The press and the media especially. Why, the media has a right to ask any public official about anything, anywhere, anytime. The official must not hesitate to think about his answer, lest his hesitation indicate his guilt immediately.

Judging from their behavior, you'd think the media has the right to know our official's medical history, his business dealings for all time, and to inquire diligently about his sex life and any affairs that he may have had, or that he may be having, or that he may be thinking about having. Congressmen are worn out fighting each other and are unable to give their full energies to running our government, fighting corruption and drugs.

Now I will be the first to admit that I have exaggerated a bit and have overstated the situation to make a point. But I think that all sane and thinking Americans will agree that there is a fair amount of truth in the point that I have been trying to make.

I honestly believe that the carpenter of Nazareth had it exactly right when he spoke to the crowd one day. The men in the crowd were taking up stones to crush out the life of a woman of the street and Jesus suggested that the man without sin cast the first stone. Some of those men, no doubt, had helped her to establish her bad reputation. They, of course, considered themselves guiltless. Perhaps this thought might dampen the enthusiasm of the sharks out there who are circling and waiting for food. It is so easy and we all are so prone to see a speck in the eye of a friend when we have a boulder in our own eye. I have noticed in dealing with children, even my own, that inconsistency is not uncommon. The very transgression that one child will accuse a sibling of, is sometimes minor compared to his own. A child will accuse a brother of accepting too many favors from the parents and at the same time overlook the fact that he has been given far more at an earlier date.

The bottom line of what I am saying is simply this, few of us have the right to get up on a stump and preach. We are everyone sinners, and our lives have many inconsistencies. Of course, we have a responsibility to point out error, mistakes and stupidities under proper circumstances and especially under oath in an investigation. But let us do so with humility, remembering that if we haven't made a fool of ourselves before, we likely will in the future.

The Launch Pad and the Shuttle

Only those who await the countdown locked inside the shuttle on the launch pad can possibly understand what lift-off is all about. I can't and you can't; we have not been there and we are not likely to be there in the future. One can't possibly understand that experience till he has been there. Nevertheless, we have all been on the launch pad in our life of one kind or another. The soldiers on D-Day awaiting the signal to go for it across the channel can relate to launch pad syndrome, as I shall call it for this story. The syndrome is excitement, uncertainty, expectation, hope, fear, joy, fast heart, tremor. Whatever, that moment gets your full attention. The syndrome is experienced as the bride and groom do down the aisle and say their vows. The expectant father has it when he passes the hospital corridor during a difficult delivery of his baby. The wife knows about that when her husband goes to the operating room for open heart surgery.

And then there is the syndrome cropping up again as husband and wife feel compelled after years of unhappiness to end a dead marriage. Uncertainty, fear, excitement, hope, joy and sadness. There will be denunciation by many and acceptance and love by a few. Whatever else is felt at a time of divorce, it is a time of chance and change. It can never be an easy time. Change is always difficult. The rut requires less effort in many ways and to steer the ship of life out of the rut is another direction requires energy, skill, determination, courage and a willingness to face rejection and even rupture of relationships that once were supportive and good. Most of the time we are accepted and loved because of who we are and what we are, what we believe, how we think and on whose side we are. Our true friends, real friends, those who really love us, will give us the freedom to make our decision to try to do what we have to do, to try to be what we have to be and to try to go where we have to go. True friends are rare. Fair weather friends may be many. And especially do we have "friends" when we are in a position to give. But all of this is nothing new. It is as old as society, as old as time has included people. And this is what makes true friendship beautiful. Rare like a diamond and beautiful like pure gold.

A ship is launched and the captain has a big burden on his shoulders. But the captain has the executive and the officers who give him advice and comfort. The president is sworn in on the steps of the Capitol building and the ship of state is launched. But the new president has the cabinet to give advice and to give comfort. A new corporation, a new college, a new church, and in the launching someone has a big burden. In every case, there are those along side the "main man" to give advice and comfort. Ah, the launching syndrome — the first operation, the first sermon, the first sail, the first lesson taught, the first race, the first play, the first anything, the first step, the last step. It is all the same.

Yes, I have seen many a patient on the launch pad locked in the shuttle. I see it as I tell my patients they have cancer. I see the launch pad syndrome when my patient goes to the operating room facing an uncertain outcome. I see it when my patient faces the nursing home and realizes it is the last step on life's journey before the grave. As a patient, I have been on the launch pad awaiting an uncertain future. I felt the syndrome coming on as I started on my journey at Homeplace Clinic, green and untried. I felt it when I went to the psychiatric hospital the first time and faced the unknown. I felt it when I thought my daughter might die during childbirth. And I know how reassuring, how comforting it is to have someone walk to the launch pad with you and maybe even slip into the shuttle before the door is closed. As a physician for many years, I have gone to the launch pad with my patients and with some, crawled into the shuttle. It is a delight to be able to do this and it is a privilege. I also know what it is to have someone walk to the launch pad with me, and some have even crawled into the shuttle. That is the bottom line of what life is all about.

Family Holiday Gatherings

You may like them, you may not, but for sure you have been to them. Today is Mother's Day and all across America, families are together. Food, drinks, talk, laughing, fussing and kids running helter skelter. Snapshots, TV, ballgames, stories, yarns, bragging, complaining and generally, giving advice on how to run the country. Then saying good-bye and everyone goes in a separate direction, highways are filled, and we head for home and tomorrow to work. Family can be wonderful, can be terrible, but generally, in between. The loud mouths, the braggers, the liars, the wise, the good ones, the bad ones, the ones we can relate to, the ones we put up with, the ones we can hardly tolerate. Some of these talk endlessly about themselves, especially their operations.

I suppose children are God's greatest blessing, or perhaps greatest curse to us depending on how it goes. Our children are an extension of ourselves and much of what we have is invested in our children. Their triumphs are ours, their defeats, too. So often their equipment to tangle with life has come from us. They are made of the same stuff as we are. They have watched us and have learned from us. If kids want to know what diseases they will have to face, look at mom and dad. If our parents lived long and were productive, then our chances of doing the same are pretty good, unless we get shot or run over. If mom or dad or both were alcoholic, then look out. If heart disease riddles the family, you better get your cholesterol checked. If cancer is prevalent, bear that in mind. In med school, I chafed at having to fuss around and take a family history of diseases, but let me tell you, it is vital to a doctor in making a diagnosis, at times, in any given patient. Emotional illnesses run in families, generation after generation. Obesity, too. Physical characteristics are handed down as well as intellectual. We all know that.

And so, our children, extensions of ourselves, can bring us intense joy or the bitterest of sorrow. We quite naturally want our children to succeed. We want them to be healthy. We want them to be happy, and especially we want them to adopt our value system if we are proud of ourselves. We want them to adopt our beliefs, our religion and we want them to be law-abiding and productive citizens of which we can be proud. When things don't work out this way, and they often don't, then we handle it in various ways. Some children feel they are only really loved and fully accepted when they are successful, when they meet their parents' expectations and sometimes this is exactly the way it is. Unfortunate, but true. If somehow we could only love and accept our children, regardless. Our belief system may say God is like that, but precious few of us mortals are. So often our love is conditional. Our kids pick up on this and handle it in various ways.

In dealing day to day with stress in the life of so many of my patients, the problems often arise in family relationships. Spouse entanglements and child-parents disharmonies. To be a good parent, really good, is a tough assignment and not all of us do too well. To grow and mature from childhood to responsible adulthood is a formidable task. In modern America, one of the very toughest assignments is to be a good parent and at the same time pursue one's professional life or earn one's income in such a way that it is fulfilling and reasonably satisfying. Especially is this a challenge to the modern housewife, caught up in the professional world, trying to find fulfillment and at the same time, be a good mother and wife. For the child and the teenager, the tensions arise as peer pressures clash with parental expectations and values. Boil it all down, life is full of challenges and difficulties. Baffling, frustrating, devastating, joyous, fulfilling, rewarding and exciting. Family gatherings? I am for them. They can be and so often are a satisfying interlude in a busy world. Children? I will take the risk anytime. Would I go to medical school again if I had to start over? Yes, Yes, Yes! Even in the changing world, even with land mines out there that I might step on, even with the endless pressures. It has been, and still is, a marvelous experience to look into the eyes of one you have helped pull out of a very deep ditch and see the gratitude and sometimes the love.

Props and Braces

We all admire the "self-made man," the adventurer, the explorer, the fearless, the strong and the brave. History has recorded their feats for our admiration. No doubt along with our feelings there is some jealousy at times as we attempt to identify with these in the winner's circle. Many have the ability to be winners, too, but uncontrolled anxiety is the monster that keeps them from stardom. Anxiety — yuck — the mere word is upsetting to us. It is a feeling — very unpleasant — that we get when we see an unavoidable motor vehicle crash coming. We feel it when a coiled rattlesnake is ready to strike us; when we are handed an exam booklet and we are unprepared; when we are promoted to a new and more responsible position or when we come home and our spouse is gone and unaccounted for. Life is filled with situations that provoke anxiety. Our heart races, we breathe faster, we may tremble. We feel inadequate and unsure of ourselves. I see it in the face of my patients when I tell them the diagnosis is cancer. I see the face of terror when I emerge from the emergency room and tell the wife that her husband has had a life-threatening heart attack and the outcome is in doubt. The alcoholics are basically treating their own anxiety with the world's oldest tranquilizer — whiskey. I see the patients with chronic anxiety who present with a multitude of symptoms which finally boil down to chronic anxiety.

In all of our attempts to cope with this monster that attacks, in one way or another, most every person, we generally try to reach out for a prop or a brace. We can call it a support system if we wish to be academic. Children have their mother's or dad's hand. Children have their security blankets. Adults are just as needy as children, but we are a bit more sophisticated as we reach out. As we go through a life crisis, we so desperately need a brace — someone to talk to who accepts us and loves us and understands us. The doctor is in a position not only to be a diagnostician and a therapist, but a friend and a confidant. Herein, of course, lies a danger; as the

physician becomes, at times, caught up in the emotion of someone's problem, he can lose his objectivity and balance.

Generally speaking, most of us want to stand alone 100
percent of the time. Not many can be admitted to that club.
Most of us need desperately in our lives support systems, props,
braces, the whole works on occasion, and that is okay. It is
a wonderful thing to be able to help a fellow-traveler and get
him out of a ditch. It is a great thing to be pulled out of a
ditch. I have been pulled out of several myself and put back
on the track.

The shuttle crew on the launch pad has a support system
so complex it is mind boggling. The Indy car has a pit crew
ready to assist in a moment's notice with lightning speed. The
heart surgeon has his support team all gathered around. The
truth is, few of us could single-handedly get our jobs done
without supports of one kind or another. The problem is cen-
tered on the question, when do we need help and when can
we go it alone? This is tough and each of us must answer this
for ourself. It is indeed one of life's greatest joys to find a
fellow-traveler in this world that we can relate to, with whom
we can share our lives, and who will cry with us and shout
with us. That person can take our hand when we need it most
and with that confidence and with that love, we can be a winner and face the unknown.

Carmen

Here I am with a Medicare card and I have never been to
the opera. How musically retarded can you get? I am ready
to confess that I have missed out on a lot of life because of
my occupation; being on call twenty-four hours a day, seven
days a week. I have been like a dog on a chain. I wander out
a little piece and suddenly the chain jerks and I become aware
of reality. Anyhow, I am out here doing more things and trying

to live like an average American. I am trying to go places and do things. So when my wife suggested, or rather, informed me that she had bought two tickets to Carmen, the die was cast. I read up on the story ahead of time. I knew I should. I can't understand operas in English, much less in French.

To Louisville we went to the Kentucky Center for the Arts and into Whitney Hall. Lots of people. Pretty fancy bunch of folks. All opera-lovers, no doubt. Maybe a few opera initiates like me, and maybe a few were there out of a sense of duty. Perhaps some were told that going to the opera would do them good, like taking cod liver oil, for example. Anyhow, we got seated and I read through the program and noted all the people who had given certain amounts of money to subsidize the opera. The $10,000 class of people were listed and then the $5,000 class and then the $1,000 class. If you have less than that, you didn't get mentioned.

The lights flickered and the inevitable late-comers came in trampling over our feet and stumbling around in the darkness. The lights went out and a few more straggled in and stumbled around. These people all were so busy and important that they couldn't possibly spare an extra five minutes and get there on time and spare us the difficulty. The Louisville Orchestra had tuned itself up and the conductor bowed and the music of Carmen began. Wow! I had heard that number before and recognized it. I guess I wasn't quite so ignorant as I thought I was. The curtain went up and the big show was on. The staging was marvelous and the costumes were brilliant. The music was delightful and the voices of the chorus and the leading people were all that we could expect and more. There were four acts. We were well along the first act and I couldn't get it all together when suddenly my eyes went up and I saw the English version of the activity on a screen to guide along the ignorant. Like a seeing-eye dog with his blind master; from there on it was a breeze. I got it!

The story of Carmen was sung and acted out and we watched for three hours what took perhaps many weeks to produce. And this not to mention the years of intense training

266

on the part of the leading singers. Operas are tragic for the most part. Carmen was a prime example of that. Carmen, oozing with sensuality, lures a good soldier away from his girlfriend and his mother and they together enjoy briefly the life of love and ecstasy. But it didn't last. It never does. Problems arose and conflicts between loyalty and passion carried Don Jose from the heights of heaven to the pits of hell. Jose wavered when Carmen had him under her control and he lost his nerve and his commitment to pleasure. He felt the call of duty and loyalty and as he made his decision, the sensuous Carmen became a tiger and he beat a hasty retreat. Carmen was back on the prowl and fell madly in love with the toreador of Seville. And then before the bullfight of fights, Jose encountered Carmen and made one attempt after another to lure her back. She was resolute. "I would rather die than go back with you," she insisted time after time, and she did just that. Jose drew back the lethal weapon and thrust the knife deep into her heart and she lay dead as the curtain came down.

Now I must confess that I don't like tragedies. I simply don't. I have for over forty years dealt with suffering and death. I don't want to see it again in the movies or in the opera or any place else that I can avoid it. I want to see something happy like Sound of Music. I am not going back to the opera. I can't handle that.

Some things in life change and change and change. Take science or the practice of medicine or surgery, for instance. But some things never change. Like beautiful and sensuous women and the men that succumb to their advances. When love and loyalty clash, love usually wins and that never seems to change. A beautiful woman is just about irresistible under certain of life's circumstances and so loyalty and discipline go out the window. And then such love affairs often are brief and turbulent and complicated and almost always tragic.

Carmen portrays perfectly that purely sensuous erotic love is usually selfish, possessive, jealous and paranoid. And so it is. It is sort of like cotton candy, gorgeous, exciting, tasty, but gone in a flash. The love that can endure has to have both Cupid and Psyche. The sensuous and the soul. The body and the mind. Such a relationship has a chance for survival and growth into maturity.

Carmen also reminds me of a phenomenon which my father used to refer to as barnyard morality. I shall call this the Carmen syndrome. I am sure the point is obvious without much need for clarification; that whoever around you appeals to you, you go for without invitation and proceed as best you can. I do feel that such behavior can be pathological at times and can even be elevated to the respectable position of uncontrollable behavior called disease. Alcoholism we now call disease and have dropped the word "sin." And so I suppose we could now popularize the term "barnyard syndrome" and simply look at it as a disease instead of a behavioral disorder.

There is one characteristic of male behavior which I must confess I have no patience for and I suppose part of the reason is that it has never been a problem of mine. I have mine, believe me, but that is not one of them and never likely to be. I am now referring to what I call the Don Jose Syndrome. Jose continued to beg and plead with Carmen to return to him, to be his lover and to give herself to him despite the fact that she was not the slightest bit interested in him, sexually or otherwise. That didn't seem to make any difference to Jose. All he wanted was for Carmen to return to him no matter how she felt about it. He seemed to care less about how she felt about him so long as she would return to him. I hear this scenario in the office from time to time. It seems that some men insist on three things and three things only. One is sex, the other is food, and the third is to keep the washing done. Aside from that, some men really don't care how their wives feel about the relationship. Some women are obviously locked up in prison in this situation and remain there because of fear or the inability to escape. As far as I am concerned, this is nothing but rape — legalized. I can put up with men with their stubbornness and their stupidity, and I have my share, certainly, of inconsistencies, head strong behavior and selfishness. But I am not afflicted with the Jose syndrome and not likely ever to be.

The Bust Part of Life

I got my free copy of *Life* Magazine today, advertising a well-known drug, and it caught my eye and perfectly performed its intended purpose. Here on the front cover was a good-looking girl with a better looking bust, neatly covered in part by a delicate bra. The caption read, "One hundred years of the bra." Now why on earth am I writing about this? Is there anything new about sexy pictures or their ability to get the eye? Of course not.

Well, anyhow, let's think about the subject of sexy pictures. Fact number one, America is soaked in sexy pictures coast to coast. What else is new? Reason? It gets our attention. Reason? Bottom line is money. We have something to sell for a profit and we have to have a buyer. To get a buyer, you have to get his attention. To get attention, you get a pretty girl, sort of scantily clad, in a provocative pose and bingo — you have your prospective customer's attention and you are on first base to get a sale. Back to the bust. I am not sure if the average American male is more easily trapped by a pretty face or the anatomically perfect breast partly concealed by the lacy bra. It seems that the female breast in America is primarily a sex symbol and no longer the lunch counter for the newborn. There are still a few exceptions to this, but not too many. Cosmetic surgeons are making lots of money fixing up American breasts to allure the boys.

Now I want to go on record as occupying a non-judgmental stance here. If a gal's self-esteem is shot because she is

269

flat-chested and if she can scrape up the dollars, I say go find a good cosmetic surgeon and get fixed. It might turn her around, who knows? If a lady has lost a breast by surgery, let her have a new breast shaped by cosmetic surgeons if she feels she wants that. Fine — go for it.

Any red blooded and alive American male appreciates a beautiful woman. The trouble is that sometimes we see only the body and fail to take note of what goes on above the eyebrows. A curvaceous lady with minimal brain does seem to satisfy the expectations and appetites of some males over an extended period. Most of our communications and relationships are spent in pursuit of activities not requiring a bed, however. Consequently, if the girl's brain is not in gear, the whole relationship might go bust. At least it would for me.

Body Traps

Booby traps are well understood by our combat soldiers. Many a leg has been blown off when the shoe sole pressed against the triggering device. But today, I am talking about body traps rather than booby traps. Recently, my wife and I attended a dance recital simply because our grandchild, Annie, was a participant. Annie is four years old. She is Shirley Temple, for sure, and she knows it. We had our tickets and to the school auditorium we went. The parking lot was full. The house was almost filled as we entered and by the time we got seated it was standing room only. Then the dancers appeared and for over two hours the show went along smoothly and efficiently. All ages of girls appeared, going through their routines, from three years old and up. All girls. Beautiful costumes. Tights, all colors of the rainbow. Some of the kids were pretty, real pretty. Some were gifted in their performance. All to dance for us and let us have a good relaxing evening of entertainment. Now there just isn't any better way to entertain the average male than to watch a pretty dancing girl with tights go through her routine. This sort of entertainment brings in the high ratings. It always has and I guess it always will. That is the way we were made. The entertainment world is saturated with this kind of activity because it is in demand.

Now at the same time society says to our youth certain things. They say that it is best to wait for sex until marriage. They say you should not have sex with anyone but your spouse. Society says a lot of things that are supposed to be for our own good and no doubt this is true. We have come to understand the hard way that sexual promiscuity may lead to disease and possibly to death. Medical science is working feverishly to try to halt the oncoming horror of AIDS.

If we could learn to discipline our sexual freedoms and appetites that would help. But with dancing girls all around us, it is not so easy. Then of course we have the opportunity to engage in safe sex, but many are in no mood to go to the trouble. It is sort of like riding a motorcycle eighty miles an hour without a helmet. It is a great thrill as we go up and over the hill. If a crash occurs, a great big bill — hospital or undertaker or both.

And so the booby traps are set awaiting our youth to make a wrong step. It never was easy to grow up. It is plumb dangerous to be a youth these days. Always was, of course. But it is getting more stressful. Maybe we should all surrender our freedoms, sell out, get black suits, get black dresses, get bonnets and hats and finally get our buggies and our horses and join the Amish. Maybe that would solve a lot of problems. If we did, we sure wouldn't have to worry about the effect on us of dancing girls in tights.

■————————————————————■

Decision Dilemma

To be or not to be — that is the question. Along with its beauty and joy, life is also a struggle, is complex and the challenges are great. Perhaps one of the thorniest problems of life has to do with decisions, decisions, decisions. There are people who make up their minds quickly and easily and readily and don't carefully weigh all the issues before making an important decision. Bamm! An answer is given. No sweat. Under these circumstances, anything can happen and it isn't always good. Too quick. Impulsive. Impatient. Then there is the man who simply takes forever to make up his mind. He tediously and cautiously weighs all the evidence and still can't seem to come to a decision about anything. It is plumb pathetic to observe such a person struggle and struggle. Then there are those who carefully survey the situation, weigh all the evidence and come to a decision with caution and yet with reasonable speed. It would be nice to be always like that. It seems to me that generally I make decisions fairly rapidly and sometimes I go too fast. Sometimes, though, I get stuck and get all bogged down and find it extremely difficult to come to a decision.

Much of life, however, sort of runs on automatic pilot. We don't have to make decisions. In a sense they are made for us. We have to go to work. We must get up at a certain time. We have to bathe, dress, shave and eat one to three meals a day. We have to go to work and do our job and pay the rent. We have accepted many responsibilities and so we carry those out in one way or another. Life, for many of us, is filled with responsibilities that basically require no decision-making — we simply do our job and carry out our responsibilities.

But now let's talk about those decisions that are not on automatic pilot but are on manual control. Decisions that must be made, some immediate, some a bit delayed and some that can be put on the back burner. It is 5:00 a.m. at this writing and I am down on my dock at the lake. Mist is rising from the lake. The air is cool even though it is the eleventh of June. This morning, alcoholic victims all over America are going to awaken to a terrible hangover and have to make a decision. Will they continue on or will they reach out for help? The heroin addict, likewise I suspect on many occasions, faces the decision of continuing in hell-bound behavior or making an effort to do whatever is necessary to come clean. The inmate in prison, soon to be released, has to decide if he can make it straight or continue his destructive behavior. The couple on the verge of divorce has to make a decision, sometimes repeatedly, whether to struggle on together or face divorce and its consequences. The couple who has a wedding date set, and one becomes uncertain about it and a decision has to be made to go through with it and hope for the best, or face the embarrassment of a broken engagement after the wedding invitations have been sent out. The soldier in the front lines in the heat of the battle has a chance to go to the scene of a wounded buddy and help him, but to do so would put him at great risk. Will he do it or will he run for safety?

The physician's life is filled full of decisions, the importance of which requires no elaboration. This applies to the executive, the building superintendent, the superintendent of schools, the presidents of corporations, the president of the United States of America, the housewife, the school boy, the firefighter, the farmer, the construction worker, the foreman, the priest, the minister and the list goes on and on. All of these face decisions.

As a physician, my life has been filled with decision-making, important ones, ones that could affect the very life of my patients. This is so obvious that I need not belabor the point. Some of the very difficult decisions relate to the patient present in the emergency room with a diagnostic problem. Are they sick or are they mainly frightened? This can be a very tough question to answer. Sometimes one cannot immediately decide. It may take a period of observation to be sure. Is the chest pain of this sixty-year-old man coming from an impending heart attack or is it his gallbladder or is it his hiatus hernia? A girl comes in with lower abdominal pain. Is it appendicitis, is it pelvic inflammatory disease, is it urinary tract infection, is it an intestinal virus, is it who knows what? These decisions are tough at times, very tough.

The confident person surely has an easier time at decision-making than the one who suffers from the continual agony of insecurity. There are those who are strong and secure and make their decisions with apparent ease and we stand in awe and admiration. Then there are those who seem to make a decision after only the most agonizing delay and the frustration of those whose actions depend on those decisions is terrible to endure. The person who comes to a decision with great difficulty is as we know the person with pretty serious problems. Then there is the person who comes to a decision too quickly — impulsively — shoots from the hip without careful aim. That person has a major problem, too. Blessed are those who can make decisions after reasonable consideration, weighing the evidence, and coming to a conclusion with reasonable speed and who are willing to make a mistake, if they must, in order to reach a decision. So often our fear of a mistake causes us to be indecisive and operate in a grey zone much of the time, driving everyone around us bananas.

My decision to go to medical school was made in the ninth grade and I never wavered from it. My decision to follow the religious conviction of my parents never wavered until I was in my fourth decade and I began to think for myself after I had had some experience in life. Now I have moved away from my basic faith and where I was once a fundamentalist of the Christian faith, I would now be branded a liberal. This comes as a result of multiple decisions regarding experience and observation, which seem to run counter to my religious indoctrination.

At one time I was planning to go to Africa and become a missionary doctor. My first disabling clinical depression struck me and I lost my nerve. I resigned from the Mission Board. Instead I decided to do home mission work in a medically impoverished area in the coal country of eastern Kentucky. It looked like a good match. They needed me and I needed them. When the time came to go, I wavered. The responsibility would be great and at times I would run the hospital alone. The echoes of the horrors of my depression kept coming back. I lost my nerve again and my dear wife with strong resolve and a bit of disgust, kicked me in the seat of the pants and simply said, "We're going now and that is all there is to it." Her resolve and her faith in me was just what I needed. I went and I flourished and I won. No, we won. And so it is in life, at critical times there are those significant people about us who care for us and enable us to make decisions when we seem to be frozen in our tracks.

Leaving Homeplace after twenty years has to have been the hardest decision in my entire life. That place answered my needs and I answered their needs. We fit. But there was a problem. Living in relative isolation and the family facing problems that I did not have to face, made for very serious difficulties and ultimately it became necessary for me to leave. I did leave with the clouds of depression hanging over, but I prevailed and the transplantation was successful.

A year ago I faced another decision. I am a workaholic and I realized I needed to slow down. My engine had overheated on a number of times previously and had broken down three times. I felt another one coming on and I had to decide whether to keep the throttle wide open and wait until I had thrown a rod or slow down and let the engine cool. Common sense finally prevailed and I decelerated and my engine cooled and I am so much happier. I am amazed.

Decisions are at our doorsteps all the time. From the moment we leave the nest on our own until we die or until dementia gets us, we cannot escape the responsibility of decision. But I love the game of decision-making for the most part. It is wonderful to live in a land where we are free to make decisions. It is wonderful to be competent and able to make decisions. It is grand to have friends and loved ones who can at times help us to make decisions. It is great to be strong enough to allow ourselves to make mistakes and incidentally that is how we learn, for goodness sakes.

At sixty-five, you would think that the worst of the decisions were over and that I could settle down into automatic pilot and relax. Not so, I found out. Each stage of life brings with it its own special problems requiring a decision.

Temptations of youth are not the temptations of maturity, but each stage has its share. Decision-making does not, for me, get any easier. But this is what makes life exciting, adventuresome, rewarding, and at times, devastating. We decide and live with the consequences. The game of life, ah, the thrill of it all! The uncertainty. The joy of winning, the agony of defeat. The opportunity to try again. I am so glad I am still in the ballgame. I am so glad that I am on the team. I rejoice that the whistle has not blown for me. I will play and play hard until the end. I look forward to scoring points still, maybe some big ones. Yet, the best part of the game may still be down the road, who knows? But this one thing I know, as long as I can wiggle a finger, I will not give up.

―――――――――――――――――――――――

The Tie That Binds

It was early December, 1941, and I was studying zoology at my desk at Bartlett Hall, Wheaton College. I needed a break. I turned on my desk radio and soon the program was interrupted by the never to be forgotten announcement that Pearl Harbor had been bombed by the Japanese and America had been dealt a dreadful and humiliating defeat. Our ships were sunk, our sailors were killed, and our planes couldn't even get in the air in order to fight. Devastation such as we had never known was our bitter medicine on that day. Only twenty-two years earlier the Armistice was signed ending a world war such as the earth had never known. This event signaled the Second World War for America and we were soon locked in a life or death struggle with Japan and Germany. America was united and welded together overnight. We had one purpose — survival at whatever the cost. Patriotism was no joke. It was real. The flag took on a new meaning. Men in uniform were cheered and helped in every conceivable way. Women left their homes and went to the factories and to the powder and ammunition plants to work. Boys left college by droves and enlisted in the armed forces. Automobile assembly lines soon began to produce tanks and military vehicles instead of cars. Luxury items for civilian use dried up and military hardware became number one. America became one nation, struggling for a single purpose — survival and victory. A common enemy is perhaps the greatest unifying force in the world — always has been and always will be. When survival is at stake, you forego the foolishness of selfishness and petty bickering and work together as a team.

I recall vividly the camaraderie that existed among those of us who were patients in psychiatry. Each time I found friends and established close bonds to fellow sufferers. We struggled together, we fought the monster together, and we won together.

In any hospital there is a marvelous spirit of unity and togetherness among patients who are in a rehabilitation center. These folks suffer all kinds of disabilities and fight together, cry together and laugh together. Alcoholics Anonymous is a marvelous example of the tie that binds men and women together as a struggle against the common enemy of alcohol. Narcotics Anonymous, likewise, is a support group that is meeting a real need in the lives of many people. Support groups of every description have arisen in recent years, bringing together divorced people, lonely singles, stressed out and depressed folks, and you name it, there is a support group out there to help.

All of this kind of support activity gives me hope for mankind. We now face the common enemy of total extinction. We can already see the signs of cooperation among nations instead of confrontation. The ice is beginning to thaw. Rationality instead of insanity is becoming evident among nations. Commonality is developing. Hope is rising as the sun rises in the eastern sky. I can see it — I can see it — I can see it!

The Tie That "Don't Bind"

Dr. Farra VanMeter had a fatherly conversation with me when I joined the staff of Homeplace Clinic. He was a member of the Board of Trustees of Homeplace Hospital and a surgeon in Lexington, Kentucky. After a brief discussion about life in general, he said to me as he reached in his hip pocket and pulled out his wallet and held it up, "Don, don't ever forget that the bottom line with most people is this." Now Farra VanMeter was a good, good man, not a miserly millionaire, but a man of compassion and concern. Yet, he wanted to emphasize to me that so often for so many, the main thing in life was the almighty dollar. I really didn't exactly plug into that idea of his at the time, but in the past thirty-five years since he told me that, I must confess, that he was pretty close to being right. Many of us would rather not admit that, but I am afraid, if we were pressed, we would. I still believe I can honestly say that if I couldn't do both, I would rather practice medicine with the emphasis on love rather than money. Believe me, I have done it both ways. I think I have a right to speak and be heard on this point.

Money, so often, is the tie that does not bind, rather it rips us apart! Families are torn apart many times when a will is read. An attempt is made to break the will, chaos results, and people are hurt and healing never occurs.

References to disputes over the greenback could go on and on and on. Families get into it over how money is spent, unions and management have their wars, and at divorce time, money is apt to be of utmost importance. Congress often is at war because of the budget and the allocation of funds. When we think we are overcharged, we fume and sometimes with good reason. When some slick operator pulls the wool over our eyes, takes our hard-earned money on a slimy deal and pulls a financial rug out from under us, we are humiliated and enraged. We have visions of parting this character's hair with a two by four.

And finally, as I have so often said, and as most of you realize, it is indeed more blessed to give than to receive. For one thing, to be in a position to give simply means that we have more than enough and can give. To be only in a receiving position, for one reason or another, means that we don't have enough. Yes, I'd rather be a doctor than a patient. I'd rather have to pay taxes than receive a handout from the government that came from tax dollars. For sure, money separates us. The rich and the poor. The landowner and the slave. The powerful and the weak. Money separates — but love binds us together. I know full well that in this real world it is often very hard and sometimes impossible to love. But I am going to keep on trying and I do often succeed, and when I do, I have a ball.

"This World is Not My Home, I Am Just A Passin' Through"

These words are from a familiar song, originated with our black community, and have become popular through the years because they express what so many of us feel. They express the fact that so often we feel dissatisfied, unfulfilled, unloved unappreciated and often, forsaken. They say that there is something better coming for us, that there is a land where wrong will be made right, where we will be loved and appreciated, where there will be no more pain, separation, frustration and struggle. In short, it says whereas much of this world has been hell, there is a heaven to come and to enjoy. I think we can all relate to this. The rich and the poor, the bound and the free, the smart and the not too smart, the hungry and the filled, the white and the black, the American and the Russian and the African. It says that life at best is a constant struggle for survival in some way or another. It says that everything has something "eatin' on it." It says that there is many a slip between the cup and the lip. It says that tomorrow is uncertain. It says that in this world we can expect along with the possibilities of joy, fulfillment and pleasure, that there will inevitably be pain, heartache and maybe tragedy. It says that there is much to endure, to suffer and simply "put up with." And tonight, as I relax on the couch in front of the fire, I would like to talk about struggle. I have been with sick people struggling with illness and injury for forty-four years, actually since my junior year in medical school. I have struggled with illness myself. I have watched people react to their losses, their pain, to their frustrations to their disappointment. I have watched people die. I know this for sure, if you have a good body and a sound mind, you are a millionaire, and if you don't, you have a major problem for sure.

The common fabric of our lives is struggle. The experience of struggling at the time can be agonizing, can be frustrating, can be hellishly difficult. If we master the enemy, if we gain the upper hand, if we achieve the victory, oh how precious and exhilarating the triumph is. How much we learn by the fight, how strengthening the fight was for us and we are enabled to rise to new heights because of the struggle. The very essence of all of life is conflict and struggle. If the theory of evolution is correct, life as we know it today, is the product of the survival of the fittest. There is struggle and uncertainty in our lives from the moment of conception. If we make it through the gestation period and if we withstand the trauma of delivery, then we are on first base so to speak. Miscarriage, abortion and death during the trauma of labor and delivery get a number of our brothers and sisters. After delivery, there is the struggle with germs and viruses. Either of these offenders get a number of the human family despite the marvels of medical advancement. If we are born today in the third world, malnutrition or starvation will claim some of us. If one's parents are drug addicts or incompetent or for some reason do not or cannot take adequate care of us and love us, then we may die of neglect. It is a dangerous world and some toddlers will be killed cruelly by accident of one kind or another or crippled in brain or body permanently. It is a world of booby traps and in our youth we may step on the trap of drug addiction or alcoholism and suffer great loss. In all of our lives there is the struggle against disease and possible injury. There is the struggle to be successful in a highly competitive world. There is the possibility of emotional illness and stress-related problems that may overwhelm us as we struggle for survival and happiness. There is a struggle for intimacy, for true companionship, and for love. There is a struggle for fulfillment, for acceptance and for a reason to live. There is a struggle to live on and push ahead when we are in prison of one kind or another, whether it be the state reformatory or the situation in life which locks us up and from which there is no escape. There is the struggle that so many in a monogamous relationship deal with, that is, to find compatibility and fulfillment and to be able to weather the storm of life that threatens its very existence. There is the struggle the widow has as she grieves her loss and makes her necessary adjustment. There is the struggle with despair as a child dies, as a lover says good-bye forever, and as we deal with a thousand and one other losses and disappointments.

How do we cope with our problems, our temptations, our frustrations, our grief, our disappointments, our prisons. The libraries are full of books of advice. The magazines, TV shows and the media in general have generous advice. How do I cope? Sometimes I don't. Sometimes I fail miserably just as you do, but sometimes I succeed. I think by virtue of my genes, I was given some advantage. I, by nature, like to work hard and I have a determined, competitive spirit, and I have reasonable intelligence. I was reared in a religious atmosphere in which principles of behavior were firmly implanted and this does help a great deal in dealing with temptation to violate our conscience. I have found it true, as many have said, that being busy at a job helps tremendously. I have found that helping someone in a mess helps me with my messes. I have found that giving is better than receiving, for in giving you often receive back a lot. I have found that when I love others many will reciprocate and love me. I need that. I have found that if I am generous, I like myself. When I am loving, I like myself. When I succeed and overcome a struggle, I like myself.

I have learned to be more tolerant and understanding of my fellow-traveler who has made what appears to be a mess of his life. Knowing these things helps me to be tolerant, understanding and reach out to my fallen brother or sister with an arm of help rather than utter a snide remark and pass them by as did the priest and the levite in Jesus' story of the Good Samaritan in the long ago.

Mountain Climbing

Now, forget it, I am not discussing my personal exploits on Mt. McKinley, Anapurna or Mt. Everest. The dirt and rock mountains that I have climbed have been on the Appalachian Trail of Eastern United States and those have been negotiated with a thirty-pound pack on my back, my legs, a walking stick, grunts and groans when I was forty-five years of age. No, today, I am talking about our personal mountains that we all inevitably have to climb if we are to succeed in anything at all. Life at its best requires climbing, climbing, climbing; blood, sweat and tears. When we hit the summit along the way, the view is gorgeous, enduring, precious and all ours for the moment. We can avoid the steep climbs if we like and go around the mountains and take the easy way in life. But we will miss so much, we lose so much, life simply becomes a bit drab as a result.

A mountain to be climbed is that of breaking a life-threatening habit that has had us in its grip for years. When the heart attack hits and we are struck with tornado force, finally about fifty percent of smokers succeed in saying good-bye forever to cigarettes. The alcoholic starts to vomit blood one day only to be told he has varicose veins in his esophagus, the result of liver cirrhosis from his alcohol. He goes on the wagon and the mountain he faces is about like climbing Mt. Everest. It is terribly difficult and impossible for some. The 100 pound overweight person develops diabetes and is told to lose it or else. It is simply continuing to eat and die younger with diabetes or lose the weight and live longer. Very few can climb this mountain without giving up and sliding back down.

There are so many other mountains to climb which can bring us reward and success and fulfillment. The housewife who goes back to college, gets her degree, enters the professional world — what a marvelous view from this mountain. The disabled person who accepts the challenge of rehabilitation and struggles day after day against great odds and makes the recovery beyond expectation — what a view from this mountain. The young athlete with unusual talents decides to go for broke. After years of training, discipline and denial, the Olympic Gold is awarded. What a view from this height! The scientist who finds the missing piece in the jigsaw to complete the picture and conquer AIDS will indeed have a commanding view from this mountain.

All through life there are mountains to be climbed. Some are fun, some are terrible, some are boring and some are ridiculous. All require determination, commitment, persistence and hard work. All of us have a number of mountains that we are climbing at this very moment. Some of these we will conquer. Some will beat us. We don't win them all by any means. Some we simply have to abandon for one reason or another. There is the mountain of morality. Sometimes temptation overwhelms us and we slide off the mountain. There is the mountain of an advanced degree and we run out of gas. There is the mountain of the pursuit of excellence in whatever, and then we settle for mediocrity.

You face your mountains and I face mine. I don't have any special formula, secrets to success or "take my advice and you can't fail to succeed" road maps. But I do know this from experience — the view from the mountain top is breathless, rewarding and worth it all. If, however, you slide off the mountain and land abruptly at the bottom, you will have lots of company there, don't forget that. I have climbed some big ones and made it. I have tried to climb others and flunked.

Sunset

It is mid-May and I am alone at my lake house. The sun is setting over the lake and it is quiet, very quiet. Not many houses here. Solitude. The sunset is gorgeous. Squirrels play in the big oak tree. I am tired and sleepy. Usual Saturday. Up at 5:30 a.m., exercises, breakfast, social rounds at the hospital. I gave up medical rounds and my colleague does the work and worrying for me now. I see my patients now in the hospital in a relaxed fashion and I call them grandfather rounds. All fun and no responsibility. Then on to the office where I saw the usual forty patients for a short Saturday. Two hours of hard work at my duplex complex on the edge of town. It is fun to shovel dirt and cut grass. The pay isn't so good as doctoring, but it is a lot of fun. A fifteen minute run to my lake house. Fast food picked up en route and I have just eaten the last bite. The sun is almost gone down. Darkness is settling in and it is peaceful, telephone not ringing, no one seeks me out. What a relief! I love it, I love this place.

Sunsets are beautiful the world over. I have seen sunsets on the Appalachian Trail while backpacking. I have seen sunsets on the ocean standing on the fantail of the USS Delta. I have seen sunsets in Israel, but the sunset here at the lake I love best of all. You know at sixty-five I am thrilled to even be in this world to enjoy a sunset. Some of my colleagues are gone. I have got my eyes to see it. I have got my brain to appreciate it. I expect to see many more. But there are no guarantees, so I will look at this one tonight and drink in its beauty.

Sunset means the day is almost over and work is done for many of us. For others, it is just starting. The people on death row don't see any at all. The many people in intensive care units tonight don't see any sunset. The thousands in nursing homes with dementia don't appreciate sunsets. The suicidal don't either. The alcoholic doesn't notice the sunset. The starving in Africa don't really see the sunset though they may be looking west. The homeless are cut off from the sunset by the tall buildings of the inner city.

Sunset of life is here for many. It can be a beautiful time. As the colors play on the clouds and shine in their grandeur, so do our experiences in life give color, richness and beauty to our lives. I am so glad that I am still alive. I am so gladl that I can still love and be loved. I am so glad I can still give and receive. I am so glad life is not over. Sunset time for me is indeed a beautiful time. I am happy, I have learned to live. I want to fully live till the whistle blows and the time clock runs out. And then when the night comes, I know morning will not delay.

A Look Ahead

Medical Practice. Today we have made great medical and surgical advances beyond our wildest imagination when we think of the medical team 100 years ago. In another hundred years we will look back to this day as a day of ignorance, relatively speaking. Research will have the answers to cancer, antibiotics will be available for viruses, causes of mental illness will have been discovered and proper treatment available. No doubt we will understand the cause of hypertension and find ways to prevent or cure it. The population will continue to age and likely the average age span will be 100 years or more. The government will be in control of the health care delivery system. Medical care will be available to all, but bureaucracy will be a dominant factor to reckon with. The quality of medical care will likely deteriorate to some degree. Doctors will earn less money and be stripped of much of their power.

One world. The future will see many changes in the social and political framework of the nations. Truly we will be much more one world than we are today. It is either this way or perish. Every nation will gradually become a home for nationalities from all over the world. This will provide for understanding and cooperation in the long run. For the short run, it will bring new problems but they can be worked out. There has been and will continue to be political gravitation for the democratic form of government. America will finally have a swing back toward respect for authority as we become disgusted with our freedoms gone wild and out of control. Arms control will be high on the agenda of all nations for discussion and problem solving. Racial intolerance will gradually diminish.

Religions. There will be increasing understanding among religious leaders of the world and greater tolerance. Distinct religions will continue to exist and even flourish, but I suspect less emphasis will be placed on missionary activity and proselytizing. There will be attempts to refine religious philosophy and practice to make it more in tune with the real world without the loss of its basic message. Catholics and Protestants in the Christian world will cooperate more and more. Non-Christian religions along with the Christian faith will come together gradually and will seek ways to cooperate and bring more understanding rather than competition.

AIDS. There will be a world-wide epidemic of AIDS of agonizing proportions and some nations may be depleted in population to a marked degree. A cure for AIDS will come and likely a vaccine as well.

In conclusion. I have described a better world to come. I honestly believe this. Man will not change his basic nature. We still are made up of good stuff and bad stuff. We are all made up of the angel and the demon in different ratios, but I believe that science and religion working together can make possible a better future for us all. Learning from experience, nations can cooperate as never before. Of course, a great miscalculation along the line can bring disaster to the world and the nuclear holocaust we fear can be upon us. This is the risk we live with, but life has always been risky. There will always be the potential for victory or defeat, cooperation or destruction, living together or dying together. We are on the tightrope going across Niagara. I believe we will make it. It is truly a fascinating trip, but we can see and probably arrive at the Promised Land together.